THE END OF PROGRESS

NEW DIRECTIONS IN CRITICAL THEORY

New Directions in Critical Theory

AMY ALLEN, GENERAL EDITOR

New Directions in Critical Theory presents outstanding classic and contemporary texts in the tradition of critical social theory, broadly construed. The series aims to renew and advance the program of critical social theory, with a particular focus on theorizing contemporary struggles around gender, race, sexuality, class, and globalization and their complex interconnections.

Narrating Evil: A Postmetaphysical Theory of Reflective Judgment, María Pía Lara
The Politics of Our Selves: Power, Autonomy, and Gender in Contemporary Critical Theory, Amy Allen
Democracy and the Political Unconscious, Noëlle McAfee
The Force of the Example: Explorations in the Paradigm of Judgment, Alessandro Ferrara
Horrorism: Naming Contemporary Violence, Adriana Cavarero
Scales of Justice: Reimagining Political Space in a Globalizing World, Nancy Fraser
Pathologies of Reason: On the Legacy of Critical Theory, Axel Honneth
States Without Nations: Citizenship for Mortals, Jacqueline Stevens
The Racial Discourses of Life Philosophy: Négritude, Vitalism, and Modernity, Donna V. Jones
Democracy in What State?, Giorgio Agamben, Alain Badiou, Daniel Bensaïd, Wendy Brown, Jean-Luc Nancy, Jacques Rancière, Kristin Ross, Slavoj Žižek
Politics of Culture and the Spirit of Critique: Dialogues, edited by Gabriel Rockhill and Alfredo Gomez-Muller
Mute Speech: Literature, Critical Theory, and Politics, Jacques Rancière
The Right to Justification: Elements of Constructivist Theory of Justice, Rainer Forst
The Scandal of Reason: A Critical Theory of Political Judgment, Albena Azmanova
The Wrath of Capital: Neoliberalism and Climate Change Politics, Adrian Parr
Media of Reason: A Theory of Rationality, Matthias Vogel
Social Acceleration: The Transformation of Time in Modernity, Hartmut Rosa
The Disclosure of Politics: Struggles Over the Semantics of Secularization, María Pía Lara
Radical Cosmopolitics: The Ethics and Politics of Democratic Universalism, James Ingram
Freedom's Right: The Social Foundations of Democratic Life, Axel Honneth
Imaginal Politics: Images Beyond Imagination and the Imaginary, Chiara Bottici
Alienation, Rahel Jaeggi
The Power of Tolerance: A Debate, Wendy Brown and Rainer Forst, edited by Luca Di Blasi and Christoph F. E. Holzhey
Radical History and the Politics of Art, Gabriel Rockhill
The Highway of Despair: Critical Theory After Hegel, Robyn Marasco
A Political Economy of the Senses: Neoliberalism, Reification, Critique, Anita Chari

THE END OF PROGRESS

DECOLONIZING THE NORMATIVE FOUNDATIONS OF CRITICAL THEORY

Amy Allen

Columbia University Press New York

Columbia University Press
Publishers Since 1893
New York Chichester, West Sussex
cup.columbia.edu

Paperback edition, 2017

Library of Congress Cataloging-in-Publication Data

Allen, Amy.
The end of progress : decolonizing the normative foundations of critical theory / Amy Allen.
pages cm
Includes bibliographical references and index.
ISBN 978-0-231-17324-7 (cloth : alk. paper)—ISBN 978-0-231-17325-4 (pbk. : alk. paper)—ISBN 978-0-231-54063-6 (e-book)
1. Critical theory. I. Title

B809.3.A45 2015
142—dc23 2015018980

∞
Columbia University Press books are printed on permanent and durable acid-free paper.
Printed in the United States of America

Cover design: Black Kat Design
Cover image: "Shibboleth" by Doris Salcedo; photo by Shaun Curry/AFP/Getty images

For Chris

Progress occurs where it ends.

—Theodor Adorno, "Progress"

I would like to say something about the function of any diagnosis concerning the nature of the present. It does not consist in a simple characterization of what we are but, instead—by following lines of fragility in the present—in managing to grasp why and how that-which-is might no longer be that-which-is. In this sense, any description must always be made in accordance with these kinds of virtual fracture which open up the space of freedom understood as a space of concrete freedom, that is of possible transformation.

—Michel Foucault, "Critical Theory/Intellectual History"

The subaltern fractures from within.

—Dipesh Chakrabarty, *Provincializing Europe*

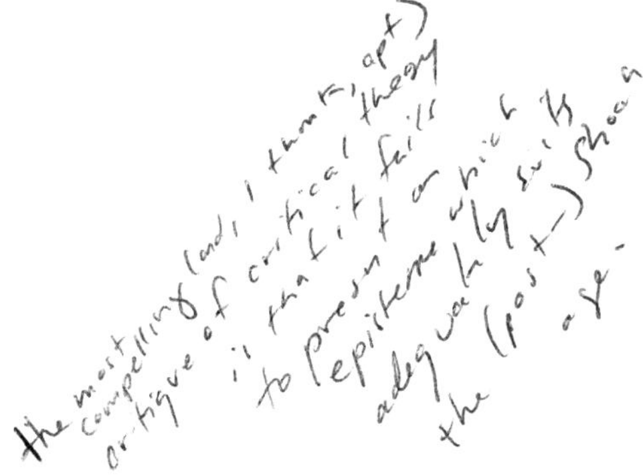

CONTENTS

PREFACE AND ACKNOWLEDGMENTS

This book aims to make a contribution to the ongoing project of critical theory. But construing the aim of the book in this way already raises a difficulty, for the term "critical theory" is contested and unstable, and can refer to a wide variety of theoretical projects and agendas. In its most narrow usage, "critical theory" refers to the German tradition of interdisciplinary social theory, inaugurated in Frankfurt in the 1930s, and carried forward today in Germany by such thinkers as Jürgen Habermas, Axel Honneth, and Rainer Forst and in the United States by theorists such as Thomas McCarthy, Nancy Fraser, and Seyla Benhabib. In a more capacious usage, "critical theory" refers to any politically inflected form of cultural, social, or political theory that has critical, progressive, or emancipatory aims. Understood in this way, "critical theory" encompasses much if not all of the work that is done under the banner of feminist theory, queer theory, critical race theory, and post- and decolonial theory. A distinct but related capacious usage of the term refers to the body of theory that is mobilized in literary and cultural studies, otherwise known simply as "theory." Here critical theory refers mainly to a body of French theory spanning from poststructuralism to psychoanalysis, and including such thinkers as Michel Foucault, Jacques Derrida, Gilles Deleuze, and Jacques Lacan. Obviously there are significant overlaps and cross-fertilizations between these latter two senses in particular, and my point here is not to attempt to draw hard and fast distinctions between them. Rather, my point is simply to map some of the complicated and shifting terrain on which this book is situated.

For once we have at least provisionally mapped the terrain in this way, it is striking how fraught and contested the interactions and dialogues between "critical theory" in the narrow sense and "critical theory" in these two wider senses of the term are. Although the former has gone some way toward incorporating the insights of feminist theory (primarily through the work of Fraser and Benhabib) and critical race theory (through the recent work of McCarthy), its long-running feud with French theory is well known. And up to now, "critical theory" in the narrow sense of that term has largely failed to engage seriously with the insights of queer theory and post- and decolonial theory. No doubt, these last two points are closely related, insofar as French theory—and the work of Foucault in particular—has been so formative for the fields of queer and postcolonial theory.

In this book, I attempt to work across the divides between these different understandings of critical theory, particularly those between the Frankfurt School approach to critical theory, the work of Michel Foucault, and the concerns of post- and decolonial theory. My main *critical* aim is to show that and how and why Frankfurt School critical theory remains wedded to problematically Eurocentric and/or foundationalist strategies for grounding normativity. My primary *positive* aim is to decolonize Frankfurt School critical theory by rethinking its strategy for grounding normativity, in such a way as to open this project up to the aims and concerns of post- and decolonial critical theory. For reasons that I discuss at more length throughout this book, I think that such an opening up is crucial if Frankfurt School critical theory is to be truly critical, in the sense of being able to engage in the ongoing self-clarification of the struggles and wishes of our postcolonial—by which I mean formally decolonized but still neocolonial—age.

In light of this complex and divided terrain, it might be useful for me to spell out at the outset how I deploy the term "critical theory." As I understand it and as I practice it in this book and elsewhere, critical theory refers simultaneously to a tradition, a method, and an aim. My approach to critical theory is situated in the intellectual tradition of the Frankfurt School. What I find particularly attractive about this tradition is its emphasis on social theory and on the understanding of the social as the nexus of the political, the cultural, and the individual. This focus on the social gives rise to the distinctive interplay between the critique of political economy, forms of social-cultural analysis, and theories of the self or individual that is the hallmark of the Frankfurt School critical theory tradition. As I see it, however, the best way to do justice to this tradition is not to remain faithful to its core doctrines or central figures but rather precisely to inherit it, by which I mean to take it up while simultaneously radically transforming it. I do this in what follows by bringing Frankfurt School critical theory into sustained conversation not only with the work of Michel Foucault but also with the work of feminist, queer, and post- and decolonial critical theorists.

But critical theory is more than a distinctive intellectual tradition of social theory. It also consists in a distinctive method for doing social theory. This method is outlined clearly in the famous programmatic essay that inaugurates the critical theory tradition, Max Horkheimer's "Traditional and Critical Theory." In this essay, Horkheimer situates critical theory between political realism—which analyzes the empirical conditions and power relations that structure our existing social, cultural, economic, and political worlds—and normative political theory—which articulates ideal, rational, normative conceptions of justice that it takes to be freestanding. In contrast to both of these methods, critical theory understands itself to be rooted in and constituted by an existing social reality that is structured by power relations that it therefore also aims to critique by appealing to immanent standards of normativity and rationality. The difference between traditional and critical theory, Horkheimer notes, "springs in general from a difference not so much of objects as of subjects."[1] On this way of understanding it, what is distinctive about critical theory is its conception of the critical subject as self-consciously rooted in and shaped by the power relations in the society that she nevertheless aims self-reflexively and rationally to critique. As I see it, preserving this distinctiveness requires critical theory to hold open the central tension between power, on the one hand, and normativity and rationality, on the other hand, for to resolve it in either direction would mean collapsing into either political realism or what is now called ideal theory.[2]

But critical theory is not just a distinctive method that emerges out of a particular intellectual tradition. It also has the practical and political aim of freedom or emancipation. Again, to take Horkheimer's classic statement, the goal of critical theory is not merely the theoretical aim of understanding what constitutes emancipation or the conditions under which it is possible but also the ambitious practical aim of "man's emancipation from slavery."[3] But here a potential tension emerges between the method of critical theory and its aim, for theoretical attempts to identify the ideal conditions under which genuine emancipation would be possible inevitably run up against charges of normative or rational idealism and complaints that they are insufficiently attentive to the complexities of power. For this reason, as I have argued in more detail elsewhere,[4] a negativistic conception of emancipation, where emancipation refers to the minimization of relations of domination, not to a social world without or beyond power relations, is most compatible with critical theory's distinctive method.

Particularly in light of its practical-political emancipatory aim, the failure of Frankfurt School critical theory to engage substantively with one of the most influential branches of critical theory, in the broader sense of that term, to have emerged in recent decades—postcolonial studies and theory—is all the more puzzling and problematic. After all, if critical theory aims at the emancipatory self-clarification of the political struggles of the age, then how can it ignore the compelling articulation and theorization of contemporary struggles over the meaning, limits, and failures of decolonization that have emerged in this body of work? In many ways this book emerges out of my puzzlement about this lack of engagement.[5] Some of this failure undoubtedly has to do with the fact that postcolonial theory has been so heavily influenced by poststructuralist theory; in that sense, the ongoing family quarrel between Frankfurt School critical theory and French critical theory is likely operating in the background to shape the Frankfurt School's reception—

or lack thereof—of postcolonial theory. But there is, I think, also something deeper going on and it has to do with the way that contemporary Frankfurt School critical theorists—Habermasian and post-Habermasian—have attempted to ground their conceptions of normativity. As I argue more fully in what follows, these attempts have primarily coalesced in the work of Habermas and Honneth in a broadly speaking neo-Hegelian reconstructivist strategy for grounding normativity in which ideas of historical progress and sociocultural learning and development figure prominently. Rainer Forst, by contrast, defends a neo-Kantian constructivist strategy in which normativity is grounded in a foundationalist conception of practical reason. Given the deep connections between ideas of historical progress and development and normative foundationalism and the theory and practice of Eurocentric imperialism, however, both of these strategies are anathema to postcolonial theory. The problematic imperialist entanglements of these normative strategies also shed light on why postcolonial theorists have by and large found French poststructuralist theory—which likewise rejects both foundationalism and progressive theories of history—more congenial to its aims than Frankfurt School critical theory.

The result is that a gulf has opened up between the Frankfurt School approach to critical theory and critical theory done under the heading of postcolonial theory. I felt this gulf very acutely as I worked on this project. When presenting my work to the former sort of audience, including but not only in Frankfurt, I was criticized vehemently for challenging the various neo-Hegelian and neo-Kantian strategies for grounding normativity favored by contemporary Frankfurt School theorists and thus flirting with relativism; when discussing my project with colleagues who work in postcolonial theory, I found that they were often stunned to learn that anyone was still willing to defend either ideas of historical progress and development or normative foundationalist projects at all. This gulf is so pronounced that the very project of this book might seem quixotic. For whom, after all, is it written? Frankfurt School critical theorists are likely to think that the anti-foundationalist account of normativity that I develop here is too weak and relativistic to count as critical, and postcolonial theorists are likely to find the critiques of Eurocentric modernity discussed here all too familiar. And yet this book attempts to speak across this divide, both by showing how and why critical theory in the narrow sense of that term can and must be decolonized and by showing how a certain way of inheriting the Frankfurt School approach to critical theory, a certain way of construing and taking up its method and its aims, can be congenial to postcolonial theory, how it might even allow postcolonial theory to be criticalized.

This book took shape over a number of years and is the result of a great many public presentations of work in progress and conversations with colleagues, friends, and students. I cannot hope to mention everyone whose comments, questions, and suggestions have made an impact on this work, but I am grateful for all of the opportunities I have had over the last six years to reframe, refine, and improve this project.

Research on this book was made possible by a generous fellowship from the Alexander von Humboldt foundation, which I took in Frankfurt in the summer semesters of 2010 and 2012. I am tremendously grateful to the Humboldt Foundation and to my cohosts for that fellowship, Axel Honneth and Rainer Forst. In a gesture of true intellectual generosity, both of them fully supported this project and its author despite the trenchant criticisms of their work pursued herein. The Forschungskolleg Humanwissenschaften in Bad Homburg v.d. Höhe provided the ideal setting for my work during those two semesters. Special thanks to Ingrid Rudolph and Beate Sutterlüty for helping to make Bad Homburg my German home away from home. I also owe a deep debt of gratitude to Dartmouth College, and particularly to former Dean of Faculty Carol Folt and Associate Dean for Arts and Humanities Katharine Conley, for providing me with an endowed research chair from 2009 to 2015. Without the extra time off from teaching and generous research funding afforded by the Parents Distinguished Research Professorship, this book would have taken much longer to complete.

As before, I have benefited enormously from my participation in three vibrant philosophical organizations—the Critical Theory Roundtable, the Colloquium on Philosophy and the Social Sciences in Prague, and the Society for Phenomenology and Existential

Philosophy—where early versions of many of the ideas in this book have been presented over the last six years. These organizations have long been my philosophical home away from home, and I remain grateful for the stimulating and challenging environments that they, in their very different ways, provide.

Early versions of various ideas, sections, and chapters of this book were presented in a variety of venues, including at the following institutions: St. Anselm College, Williams College, Michigan State University, the New School, University of Frankfurt, University of York, Miami University (Ohio), the University of Oregon, Vanderbilt University, Emory University, Grinnell College, University of Luzern, University of Jena, Humboldt University Berlin, Rochester Institute of Technology, Northwestern University, Stony Brook University, CUNY Graduate Center, Pennsylvania State University, and Columbia University. I am grateful to the audiences on each of these occasions for their insightful and challenging questions and comments. Special thanks to Maeve Cooke at University College Dublin and to the Feministische Philosoph_innen Gruppe in Frankfurt for organizing workshops on the manuscript in progress in December 2010 and June 2012, respectively.

Many people read drafts of various chapters or parts of chapters of this book and provided crucial feedback along the way. Thanks to Denise Anthony, Albena Azmanova, Steven Crowell, Nikita Dhawan, Alley Edlebi, Matthias Fritsch, Robert Gooding-Williams, Nathan Gusdorf, María Pía Lara, Claudia Leeb, Matthias Lutz-Bachmann, Lois McNay, Charles Mills, David Owen, Dmitri Nikulin, Alexander de la Paz, Falguni Sheth, Ian Storey, Ben Schupmann, James Tully, Barbara Umrath, Eva von Redecker, Kenneth Walden, and Christopher Zurn. Several others deserve a special thanks for reading and commenting on the entire manuscript, including Richard Bernstein, Chiara Bottici, Fabian Freyenhagen, Timo Jütten, Colin Koopman, Tony Laden, Thomas McCarthy, Johanna Meehan, Mari Ruti, Jörg Schaub, and Dimitar Vatsov. My Dartmouth research assistant, Benjamin Randolph, not only offered insightful comments on the content of the book, he also provided invaluable help with the copy-editing process. Thanks also to my Penn State research assistant, Daniel Palumbo, for help with the index. In January 2014,

Dartmouth's Leslie Humanities Center sponsored a manuscript review workshop on this project. I am tremendously grateful to my former Dartmouth colleagues who participated in that workshop—Leslie Center director Colleen Boggs, Susan Brison, Leslie Butler, and Klaus Mladek—and especially to the two external readers—Kevin Olson and Max Pensky—whose trenchant and careful readings made this a much better book than it otherwise would have been.

Special thanks to my editor at Columbia University Press, Wendy Lochner, for her unflagging support, patience, and cheerful good sense, and to her assistant, Christine Dunbar, for superb logistical assistance and attention to detail.

Finally, I owe an infinite debt of gratitude to my family. First, to my children, Clark, Oliver, Isabelle, and Eloise, who put up with my long work hours and elevated stress level as I struggled to bring this project to completion. And last, but certainly not least, to my husband, Chris, who has supported me and my work in all of the ways that truly matter and even when doing so has meant letting go of some of his own dreams and plans. I dedicate this book to him.

ABBREVIATIONS

WORKS BY ADORNO

CCS	"Cultural Criticism and Society"
DE	*Dialectic of Enlightenment: Philosophical Fragments*, by Theodor Adorno and Max Horkheimer
EF	"The Essay as Form"
H	*Hegel: Three Studies*
HF	*History and Freedom: Lectures, 1964–1965*
MM	*Minima Moralia: Reflections on a Damaged Life*
ND	*Negative Dialectics*
P	"Progress"
PMP	*Problems of Moral Philosophy*

WORKS BY FORST

CJ	*Contexts of Justice: Political Philosophy Beyond Liberalism and Communitarianism*
JC	*Justification and Critique: Towards a Critical Theory of Politics*
JJ	"Justifying Justification: Reply to My Critics"
NP	"Noumenal Power"
RJ	*The Right to Justification: Elements of a Constructivist Theory of Justice*

TC	*Toleration in Conflict: Past and Present*
TP	"Two Pictures of Justice"
ZBF	"Zum Begriff des Fortschritts"

WORKS BY FOUCAULT

ABHS	"About the Beginning of the Hermeneutics of the Self: Two Lectures at Dartmouth"
CT/IH	"Critical Theory/Intellectual History"
ECSPF	"The Ethics of the Concern for Self as a Practice of Freedom"
HM	*History of Madness*
NGH	"Nietzsche, Genealogy, History"
OGE	"On the Genealogy of Ethics"
OWWH	"On the Ways of Writing History"
PPP	"Polemics, Politics, and Problematizations"
PT	*The Politics of Truth*
SKP	"Space, Knowledge, and Power"
SP	"The Subject and Power"
UP	*The Use of Pleasure*
WE	"What Is Enlightenment?"

WORKS BY HABERMAS

BFN	*Between Facts and Norms: Contributions to a Discourse Theory of Law and Democracy*
BNR	*Between Naturalism and Religion: Philosophical Essays*
CD	"Constitutional Democracy: A Paradoxical Union of Contradictory Principles?"
CES	*Communication and the Evolution of Society*
DE	"Discourse Ethics: Notes on a Program of Philosophical Justification"
DW	*The Divided West*
EFK	"Essay on Faith and Knowledge"
IO	*The Inclusion of the Other: Studies in Political Theory*
JA	*Justification and Application: Remarks on Discourse Ethics*

PDM *The Philosophical Discourse of Modernity: Twelve Lectures*
PWS "A Postsecular World Society? On the Philosophical Significance of Postsecular Consciousness and the Multicultural World Society"
R "Reply to My Critics"
RR1 *Religion and Rationality: Essays on Reason, God, and Modernity*
STPS *The Structural Transformation of the Public Sphere: An Inquiry Into a Category of Bourgeois Society.*
TCA1 *The Theory of Communicative Action*, vol. 1, *Reason and the Rationalization of Society*
TCA2 *The Theory of Communicative Action*, vol. 2, *Lifeworld and System: A Critique of Functionalist Reason*
TP *Theory and Practice*

WORKS BY HONNETH

CP *The Critique of Power: Reflective Stages in a Critical Social Theory*
CT "Critical Theory"
FR *Freedom's Right: The Social Foundations of Democratic Life*
IP "The Irreducibility of Progress: Kant's Account of the Relationship Between Morality and History"
NEL "The Normativity of Ethical Life"
PDCS "The Possibility of a Disclosing Critique of Society: The *Dialectic of Enlightenment* in Light of Current Debates in Social Criticism"
R2 "Replies"
RI "Recognition as Ideology"
RR2 *Redistribution or Recognition? A Political-Philosophical Exchange*, by Nancy Fraser and Axel Honneth
RSC "Reconstructive Social Criticism with a Genealogical Proviso: On the Idea of 'Critique' in the Frankfurt School"
SDD "The Social Dynamics of Disrespect: On the Location of Critical Theory Today"

SPR "A Social Pathology of Reason: On the Intellectual Legacy of Critical Theory"

SR *The Struggle for Recognition: The Moral Grammar of Social Conflicts*

THE END OF PROGRESS

1

Critical Theory and the Idea of Progress

In 1993, in his sequel to his groundbreaking and field-defining book *Orientalism*, Edward Said offers the following indictment of Frankfurt School critical theory: "Frankfurt School critical theory, despite its seminal insights into the relationships between domination, modern society, and the opportunities for redemption through art as critique, is stunningly silent on racist theory, anti-imperialist resistance, and oppositional practice in the empire."[1] Moreover, Said argues, this is no mere oversight; rather, it is a motivated silence. Frankfurt School critical theory, like other versions of European theory more generally, espouses what Said calls an invidious and false universalism, a "blithe universalism" that "assume[s] and incorporate[s] the inequality of races, the subordination of inferior cultures, the acquiescence of those who, in Marx's words, cannot represent themselves and therefore must be represented by others."[2] Such "universalism" has, for Said, played a crucial role in connecting (European) culture with (European) imperialism for centuries, for imperialism as a political project cannot sustain itself without the *idea of empire*, and the idea of empire, in turn, is nourished by a philosophical and cultural imaginary that justifies the political subjugation of distant territories and their native populations through claims that such peoples are less advanced, cognitively inferior, and therefore naturally subordinate.

Twenty years after Said made this charge, not enough has changed. Contemporary Frankfurt School critical theory, for the most part, remains all too silent on the problem of imperialism. Neither of the major contemporary theorists most closely associated with the legacy of the Frankfurt School, Jürgen Habermas and Axel Honneth, has made systematic reflection on the paradoxes and challenges produced by the waves of decolonization that characterized the latter half of the twentieth century a central focus of his work in critical theory, nor has either theorist engaged seriously with the by now substantial body of literature in postcolonial theory or studies.[3] In the case of Habermas, this lack of attention is all the more notable, given his increasing engagement in recent years with issues of globalization, cosmopolitanism, and the prospects for various forms of post- and supranational legal and political forms.[4] Moreover, with a few prominent exceptions, critical theorists working in the Frankfurt School tradition have followed Habermas's and Honneth's lead.[5] Although the topics of global justice and human rights have been high on the agenda in recent years in Frankfurt, those topics tend to be pursued in a way that refrains from the kind of wholesale reassessment of the links between moral-political universalism and European imperialism that Said counsels. And even those relatively few calls from within the Frankfurt School camp for the decolonization of critical theory have tended to be met with an expansion of the canon of critical theory, to include such thinkers as Frantz Fanon, Enrique Dussel, Frederick Douglass, and Toni Morrison.[6] As welcome as such an expansion of what counts as critical theory is, and as fruitful and groundbreaking as its results are, this strategy for responding to the silence of mainstream critical theorists on the questions of imperialism and colonialism means that the deep and difficult challenge that our postcolonial predicament poses to the Frankfurt School's distinctive approach to social theorizing has not only not yet been met, it has not even been fully appreciated by its practitioners. This book constitutes an attempt both to articulate and to meet that challenge.

Like Said, I believe that there is a reason for the Frankfurt School's failure to respond adequately to the predicaments of our post- and neocolonial world and that this reason is connected to philosophical commitments that run deep in the work of its contemporary practitioners. The problem, as I see it, arises from the particular role that ideas of historical progress, development, social evolution, and sociocultural learning play in justifying and grounding the normative perspective of critical theorists such as Habermas and Honneth.[7] As I shall argue at length in what follows, Habermas and Honneth both rely on a broadly speaking left-Hegelian strategy for grounding or justifying the normativity of critical theory, in which the claim that our current communicative or recognitional practices represent the outcome of a cumulative and progressive learning process and therefore are deserving of our support and allegiance figures prominently. Thus, they are both deeply wedded to the idea that European, Enlightenment modernity—or at least certain aspects or features thereof, which remain to be spelled out—represents a developmental advance over premodern, nonmodern, or traditional forms of life, and, crucially, this idea plays an important role in grounding the normativity of critical theory for each thinker. In other words, both Habermas and Honneth are committed to the thought that critical theory needs to defend some idea of historical progress in order to ground its distinctive approach to normativity and, thus, in order to be truly critical. But it is precisely this commitment that proves to be the biggest obstacle to the project of decolonizing their approaches to critical theory. For perhaps the major lesson of postcolonial scholarship over the last thirty-five years has been that the developmentalist, progressive reading of history—in which Europe or "the West" is viewed as more enlightened or more developed than Asia, Africa, Latin America, the Middle East, and so on—and the so-called civilizing mission of the West, which served to justify colonialism and imperialism and continues to underwrite the informal imperialism or neocolonialism of the current world economic, legal, and political order, are deeply intertwined.[8] In other words, as James Tully has pithily put the point, the language of progress and development is the language of oppression and domination for two-thirds of the world's people.[9]

Habermas's and Honneth's reliance on a progressive, developmentalist understanding of history as a way of grounding normativity thus raises a deep and difficult challenge for their approach to critical theory: How can their critical theory be truly critical if it remains committed to an imperialist metanarrative, that is, if it has not yet been decolonized? On the flip side, how can it be truly critical if it gives up its distinctive strategy for grounding normativity? If we accept Nancy Fraser's Marx-inspired definition of critical theory as the "self-clarification of the struggles and wishes of the age,"[10] and if we further assume that struggles around decolonization and postcolonial politics are among the most significant struggles and wishes of our age,[11] then the demand for a decolonization of critical theory follows quite straightforwardly from the very definition of critical theory. If it wishes to be truly critical, then contemporary critical theory should frame its research program and its conceptual framework with an eye toward decolonial and anti-imperialist struggles and concerns. However, if, as I have suggested, contemporary Frankfurt School critical theory relies on ideas of historical development, learning, and progress to ground its conception of normativity, then (how) can this project be decolonized without radically rethinking its approach to normativity?[12] In response to this last question, I will argue in what follows that critical theory's approach to grounding normativity must be radically transformed if it is to decolonize itself and thus be truly critical.

As I mentioned, Habermas's and Honneth's emphasis on ideas of progress in the form of notions of sociocultural development and historical learning processes can be understood as part of the general left-Hegelianism or Hegelian-Marxism of the Frankfurt School, though it is worth noting at the outset that this understanding of history sets the second and third generations of the Frankfurt School apart from the first generation, whose leading members were, at least after World War II, much less sanguine about the idea of progress. The catastrophe of Auschwitz, Adorno noted in his lectures on the philosophy of history, "makes all talk of progress towards freedom seem ludicrous" and makes the "affirmative mentality" that engages in such talk look like "the mere assertion of a mind that is incapable of looking horror in the face and that thereby perpetuates it" (HF, 7). Adorno evokes Benjamin's ninth thesis on the philosophy of history, in which progress is famously depicted as the storm that blows in from Paradise and irresistibly propels

the angel of history into the future. With his back to the future, the angel of history faces the past and "sees one single catastrophe which keeps piling wreckage upon wreckage and hurls it in front of his feet."[13] Crucially, however, Adorno and Benjamin do not reject the idea of progress altogether, but rather seek to break it apart and reconceive it dialectically. Specifically, Adorno and Benjamin doubted not that progress in the future is possible or desirable but that any sense could be made of the claim that progress had already happened; indeed, on Adorno's view, progressive readings of history serve as ideological impediments that block progress in the future. Thus, as Max Pensky puts it, glossing Benjamin, "progress's first step is the enraged destruction of the discourse of progress."[14] Or, as Adorno put it in the line that serves as the inspiration for the title of this book, "progress occurs where it ends" (P, 150). What distinguishes Habermas and Honneth from the approach of earlier Frankfurt School thinkers is not their commitment to progress as a future-oriented moral-political goal—a commitment that all of these thinkers share—but rather their commitment to what Pensky calls the discourse of progress as an empirical history. Furthermore, for Habermas and Honneth, these two aspects of progress are deeply intertwined in their critical theory, and it is this intertwining that makes their critical theory so greatly in need of decolonizing.

The overall aims of this book are to critically assess the role played by ideas of development, sociocultural learning processes, and historical progress in grounding and justifying the normativity of critical theory in mainstream Frankfurt School theory, and to develop an alternative framework for thinking about history and the question of normative grounding, one that is more compatible with the urgent project of decolonizing critical theory. In this project, I draw on theoretical resources that can be found in or nearby the Frankfurt School tradition, particularly the work of Adorno and Michel Foucault. This book thus follows in the footsteps of the work of Robert J. C. Young, and could be understood as an attempt to do for Frankfurt School critical social theory what Young's *White Mythologies* did for Marxist literary criticism: namely to expose the extent to which that project is implicated at the theoretical level, by virtue of its commitment to a certain understanding of history, in the very imperialism that it condemns politically.[15] My goal is twofold: to decolonize critical theory by opening it from within to the kind of post- and decolonial theorizing that it needs to take on board if it is to be truly critical and, conversely, to show, through a rethinking of the question of normativity in the Frankfurt School tradition, how post- and decolonial theory might be criticalized, that is, how it might respond to long-standing charges of relativism and questions about the normative status of its critique.[16]

In this chapter, I begin by laying out the major conceptual issues involved in the appeal to ideas of historical learning, development, and progress as a strategy for securing normativity. First, I discuss what precisely is meant—and not meant!—by progress in the context of contemporary critical theory, and consider the main reasons that have been offered in favor of the claim that the idea of progress is indispensable for critical theory. Second, I consider the deeply intertwined epistemological and political critiques of the discourse of progress that have gained prominence in post- and decolonial theory. This discussion aims not only to establish why critical theory needs to decolonize itself, to the extent that it is wedded to a certain version of the discourse of progress, but also to motivate the particular strategy for decolonizing critical theory that I will adopt in this book. Finally, I discuss Thomas McCarthy's recent attempt to respond to such postcolonial and postdevelopment critiques of the discourse of progress, and suggest that the shortcomings of McCarthy's approach provide us with some preliminary indications of the shape that a decolonization of critical theory will have to take. Those indications will be taken up and developed further in subsequent chapters.

PROGRESS AND THE NORMATIVITY OF CRITICAL THEORY

Before exploring the role that is played by the idea of progress in contemporary critical theory, let me first say a few words about what precisely is meant here by the term "progress." In its broadest terms, the idea of historical progress refers not just to progress toward some specific goal but rather to human progress or development overall, *überhaupt*. As Reinhart Koselleck has argued, this notion of historical progress is a distinctively modern concept that emerges in the eighteenth century. Although the Greeks and Romans had terms that could "characterize a relative progression in particular spheres of fact and experience"—*prokopē, epidōsis, progressus, perfectus*—these concepts were, according to Koselleck, always concerned with looking back and were not linked to the idea of a better future.[17] Moreover, and perhaps more important, they were always partial, local; the term "progress" did not, for the Greeks, refer to "an entire social process, as we associate it today with technological practices and industrialization" (PD, 222). The Christian notion of progress, by contrast, referred to a spiritual progress that was to culminate at a point outside of time; Christianity thus opened up the horizon of the future, but the better future that it projected would only be realized after the end of history. As far as history was concerned, for the Middle Ages, as for antiquity, "the world as a whole was aging and rushing toward its end. Spiritual progress and the decline of the world were to this extent correlational concepts that obstructed the interpretation of the earthly future in progressive terms" (PD, 224). The modern notion of progress transformed the "constant expectation of the end of the world into an open future"; spiritual *profectus* became worldly *progressus* (PD, 225).

On Koselleck's analysis, the modern concept of progress, which went hand in hand with a new experience of time, consisted in several features. First, the idea of the future as an infinite horizon denaturalized the idea that the age of the world is analogous to the old age of an individual; this, in turn, led to a break between the age of world and the idea of decay or decline: "Infinite progress opened up a future that shirked the natural metaphors of aging. Although the world as nature may age in the course of time, this no longer involves the decline of all of humanity" (PD, 226). In modernity, decline was no longer seen as the pure opposite of progress; "rather progress has become a world historical category whose tendency is to interpret all regressions as temporary and finally even as the stimulus for new progress" (PD, 227). Second, in the modern concept of progress, the striving for perfection that had also characterized Christian thinking about progress became temporalized, located in human history. As a result, progress became an ongoing, never-ending, dynamic process, an infinite task (PD, 227–228). Finally, this modern concept of progress referred to both technical-scientific and moral-political progress, that is, to progress *überhaupt*. Here is Koselleck again: "Progress (der Fortschritt), a term first put forth by Kant, was now a word that neatly and deftly brought the manifold of scientific, technological, and industrial meanings of progress, and finally also those meanings involving social morality and even the totality of history, under a common concept" (PD, 229).

This modern concept of progress found its clearest expression in the classical philosophies of history of Kant, Hegel, and even Marx. There, historical progress was understood in the strongest possible terms, as a necessary, inevitable, and unified process. Whether operating through the mechanism of a purposive nature, which uses evil to produce good, or of the cunning of reason, which behind men's backs and over their heads rationalizes existing reality, or of the development of the forces and relations of production, which sows the seeds for communist revolution, these classical philosophies of history understood progress to be necessary (though they had somewhat different views on how much of a role individuals should or could play in bringing about that necessary development) and unified (as occurring more or less simultaneously across society as a whole). Moreover, these classical philosophies of history rested on metaphysically loaded conceptions of the goal or telos toward which progress aimed, whether that was understood as the realization of the kingdom of ends on earth, the attainment of the standpoint of Absolute knowing, or communist utopia.

To be clear: none of the current defenders of the idea of progress in the Frankfurt School critical theory tradition makes such strong claims. Thus, I want to emphasize at the outset that I am not claiming that either Habermas or Honneth holds on to a traditional philosophy of history or to the strong notion of historical progress that comes along with it. Already the failure of the proletariat to rise up and overthrow the bourgeoisie in Europe and the United States in the early twentieth century caused trouble for the Marxist version of the classical philosophy of history, while the regressive barbarism and moral-political catastrophes of the Holocaust and the Gulag further undermined strong Hegelian and Kantian theodicies of history. For contemporary critical theory, progress is accordingly understood in contingent rather than necessary, disaggregated rather than total, and postmetaphysical rather than metaphysical terms. To say that progress is contingent is to say that whether or not any particular culture or society will in fact progress is a matter of contingent historical circumstances, and that regressions are always also possible. To say that it is disaggregated is to say that progress in one domain—say, the economic or technological-scientific sphere—can occur simultaneously with regress in another—say, the cultural or political sphere. To say that progress is understood in postmetaphysical terms is to say that the conception of the end toward which progress aims is understood in a deflationary, fallibilistic, and de-transcendentalized way, as a hypothesis about some fundamental features of human sociocultural life—the role that mutual understanding plays in language, or that mutual recognition plays in the formation of identity—that stands in need of empirical confirmation.

And yet, I do want to argue that a certain vestigial remnant of the traditional philosophy of history remains in contemporary Frankfurt School critical theory and that it takes the form of the notions of sociocultural development, historical learning, and moral-political progress that inform Habermas's and Honneth's conceptions of modernity. In other words, Habermas and Honneth are committed to a common core understanding of social progress, such that if a society can be said to have progressed then this will be because that society has followed a certain developmental, unidirectional, and cumulative moral-political learning process. To be sure, as Habermas emphasizes, this notion of progress does not entail any simple-minded judgment about "the superiority for the actual moral behavior or the ethical forms of life of later generations" (R, 360). The crucial point, for Habermas, is the moral-cognitive one that "there is progress in the de-centering of our perspectives when it comes to viewing the world as a whole, or to making considered judgments on issues of justice" and that this type of progress, epitomized in the Enlightenment, has "become so natural for later generations" that it is "assumed to be irreversible"

(R, 360). Habermas goes further than Honneth in that he also defends a notion of technical-scientific progress, though, in line with the nontraditional philosophy of history sketched above, he sees this as wholly distinct and disaggregated from moral-political progress. Indeed, he follows Max Weber in understanding the very separation and disaggregation of moral-political discourses and institutions from technical-scientific ones as a hallmark of modernity and thus as itself the indication of a kind of progress or sociocultural learning. On this view, the ability to separate truth validity from normative validity claims is one of the hallmarks of the postconventional autonomy that becomes possible in posttraditional societies; thus, it is one of the key features distinguishing modernity from myth (see TCA1).

Insofar as the primary aim of this book is to analyze the relationship between ideas of historical progress and the problem of normativity and the impediment that this relationship poses for the project of decolonizing critical theory, my main focus throughout will be on the idea of normative or moral-political progress. Accordingly I will attempt to leave questions about technical-scientific progress aside. In defense of this move, I can only say that the issues that I am grappling with in this book are difficult enough without my having to take on board the complex debates about progress or the lack thereof in science, for which I lack the requisite expertise in the history and philosophy of science in any case. To be sure, there is an irony here, inasmuch as by accepting the separation of moral-political questions from technical-scientific ones, I could be seen as tacitly endorsing Habermas's conception of modernity at the same time as I am criticizing it.[18] If pressed, I would admit that it seems to me that there are good reasons to doubt Habermas's Weberian story. Think, for example, of Bruno Latour's argument that we have never really been modern in the sense that we have never really accomplished the purification of the realms of truth and normative validity that are taken on this view to be the hallmark of modernity.[19] We have never been modern, Latour argues, because so-called modernity is chock full of the very nature-culture, fact-value, part object-part subject hybrids that modernizers such as Habermas see—and judge as inferior—in the worldviews of so-called primitive cultures.[20] Moreover, as this example suggests and as Latour also argues, it also seems plausible to say that the separation of science, technology, and nature from politics, society, and culture goes hand in hand with the radical separation of "Us" (the moderns) from "Them" (the premoderns) that undergirds imperialism. As Latour puts it:

> The Internal Great Divide [that is, the divide between Nature and Society] accounts for the External Great Divide [that is, the divide between modern and premodern societies or cultures]: we are the only ones who differentiate absolutely between Nature and Culture, between Science and Society, whereas in our eyes all the others—whether they are Chinese or Amerindian, Azande or Barouya—cannot really separate what is knowledge from what is Society, what is sign from what is thing, what comes from Nature as it is from what their cultures require. . . . The internal partition between humans and nonhumans defines a second partition—an external one this time—through which the moderns have set themselves apart from the premoderns.[21]

With Latour's argument in mind, my restricted focus on questions of normative or moral-political rather than scientific progress or learning should be understood as a provisional bracketing rather than a hard and fast separation. The hope is that this bracketing will allow me to bring greater focus and clarity to a particular strand of the broader complex of debates about progress, a strand that has important implications for the vexing question of the normativity of critical theory and its prospects for decolonization. The question of the validity of Habermas's Weberian construal of the superiority of modernity over myth will be broached, if a bit obliquely, in chapter 2.

Turning now to the idea of moral-political progress, there are actually two distinct yet closely interrelated conceptions of normative progress at work in contemporary critical theory. These two conceptions are related, in turn, to two distinct arguments that are offered for the claim that critical theory needs some idea of progress in order to be truly critical. The first conception is forward-looking, oriented toward the future. From this perspective, progress is a moral-political imperative, a normative goal that we are striving to achieve, a goal that can be captured under the idea of the good or at least of the more just society. The second conception is backward-looking, oriented toward the past. From this perspective, progress is a judgment about the developmental or learning process that has led up to "us," a judgment that views "our" conception of reason, "our" moral-political institutions, "our" social practices, "our" form of life as the result of a process of sociocultural development or historical learning. I will call the forward-looking conception of progress "progress as an imperative" and the backward-looking one "progress as a 'fact.'"

As I said, these two different conceptions of progress correspond to two different arguments for the claim that critical theory needs the idea of progress in order to be genuinely critical. The first argument is that we need the idea of progress toward some future goal in order to give us something to strive for politically, in order to make our politics genuinely progressive. Thomas McCarthy expresses this point eloquently when he writes:

> There is no doubt that the historical record warrants the melancholy that Walter Benjamin experienced in contemplating it; nor is there any denying the disappointment of hopes for progress by the events of the twentieth century. But though these must remain central to our "postmodern" sensibility, a politics premised solely on melancholy or disappointment—or on some other form of historical pessimism, that is, on the abandonment of hope for a significantly better future—would not be a progressive politics.[22]

Progress understood in this sense is a moral-political imperative to strive to improve the human condition, and is connected to Kant's famous third question, what may I hope for? For a theory to be critical, it must be connected to the hope for some significantly better—more just, or at least less oppressive—society. Such hopes serve to orient our political strivings, and in order to count as genuine hopes, they must be grounded in a belief or a hope in the possibility of progress. The second reason that critical theory is thought to need an idea of historical progress relates to the backward-looking conception of progress as a historical "fact." "Fact" is in scare quotes here because this is not merely an empirical judgment but necessarily also a normative one.[23] To say that progress is a "fact" is typically to say that the normative ideals, conception of practical rationality, and social and political institutions that have emerged in European modernity—in particular, in the Enlightenment—are the result of a cumulative and progressive developmental or historical learning process.

A central argument of this book is that this backward looking conception of progress as a "fact" plays a crucial, if often unacknowledged, role in grounding the normativity of critical theory for both Habermas and Honneth. This follows more or less directly from the combination of two commitments: first, the desire to avoid the twin evils of foundationalism and relativism;[24] and, second, the idea that the normative perspective of critical theory must be grounded immanently, in the actual social world.[25] The desire to avoid foundationalism grows out of the resolutely postmetaphysical stance of contemporary critical theory; as Habermas puts it, critical theory must make clear "that the purism of pure reason is not resurrected again in communicative reason" (PDM, 301).[26] The attempt to avoid foundationalism gives rise to the resolution to ground the normative perspective of critical theory immanently, within the existing social world. But this commitment, in turn, inevitably raises worries about conventionalism and relativism. If our normative perspective is grounded within the social world, then how can critical theory avoid the charge of reducing normativity to an endorsement of whatever normative standards happen to be accepted at a given time and place? In other words, how can we justify the normative standards that critical theory finds in existing social reality without recourse to foundationalist premises? Habermas's and Honneth's broadly speaking Hegelian strategy constitutes an attempt to answer such questions while avoiding the twin pitfalls of foundationalism and relativism.[27] The basic idea is that the normative principles that we find within our social world—as inheritors of the project of European Enlightenment or the legacy of European modernity, which has a certain conception of rational autonomy

(Habermas) or social freedom (Honneth) at its core—are themselves justified insofar as they can be understood as the outcome of a process of progressive social evolution or sociocultural learning. The move to ground normative principles within the social world allows critical theory to avoid the charge of foundationalism, and yet, in order to avoid collapsing into relativism, critical theory relies on the backward-looking conception of historical progress as a "fact." This conception of progress enables critical theory to understand the normative standards that it finds within the existing social world—that is, within its own world, the world of modern Europe—not merely as contingent or arbitrary framework-relative standards, but rather as the results of a process of social development and historical learning.[28]

But if critical theory's immanent grounding of normative principles within the social world ultimately rests on a claim about sociocultural learning processes, then this means that the normative standards that enable us to envision a good or more just society—the discourse principle, for example, or the idea of social freedom—are themselves justified inasmuch as they are the outcome of a progressive process of sociocultural development or learning. In other words, the two conceptions of progress delineated above are intertwined in that progress as a moral-political imperative is, for Habermas and Honneth, grounded in the basic normative orientation that is undergirded by the conception of progress as a historical "fact"—at least, this is my central interpretive claim vis-à-vis Habermas and Honneth, a claim that will be developed and defended in subsequent chapters.[29] The normative perspective that serves to orient the forward-looking conception of progress is justified by the backward-looking story about how "our" modern, European, Enlightenment moral vocabulary and political ideals are the outcome of a learning process and therefore neither merely conventional nor grounded in some a priori, transcendental conception of pure reason. This normative orientation, in turn, provides us with a conception of the "good" or "more just" society that provides the basis for our moral-political strivings.

This suggests that, at least as the idea of progress is used in Habermas's and Honneth's work, these two conceptions of progress—the forward-looking notion of progress as a moral-political imperative and the backward-looking idea of progress as a "fact" about the processes of historical learning and sociocultural evolution that have led up to "us"—cannot easily be pulled apart. In other words, it isn't possible for this version of critical theory to hold on to progress as a moral-political imperative without believing in progress as a "fact" so long as the normativity of critical theory is being secured through this progressive story of sociocultural development or historical learning. This means that contemporary critical theory as Habermas and Honneth conceive it could only be disentangled from its commitment to progress by also rethinking its understanding of normativity. As I will argue in the next section, it is Habermas's and Honneth's commitment to the backward-looking story about progress as a "fact" that makes their approach to critical theory stand in need of decolonizing and also proves to be the most serious obstacle to such decolonization.

To be sure, it is conceptually possible to retain the idea of progress as a moral-political imperative without rooting that conception of progress in a developmental-historical story about progress as a "fact." For example, the Kantian-constructivist strategy for grounding the normativity of critical theory advanced recently by Rainer Forst articulates a universal moral-political standard—the basic right to justification—that is grounded not in a backward-looking story about historical progress but rather in what Forst characterizes as a freestanding account of practical reason. Forst further argues that progress is a normatively dependent concept in the sense that it is dependent on this universal normative standard, which in turn provides a clear benchmark for measuring claims about historical progress. This alternative way of understanding the relationship between normativity and claims about historical progress avoids the worries about conventionalism and the reliance on the notion of progress as a "fact" that plague Habermas's and Honneth's account. However, as I will discuss further in chapter 4, Forst's strongly universalist conception of morality and his "freestanding" account of practical reason remain vulnerable to postcolonial critique, in particular, to worries that his allegedly freestanding, universal conception of practical reason is really a thick, particular, and Eurocentric notion in disguise. Moreover, in seeking to avoid conventionalism and relativism, Forst's neo-Kantian approach ends up in foundationalism. This leads him to adopt a kind of political philosophy as applied ethics approach that sacrifices the methodological distinctiveness of critical theory. As a result, critical theorists who aim to disentangle progress as a moral-political imperative from progress as a "fact" will need to find other ways to accomplish this goal. In the end, I shall argue that the best way forward for critical theory with respect to this problem will be for it to go back, that is, to recover the insights of one of the most prominent members of the first generation of the Frankfurt School—Theodor Adorno—and of the philosopher who I will call his other "other son"—Michel Foucault.

THE COLONIALITY OF POWER: THE POLITICAL-EPISTEMOLOGICAL CRITIQUE OF PROGRESS AS A "FACT"

But why think that critical theory needs to disentangle its hope for progress as a moral-political imperative from the idea of progress as a historical "fact"? What, after all, is wrong with this idea of progress as a "fact"? In this section, I further flesh out two specific lines of criticism of the idea of progress as a historical "fact," both of which were alluded to above, and both of which are raised in pressing forms in post- and decolonial theory.[30]

The first problem is primarily political, and it concerns the entwinement of the idea of historical progress with the legacies of racism, colonialism, and imperialism and their contemporary neocolonial or informally imperialist forms.[31] In his recent work, Thomas McCarthy traces this dilemma back to Kant, where it is evident in the form of a deep tension between Kant's moral-political universalism—according to which every human being is a self-legislating member of the kingdom of ends who has an infinite worth and dignity—and his practical-anthropological particularism—according to which Africans, Native Americans, and Asians are less advanced than white Europeans and thus less capable of autonomous self-rule.[32] In light of this tension, McCarthy notes that historical progress for Kant in the sense of "cultivation, civilization, and moralization is and will continue to be a process of diffusion from the West to the rest of the world" and progress for non-European cultures is understood in terms of gradual assimilation to European culture.[33] In what McCarthy calls the "convergence model of progress,"[34] there is thus an implicit—even if not explicitly articulated—rationale offered for the so-called civilizing mission of the West, a key ideological justification for the colonial and imperial projects.[35] Kant's account of progress and development thus serves, according to McCarthy, as a solution to the problem of how to reconcile his liberal universalism with his liberal imperialism. By taking the European path of development as normative, and viewing non-European cultures and peoples as less developed or as non- or premodern, progressive or developmental theories of history serve as an ideological rationalization and justification for ongoing racism, neoracism, colonialism, and neoimperialism.

The progressive reading of history that views European modernity as developmentally more advanced than premodern cultures or societies also relies on a highly selective reading of Europe's own history, a reading that ignores the extent to which the distinctively European form of modernity that Kant and other Enlightenment thinkers valued so highly was a product not of Europe alone but of Europe's interaction with the non-West. This is true first and foremost in a material sense—that is, in the sense that the rise of capitalism in Europe was made possible by the extraction of natural resources from its colonies and the exploitation of colonized subjects.[36] As Fanon famously and succinctly put this point: "Europe is literally the creation of the Third World. The riches which are choking it are those plundered from the underdeveloped peoples."[37] Anibal Quijano echoes Fanon, referencing the earlier wave of colonialism in the Americas that began in the sixteenth century: "The constitution of Europe as a new historic entity/identity was made possible, in the first place, through the free labor of the American Indians, blacks, and mestizos, with their advanced technology in mining and agriculture, and with their products such as gold, silver, potatoes, tomatoes, and tobacco."[38] But Europe was not only materially dependent on its colonies; it was also ideologically dependent in the sense that Europe's very identity as a distinct culture was formed in response to those it perceived as its geographical, cultural, and historical others, and by the anxieties and dislocations generated by its interactions with the colonies.[39] This was one of the central arguments of Said's *Orientalism*, as he explained in his introduction to that text: "Orientalism is never far from . . . the idea of Europe, a collective notion identifying 'us' Europeans as against all 'those' non-Europeans, and indeed it can be argued that the major component in European culture is precisely what made that culture hegemonic both in and outside Europe: the idea of European identity as a superior one in comparison with all the non-European peoples and cultures."[40]

Moreover, as Susan Buck-Morss's recent work shows, the material and ideological aspects of Europe's dependence on its colonies were deeply intertwined. Even the much vaunted idea of freedom, taken by Enlightenment thinkers and contemporary critical theorists such as Habermas and Honneth alike to be the highest political value,

> began to take root at precisely the time that the economic practice of slavery—the systematic, highly sophisticated capitalist enslavement of non-Europeans as a labor force in the colonies—was increasing quantitatively and intensifying qualitatively to the point that by the mid-eighteenth century it came to underwrite the entire economic system of the West, paradoxically facilitating the global spread of the very Enlightenment ideals that were in such fundamental contradiction to it.[41]

Hence the political problem with the reading of European modernity as the outcome of a progressive historical development is not only the way in which it positions the pre- or nonmodern as less developed and therefore serves to rationalize and justify imperialism in its formal and informal, colonial and neocolonial guises; it also overlooks or obscures the extent to which the very material preconditions for and ideas of Europe and of European modernity are themselves colonized and racialized.[42]

So, to sum up the political problem: the backward-looking conception of progress as a "fact," insofar as it sees the norms or institutions of European modernity as the outcome of a developmental or learning process, and insofar as it overlooks the role that Europe's material and ideological relation to its colonies played in shaping European modernity as a racialized construct, has served and continues to serve the ideological function of rationalizing and legitimizing contemporary forms of informal imperialism, neocolonialism, and racism. In other words, the notion of historical progress as a "fact" is bound up with complex relations of domination, exclusion, and silencing of colonized and racialized subjects.

The second problem with the notion of historical progress as a "fact" is an epistemological one, and it turns on the following questions: On what basis do we claim to know what counts as progress? Does a judgment about historical progress not presume knowledge of what counts as the end point or goal of that historical development? And how could this be known without having access to some God's-eye point of view or point of view of the Absolute, ideas that go against the basic methodological assumptions of critical theory, in particular its desire to avoid foundationalism? But if we aren't willing to posit such a God's-eye point of view or to consider the standards by which we measure progress to be known sub specie aeternitatis, then we are left with the idea that we have to make judgments about what counts as progress from our own, internal, reconstructive point of view. And in that case, we must confront the worry that, insofar as judgments about progress rely on our own current beliefs and principles, they may appear, as Charles Larmore has put it, "irredeemably parochial." "Is not the notion of progress," Larmore asks, "basically an instrument of self-congratulation?"[43]

Although this epistemological worry can be framed, as Larmore does, in broad, conceptual terms, it has also been raised in a particularly trenchant way in post- and decolonial theory. The argument here concerns the original formulation and justification of the stadial or developmental-stages reading of history. In the modern period, this reading of history was developed by thinkers of the Scottish Enlightenment such as Adam Smith; later it found its way into German philosophy through Hegel and Marx, both careful readers of Smith; and through Émile Durkheim and Max Weber, both trained in the Hegelian and Marxist philosophical tradition, it made its way into the founding assumptions of sociology as a discipline. As Gurminder Bhambra has argued in her book *Rethinking Modernity*, this stadial reading of history understood society to develop through a series of progressively advancing stages based on different modes of economic organization. Colonial encounters—for example, the conquest of Native Americans in the Americas—were, Bhambra argues, "fundamental to the emergence of the idea of historical stages of development."[44] British and European thinkers of the eighteenth century formulated the stadial reading of history and its attendant notions of historical progress and sociocultural development as a way of understanding the information that was coming back to them from the colonies in the New World. They made sense of this information by hypothesizing that, as Locke put it, "in the beginning all the World was America," and then postulating a series of stages through which humanity must have passed in order to get from there to the civilized commercial society of eighteenth-century Europe.[45] The problem with this move is that, as Bhambra explains, "the chronological (and evaluative) relationship established between different types of culture emerged out of a hierarchical ranking of contemporary cultures that had no evidential foundation."[46] In other words, at its core this developmental reading of history was based on what I would call a kind of normative decisionism by means of which Native Americans were *first* judged to be inferior to—more primitive, less civilized, less developed—Europeans and then, in a second step, that inferiority was explained by means of a developmental or stadial theory of history.

As Quijano further argues, this inferiority was naturalized through the creation of invidious racial classifications that served to legitimate the relations of domination that were imposed through the colonial conquest. Quijano maintains that it is not unusual for colonial dominators to feel superior to those they dominate and to appeal to their feelings of superiority to justify their domination, but for European colonizers that feeling of superiority took a unique form, namely, "the racial classification of the world population after the colonization of America. The association of colonial ethnocentrism and universal racial classification helps to explain why Europeans came to feel not only superior to all other peoples of the world, but, in particular, naturally superior."[47] In other words, for Quijano, colonial domination came first, and then this domination was justified by means of a claim about the inferiority of the colonized, an inferiority that was then naturalized through the construction of racial classifications. Like Bhambra, Quijano also connects this process to the emergence of developmental or progressive theories of history: "The Europeans generated a new temporal perspective of history and relocated the colonized population, along with their respective histories and cultures, in the past of a historical trajectory whose culmination was Europe."[48] The colonized were not only deemed inferior, and naturally so because racially so; they were also relegated to a primitive or archaic past.[49] As Quijano sums up the idea of progress, which he characterizes as one of the foundational myths of Eurocentrism:

> All non-Europeans could be considered as pre-European and at the same time displaced on a certain historical chain from the primitive to the civilized, from the rational to the irrational, from the traditional to the modern, from the magic-mythic to the scientific. In other words, from the non-European/pre-European to something that in time will be Europeanized or modernized. Without considering the whole experience of colonialism and coloniality, this intellectual trademark, as well as the long-lasting global hegemony of Eurocentrism, would hardly be explicable.[50]

Moreover, Bhambra argues that this normative decisionism has been obscured by subsequent work in sociology, which has for the most part taken this developmental story of modernization as its starting point. Hence, Bhambra notes, "*the evidential basis for the idea of historical stages remains weak just because the idea becomes embedded in the conceptual frameworks of social science.*"[51] Thus a good deal of work in sociology, especially sociological theories of modernization, tends to "confirm" this developmental reading of history precisely because that reading also frames the basic assumptions of its research program.[52] Bhambra's argument raises a deep challenge for Habermas's work in particular. As McCarthy notes, the Habermasian view of history is an heir to Kantian and Hegelian philosophies of history but, unlike those projects, it is empirically based, practically oriented, and postmetaphysical.[53] Habermas's approach to progress is not a traditional philosophy of history but rather a reconstructive science that seeks to uncover deep sociohistorical structures that condition historical change; as a reconstructive science, it is open and fallible and dependent upon empirical confirmation from the social sciences.[54] But herein lies the rub. Insofar as ideas of historical progress and modernity are foundational for certain sociological research programs, the "openness" of a theory of sociocultural learning to empirical (dis)confirmation by empirical work in sociology seems to be not nearly open enough. Rather, the argument threatens to be self-sealing.

The epistemological problem, then, goes to the heart of critical theory's attempt to offer an immanent, reconstructive form of critique that nevertheless relies on ideas of progress, development, and historical learning processes to offer a nonfoundationalist account of normativity that avoids collapsing into conventionalism or relativism. If judgments about historical progress are not to appeal implicitly to a suprahistorical point of view—the purity of pure reason or the point of view of Absolute knowing—then they remain judgments of progress *for us*, made in accordance with our standards or by our lights. In this case they must confront the worry that they are nothing more than self-congratulatory defenses of the status quo. The post- or decolonial version of this criticism raises the particular worry that the very idea of progress or of a developmental reading of history is grounded in a normative decisionism by means of which European Enlightenment theorists congratulated themselves on being more civilized, developed, and advanced than Native Americans and other colonized subjects, and then embedded this self-congratulatory assumption into the sociological theories of modernization to which contemporary critical theorists, in turn, appeal to support their claims about progress.

These two sorts of objections to the idea of historical progress as a "fact," the political and the epistemological, are, as the reader may have already guessed, closely related to each other.[55] Quijano brings them together under the concept of "the coloniality of power." For Quijano, European colonialism as a form of political domination and economic exploitation goes hand in hand with Eurocentrism, which he defines as "a specific rationality or perspective of knowledge that was made globally hegemonic, colonizing and overcoming other previous or different conceptual formations and their respective concrete knowledges, as much in Europe as in the rest of the world."[56] A similar recognition of this deep intertwining of colonial power relations and forms of knowledge production leads Chakrabarty to ask: "Can the designation of something or some group as *non-* or *premodern* ever be anything but a gesture of the powerful?"[57]

The intertwining of the political and epistemological dimensions of colonialism, captured in Chakrabarty's question and Quijano's notion of the coloniality of power, helps to motivate the particular strategy for decolonizing critical theory that I will follow in this book. After all, one might argue, following Terry Eagleton, that it is far from obvious that taking on board the insights of "postcolonialism"—understood as a particular theoretical project, prominent in Europe and the United States, heavily influenced by French poststructuralism—is the best way to think through the challenges and injustices of postcolonialism—understood as the current social, economic, and political situation of formally decolonized states, which are still subjected to gross forms of global injustice, largely through the workings of the international financial system.[58] "Postcolonialism," according to this view, is simply a fashionable offshoot of postmodernism, and it suffers from the same excessive culturalism that plagues its forerunner. If one wants to think through the challenges of our current post- as well as neocolonial or informally imperialist age, a proponent of this view might ask, why not turn to Marxism, which after all offers ample resources for connecting the critique of capitalism to the critique of imperialism, even if Marx himself never quite connected all of those dots?[59] On this view, the retreat to the cultural that characterizes "postcolonialism" is not only insufficient for theorizing the complexities of postcolonialism; it is also best understood as one more indication of the "postsocialist" condition that coincided with its rise to prominence in the 1980s and 1990s[60]—a stance that we can ill afford to take in the wake of the financial crisis, now that the critique of capitalism is as important as ever.

This "postcolonialism" versus Marxism argument is long running—though it has flared up again very recently in a spectacular debate between Vivek Chibber and Partha Chatterjee that has been viewed over eighteen thousand times on Youtube[61]—and it could be understood as an offshoot of earlier debates about postmodernism or poststructuralism versus Marxism. It is a strange opposition, however, especially because Marxism has been very influential for much work in postcolonial theory, not only in the Subaltern Studies group but also in Latin American post- and decolonial theory, which draws frequently and heavily on the work of world systems theorists like Immanuel Wallerstein and Samir Amin. It is also strange because, as Robert Young has argued very convincingly, French poststructuralism was itself heavily influenced by Marxism—not, to be sure, by the Hegelian Marxism that was so influential for the Frankfurt School, but rather by the structuralist Marxism of Althusser and the Third World, anti-imperialist Marxism of Mao.[62] Mapping the "postcolonialism" versus Marxism split onto a split internal to twentieth-century Marxism enables us to understand why an engagement with postcolonial theory ("postcolonialism") is in fact the best way to address the challenges posed to critical theory by our postcolonial condition (postcolonialism). For the simple truth is that there is a perfectly good reason that postcolonial theorists have by and large found poststructuralism more useful than contemporary Marxist theory, and the reason is that, as Young argues, unlike poststructuralism, Western Marxism never addressed the challenge that colonialism posed to "its own political thinking *at a theoretical or philosophical level*."[63] Marxism, particularly its Hegelian variants, remains committed to the kind of developmental or progressive reading of history—historicism or History with a capital *H*, for short—that is the central target of post- and decolonial critique. As Young puts this point: "Marxism, insofar as it inherits the system of the Hegelian dialectic, is also implicated in the link between the structures of knowledge and the forms of oppression of the last two hundred years: a phenomenon that has become known as Eurocentrism."[64] Young draws the conclusion that addressing the challenge posed by what Quijano calls the coloniality of power thus requires a radical rethinking of History. I would add that if my argument about the link between ideas of historical progress and normativity in contemporary critical theory is plausible, then it further requires rethinking the strategy for grounding normativity. For this project, I will argue that the work of Adorno and Foucault, read alongside each other, proves particularly fruitful.[65] This is *not* to say that none of Marx's insights is fruitful, nor is it to say that the critique of capitalism is not important for contemporary critical theory; many of them are and of course it is. It is just to say that *for the specific project of rethinking the relationship between history and normativity that is necessary if critical theory is to be decolonized*, we are better off turning to Adorno and Foucault than to Marx.

PROBLEMATIZING PROGRESS

As we have seen, the primary target of post- and decolonial criticism is the backward-looking conception of progress as a "fact," for it is this assumption that is deeply intertwined with problematic claims about the superiority of European modernity. But notice that if, as I argued above, for certain versions of critical theory, the forward-looking conception of progress as an imperative depends on the backward-looking claim about progress as a "fact," then the critique of progress outlined above threatens to expose the normative perspective of critical theory as Eurocentric at best and, at worst, as obscuring the racialized aspects of European modernity and thereby reinforcing them.[66] How can critical theorists best respond to these charges of the ideological nature of the idea of progress as a historical "fact"? If we admit, as it seems we must, that such ideas of progress and development have served ideological uses in the past and may well continue to do so, does that mean that they are *merely* ideological and thus should be rejected?

In his recent work, Thomas McCarthy grapples with these questions. McCarthy argues that, like all Enlightenment ideals, the idea of historical development is "inherently ambivalent in character, both indispensable and dangerous," and that it can and must be subjected to an "ongoing deconstruction and reconstruction."[67] While I find much to admire in McCarthy's subtle analysis of the ambivalences and complexities of the ideas of progress and development, I want to raise some questions at the outset about whether and in what sense the ideas of historical progress and development—including the conceptions of progress as an imperative and of development as a "fact," both of which McCarthy defends—could be considered indispensable for critical theory.[68] One of the major aims of this book is to show that critical theorists can and should get by with a much more limited forward-looking notion of moral-political progress as an imperative, one that has been disentangled from the deeply problematic notion of progress as a "fact" and that rests on a thoroughly contextualist conception of normativity. Indeed, I shall argue that only by problematizing the idea of progress as a historical "fact" can critical theorists decolonize critical theory and thereby make possible moral-political progress in the future. This is how I propose to take up Adorno's suggestion that progress occurs where it comes to an end.

By contrast, McCarthy, while acknowledging the political objection to the idea of progress outlined above, and while admitting that a critical theory of development and progress "has to remain aware of the horrors historically perpetuated in the name of human development," nevertheless concludes that we can not "deny the evident advance of human learning in numerous domains and the enhancement of our capacity to cope with a variety of problems" (RED, 233). Moreover, in stark contrast to Latour's claim that we have never been modern, McCarthy maintains that we are all moderns now—in the sense that, culturally speaking, posttraditional forms of hyperreflexivity are "practically unavoidable presuppositions of contemporary discourse" (RED, 156) and that, socially speaking, certain modern institutions, such as capitalist markets and systems of positive law, are functionally unavoidable (RED, 158). On this view, no one faces the choice of whether or not to modernize; the choice that we face now is which forms and features of modernity to develop further. The range of possible "alternative" or "multiple" modernities is constrained in advance by these cultural and social "facts" of global modernity: the functional unavoidability of capitalism and positive law and the practical unavoidability of the presuppositions of contemporary discourse. This means that "a global discourse of modernity carried on at a critical-reflective level simultaneously opens up *an inexhaustible, ever-shifting horizon of possibilities for reasonable disagreement*" (RED, 160) over "what is progressive and what is regressive in capitalist modernization" (RED, 162). If all participants in such a debate are to be treated equally, then any and all cognitive and evaluative claims about culture and society will have to be essentially contestable. In particular, any and all claims to specify the end point of development or of history will be subject to ongoing contestation and critique for, as McCarthy puts it, "it certainly makes good sense to doubt that modernity as it has developed in the West and through its relations with the rest of the world is a perfect ending to the story of human development" (RED, 165).

McCarthy's response to the political objection also suggests a potential response to the epistemological one, for responding effectively to this problem requires us to understand the normative status of the resources handed down by our tradition in a more modest and contextualist way than, for example, Habermas tends to do, with his stronger notion of context-transcendence. As McCarthy is fond of insisting, we have to start from where we are (where else could we start?) and this means, at least, that we have to draw on our existing normative standards (what other standards could we use?). For those of us situated in the context of late modernity, those resources include Enlightenment notions of freedom, autonomy, reflexivity, inclusiveness, and equality. Of course, once we acknowledge, as we must, that traditions or forms of life are not closed but instead open and interconnected, then we don't have to think of ourselves as limited to these particular resources, nor are we permitted to think of them as uniquely "ours," as if no one else can make use of them. As McCarthy puts it,

> learning how best to be modern in a world in which "we are now all moderns" will require going beyond Eurocentric modernity by

> going forward, that is, by superseding it both in theory and in practice. While universalism certainly does not become superfluous in such a setting, it entails intercultural discussion and negotiation of the universals we have to bring into play in shaping our common human lives, ongoing contestation of their meaning in practice.
>
> (RED, 165)

By offering responses to the political and epistemological challenges posed by postcolonial theory to critical theory's reliance on ideas of historical progress and development, McCarthy's work suggests a possible path for decolonizing critical theory. And yet, I want to argue that his work does not go far enough, since new versions of the political and epistemological challenges to the idea of progress as a "fact" can be posed even to McCarthy's much more modest and chastened formulation of it. For even if McCarthy defends the idea of progress as a "fact" in a more chastened way, acknowledging the ideological misuses of the concept, and in a more contextualist form, acknowledging the essential contestedness of any and all claims about what counts as progress or development, he nonetheless preserves certain problematic elements of this idea. This is evident, for example, in his formulation of the "fact" of cultural modernity, according to which there is no viable alternative to the hyperreflexivity of modern forms of discourse. "One can argue against these basic features of posttraditional culture [such as hyperreflexivity]," McCarthy writes, "only by drawing upon them; and this is a good indication that they are practically unavoidable presuppositions of contemporary discourse" (RED, 156). Similarly, he contends that "we are constrained, on pain of incoherence, to regard any worldview which remains largely untouched by the second, historicist enlightenment—that is, which does not reflectively comprehend itself as one possible interpretation of the world among many others—as deficient in that respect, as not evincing adequate awareness of something that we know to be the case" (RED, 156). In other words, critics of modernity have no choice but to tacitly acknowledge the superiority of posttraditional forms of discourse even in the process of trying to call them into question, and "we" have no choice but to judge traditional forms of life to be inadequate and inferior to ours insofar as they do not regard themselves as simply one point of view among others. As Tully argues and as I will discus further with respect to Habermas in chapter 2, the problem with this kind of "neo-Kantian imperialism" is that it "cannot approach another people's way of life as an alternative horizon, thereby throwing their own into question and experiencing human finitude and plurality, the beginning of insight and cross-cultural understanding."[69]

To be sure, McCarthy acknowledges that macrolevel narratives of historical development and progress are never value-neutral and are always told from a particular point of view; hence any and all claims to their value-neutrality should be met with suspicion. Because that point of view has up to now primarily been a Western one, it is no surprise that most stories of historical development and progress have turned out, upon further reflection, to be Eurocentric. The antidote for such Eurocentrism is, McCarthy argues, "not merely gathering more data but further opening the discourse of modernity to non-Western voices" (RED, 225). And in fact, McCarthy continues, this process is already underway, with the emergence of postcolonial voices in the global discourse of modernity, and the decentering effects of such an opening are starting to make themselves felt. However, on the other hand, McCarthy insists, contra some postcolonial theorists, that "the theory and practice of development cannot simply be abandoned in favor of some postdevelopmental thinking of difference. Not only do the facts of cultural and societal modernity weigh theoretically against that, but the pressing need for organized collective action on behalf of the poorest and most vulnerable societies also make it practically objectionable" (RED, 226).

Note that what McCarthy calls for here is not organized collective action *on the part of* or even *in solidarity with* the members of the poorest and most vulnerable societies, but rather action *on their behalf*. This is a telling moment, indicative of the extent to which McCarthy, notwithstanding his extremely laudable attempt to frame a genuinely open and open-ended intercultural dialogue on the costs and benefits of capitalist modernization, ends up recapitulating certain features of Kantian-style liberal imperialism. One also hears here distinct echoes of Marx, who while politically quite distinct from Kant nevertheless shared his broadly speaking developmentalist understanding of history, and who once wrote of the small peasants that "they cannot represent themselves, they must be represented."[70]

Moreover, McCarthy's claim that we are all moderns now undergirds his reliance on the "multiple modernities" paradigm, which was introduced in an attempt to overcome the Eurocentrism of previous conceptions of modernity. However, as Bhambra has argued, and as I will discuss in more detail in chapter 2, "theories of multiple modernity continue to rest on assumptions of an original modernity of the West which others adapt, domesticate, or tropicalize. *Their experiences make no difference to the pre-existing universals.*"[71] There is a kind of all roads lead to the same end logic to McCarthy's talk of multiple modernities, even if he grants that societies take different paths along the way and instantiate capitalist economic and democratic legal and political institutions in very different cultural forms of life. Moreover, there is an assumption that openness to postcolonial difference requires mainly that the normative universals that were developed in European modernity must now be opened up to contestation by those who were previously excluded from them—but always, to be sure, on terms set by the demands of posttraditional, hyperreflexive, modern discourse.

What this account leaves out is the idea that a reciprocal elucidation (to borrow James Tully's felicitous phrase)[72] between different traditions might require not only that we construe certain aspects of our own history as forms of sociocultural learning but also that we be willing to *unlearn* certain aspects of our own taken-for-granted point of view in order to engage in a genuinely open way with various participants in debates about global modernity. As David Scott argued in his response to McCarthy's book, even if it is true that we are all moderns now, in the sense that our lives are conditioned by the practical, discursive, normative, and institutional structures of a global modernity, it is not at all clear what follows from this normatively. From McCarthy's point of view, what seems to follow is that we have no choice but to draw on the epistemic and normative resources supplied by the point

of view of modernity. Without denying this, Scott suggests that something else follows from it as well, namely, that "Europeans and Euro-Americans" have a responsibility to be willing to "*unlearn* the taken-for-granted privilege of their traditions and *learn* to think inside of the moral languages of their historical others."[73] Moreover, I would add that this openness to unlearning is properly understood not as a rejection of the reflexivity afforded to us by the epistemic and normative resources of modernity, but rather as a further elaboration of it.

For the task of unlearning, however, critical theory will need normative and conceptual resources other than those afforded by the left-Hegelian theory of historical progress and sociocultural development as a "fact." Such a theoretical project has, as I've already suggested and will argue at greater length in chapters 2 and 3, a tendency toward self-congratulation that remains even after it has acknowledged the contingency and fragility of the achievements of its own posttraditional, Euro-modern form of life and even once it has opened itself up to contestation (on terms set by itself) with its "others." The proper antidote for such a tendency to self-congratulation is, I suggest, an alternative way of thinking about history in relation to normativity, an alternative represented by a distinctive understanding of genealogy as critical theory. For, as I shall argue in more detail in chapter 5, building on the work of Colin Koopman,[74] a genealogy that aims neither at the subversion or debunking nor at the vindication or defense of our normative point of view, but rather more ambivalently at its critical problematization, is an important tool for this kind of unlearning. Although McCarthy too argues that genealogy has an important role to play in critical theory, he conceives of this role in an overly circumscribed way. For McCarthy, genealogy, which he equates with subversive genealogy, represents a "metacritical" moment of critique by means of which "past and present forms of 'existing reason' have to be ongoingly interrogated with regard to the elements of power invested in them" (RED, 14). For McCarthy, genealogy's restricted focus on "historical and contemporary forms of existing reason" as distinct from the context-transcendent reconstruction of the values, ideals, and principles embedded in a discourse-ethical conception of practical reason suggests that the relevance of genealogy is relegated to the empirical domain (RED, 14).[75] In later chapters, drawing on Foucault and Adorno, I present an alternative conception of genealogy, according to which genealogy is not merely subversive but problematizing, which means that it contains *both* subversive *and* vindicatory moments but that its aim is *neither* merely to subvert *nor* to vindicate but rather to problematize. I further argue that the proper scope of genealogy includes not only the empirical applications of our normative ideals and conceptions of reason but also the kinds of epistemic violence contained within those normative ideals and conceptions of reason themselves. However, in a further reflexive twist, I contend that this problematizing mode of genealogy plays an important role in realizing the kind of genuine respect for and openness to the Other that would allow us to move beyond progressive, developmentalist conceptions of history and hence to decolonize critical theory from within.

Insofar as problematizing genealogy represents an alternative to progressive readings of history, adopting it as a method for doing critical theory requires us to give up on this backward-looking conception of progress as a large-scale, macrolevel narrative about historical learning or sociocultural development. This does not mean that any and all backward-looking claims about progress in some specific context or local domain are thereby undermined. In order to make judgments about progress, historical or otherwise, all that one needs is a standard or benchmark against which progress is to be measured; thus, it is perfectly compatible with this approach to thinking about history that we could continue to make such judgments with respect to particular events or political transformations. In other words, the issue here is not so much about specific claims vis-à-vis progress in particular domains but rather about how claims to broad-based historical learning and sociocultural development serve to underwrite the normative perspective of certain approaches to critical theory. One can reject the latter while still admitting the possibility of the former; in other words, one can reject the idea of *historical progress* as a "fact" and the role that this idea plays in securing the normative perspective of critique while still admitting that in certain specific cases or domains it makes sense to say that there has been *progress in history*, by which I mean progress in a specific domain as judged by standards that are themselves historically and contextually grounded. However, in general I think that we should be cautious about even such local and contextually grounded claims precisely because the seductions of self-congratulation can be so difficult to resist and so dangerous for critical theory. Indeed, I would suggest that the pressing need to avoid such seductions is precisely what makes a problematizing genealogical approach to history so valuable for critical theory. Such an approach shares the sense that, as Samuel Moyn puts it, "the past is more useful for challenging rather than confirming our certainties."[76]

Nor does rejecting the backward-looking notion of progress as a "fact" mean that we have to give up on the forward-looking notion of progress as a moral-political imperative. The trick here is disentangling the latter from the former. As I have already indicated, I will draw on Adorno's idea that progress occurs where it comes to an end to think through this disentanglement. Somewhat paradoxically, perhaps, I also follow Adorno in claiming that disentangling the forward- from the backward-looking conception of progress is required if we are to live up to the normative inheritance of modernity, particularly to its notions of freedom, inclusion, and equal moral respect. Although this might seem to suggest that I end up falling back on the assumption that European modernity is uniquely tolerant, open-minded, and respectful of other cultures, and thus in that sense that it is in fact "superior" to pre- or nonmodern cultures, I understand Adorno's lesson differently. The normative point of genealogical problematization, as I see it, is to compel us to adopt a stance of modesty or humility, not one of superiority, toward our own moral certainties.

Insofar as the conception of progress as a "fact" is doing important philosophical work for critical theory by grounding its normative claims, substituting a problematizing genealogy for a progressive, developmental reading of history will also require us to adopt a different approach to the question of normative grounding. If we accept the idea that critical theory is an immanent and reconstructive project that draws its normative content from within existing social reality,[77] and if we reject Habermas's and Honneth's Hegelian strategy for affirming this stance while avoiding foundationalism, then we are left with the option of developing a more contextualist metanormative position. However, accepting a contextualist moral epistemology does not leave us mired in a substantive or first-order moral-political relativism. On the contrary, metanormative contextualism is perfectly compatible with the kind of moral-political universalism that Habermas and others hold so dear. In other words, the normative principles and ideals on which we rely in our judgments about what could or would count as progress in the future may rest on a contingent foundation, but they are no less powerful for that. Or, at least, so I shall argue.

OUTLINE OF THE BOOK

In chapter 2 I consider in detail the role that the idea of historical progress plays in grounding normativity for Habermas. Against those who read Habermas as neo-Kantian constructivist, I read him as a neo-Hegelian reconstructivist, by uncovering the role that Habermas's theories of social evolution and of modernity play in grounding and justifying his later work in discourse ethics. Once this connection has been uncovered, it becomes clear why the charge of Eurocentrism emerges in such a seemingly intractable form for Habermas. I also discuss his various attempts to respond to this charge, particularly through an engagement with his recent work on multiple modernities and on the idea of postsecular reason. Habermas's quasi-Hegelian strategy for grounding his discourse ethics also raises difficult questions about whether he can maintain his metanormative position without either appealing to foundationalism or collapsing into the contextualism that he strives so strenuously to avoid.

My critique of Habermas in chapter 2 suggests two possible strategies for critical theorists in thinking about the relationship between normativity and history. The first strategy is to double down on the historicist strand of Habermas's thinking to embrace a more consistently contextualist account of normativity; the second is to avoid the dangers of historical and normative contextualism by taking a constructivist route for grounding normativity. In chapters 3 and 4 I present the recent work of Axel Honneth and Rainer Forst as exemplifying these two strategies, respectively. The danger of Honneth's version of the first strategy is that it tends toward a defense of the (informally imperialist) status quo; the danger of Forst's strategy is that it secures its grounding of normativity in a "freestanding" conception of practical reason that not only stands in need of decolonizing but also sacrifices the methodological distinctiveness of critical theory.

In chapter 5 I then turn to Adorno and to Foucault to construct an alternative framework for thinking through the relationship between history and normativity. I read both Adorno and Foucault as attempting to historicize and to problematize the very notion of History—the historicist, Hegelian notion of historical progress—upon which contemporary critical theorists such as Habermas and Honneth still implicitly or explicitly rely. The aim of this problematization is to theorize the possibility of moving beyond (or, perhaps it is better to say, outside of) this conception of history. Thus, I find in Adorno and Foucault indispensible methodological tools for the kind of problematization of History that is crucially needed if critical theory is to be decolonized.

In the final chapter, I conclude the book by offering some further reflections on metanormative contextualism, including considerations of how this contextualism transforms our understandings of practical reason and normative justification while avoiding first-order moral or political relativism. This enables us to see not only how the normative foundations of critical theory might be decolonized, but also how post- and decolonial theory might be criticalized through the articulation of a contextualist but nonrelativistic account of progress as a moral-political imperative.

This book attempts to weave three strands of argument together, each strand focusing on a different concept: progress, normativity, and decolonization. At different times throughout the book, one strand moves to the foreground while the others recede to the background. But I ask the reader to keep in mind throughout that the three strands are interwoven in the following way: critical theory stands in need of decolonization insofar as its strategy for grounding normativity relies on the notion of historical progress; thus, if critical theory is to be decolonized, it will have to find another strategy for grounding normativity and another way of thinking about progress.

2

From Social Evolution to Multiple Modernities

HISTORY AND NORMATIVITY IN HABERMAS

It is widely recognized that a—if not *the*—central aim of Habermas's work over the last fifty years has been to put critical social theory on a secure normative footing. Mindful of what he saw as the failure of the first generation of the Frankfurt School to ground its own normative perspective, Habermas set himself the ambitious aim of developing a critical social theory that could, as he put it in the preface to his magnum opus, *The Theory of Communicative Action*, "validate its own critical standards" (TCA1, xli). And yet, despite the centrality of this goal, Habermas's strategy for grounding normativity remains unclear and open to conflicting interpretations.[1] As Seyla Benhabib has noted, a series of "normative puzzles" have perplexed an entire generation of Habermas scholars, including the following: "What is the relationship of universal pragmatics to the 'ideal speech situation'? Of the ideal speech situation to communicative ethics? Is communicative ethics a theory of justice, a theory of universalist morality or rather, a meta-theory of normative justification?"[2] To this list of puzzles, we might add the following related set of puzzles that are central to the argument of this book: What is the relationship between Habermas's universal- or formal-pragmatic analyses of language and discourse, on the one hand, and his theory of modernity as the outcome of a process of social evolution, on the other hand? Does the former provide justificatory support for the latter, or vice versa?[3] Or do formal pragmatics and the theory of modernity provide mutual support for each other?

Equally unclear and contested is Habermas's stance toward the project of philosophy of history. For example, Habermas claims in the conclusion to *The Theory of Communicative Action* that his work constitutes an *alternative* to the Marxist philosophy of history presupposed by first-generation critical theorists (TCA2, 396–97). Critics such as John McCormick have taken Habermas at his word here and claimed that he "professes to be completely free of philosophy of history altogether."[4] And yet, as other commentators have noted, there is a sense in which a modified understanding of the project of philosophy of history—what McCarthy calls, in his introduction to Habermas's *Communication and the Evolution of Society*, an "empirical philosophy of history with practical (political) intent" (CES, ix)—plays a crucial role in Habermas's argument.[5] When Habermas says that he is offering an alternative to the philosophy of history, it is important to keep in mind that he is referring to a particular version of philosophy of history, namely, to a theory of history that presumes a metaphysical, teleological, and necessary progression of a unified historical subject. Just to be perfectly clear: *Habermas does not and never has practiced philosophy of history in this sense*, and I am not saying that he has. And yet, a pragmatic, postmetaphysical, and deflationary but nonetheless progressive understanding of history plays a crucial role in Habermas's critical theory and, as I will argue, particularly in relation to his account of normativity. The key here is Habermas's ongoing commitment to a theory of social evolution that positions "modernity" as the outcome of a process of moral-practical learning. Even if Habermas has left behind many of the trappings of traditional philosophy of history, his theory of social evolution nonetheless commits him to the idea that has always been central to that project: the idea of historical progress. The remainder of this chapter will attempt to spell out how, in what sense, and to what extent he is so committed, and also to explore some of the implications of that commitment.

For the purposes of this book, the most important implication of Habermas's ongoing commitment to ideas of social evolution and modernity as progress is the problem of Eurocentrism, which thus turns out to be closely related to the normative puzzles that I just sketched. Indeed, I want to suggest that the problem of Eurocentrism continually plagues Habermas not merely because he just so happens to be a staunch defender of the ideals forged in the European Enlightenment, but also because the theory of social evolution—along with the theory of modernity to which it gives rise—plays a crucial role in validating the critical standards of Habermasian critical theory. In other words, the vestigial commitment to a progressive reading of history that Habermas retains from more traditional approaches to the philosophy of history is neither incidental nor peripheral to his theory: rather, it is a central metanormative, theoretical commitment. In conjunction with the theory of formal pragmatics, the theories of social evolution and of modernity do real work in grounding his normative project. And this fact, more than anything else, explains why the problem of Eurocentrism emerges in such a seemingly intractable form in Habermas's work. The fact that the theories of social evolution, modernity, and progress are doing real work in grounding the normativity of Habermasian critical theory means that there is only so far that he can go in rethinking or revising those theories in response to postcolonial critiques of the colonial and informally imperialist logics of such theories. In recent years, Habermas has attempted such a rethinking by adopting the multiple modernities paradigm developed in sociology by Shmuel Eisenstadt.[6] Although this is in many ways a positive step, it does not, in my view, go far enough.

This chapter thus turns around two axes: it both addresses the normativity puzzle in Habermas's work and shows how Habermas's chosen strategy for addressing that puzzle leaves him vulnerable to postcolonial critics who charge him with Eurocentrism and informal imperialism.[7] The thread that connects these two strands of argument is the role that a nontraditional but still progressive philosophy of history—represented in Habermas's work by his theory of social evolution and his closely related theory of modernity—plays in grounding normativity for Habermas. With respect to the normativity puzzle, and against those who read him as a neo-Kantian constructivist,[8] I read him as a neo-Hegelian reconstructivist, in the sense that the developmental story about modernity as the result of a historical learning process at the very least plays a crucial role in Habermas's attempts to validate his own critical standards. In the final section of this chapter, I critically assess Habermas's repeated attempts to respond to the charges of Eurocentrism that this developmental story invites, particularly through his recent work on multiple modernities, and find them wanting.

THE LAST MARXIST? SOCIAL EVOLUTION AND THE RECONSTRUCTION OF HISTORICAL MATERIALISM

In a discussion in 1989 of the English translation of his book *The Structural Transformation of the Public Sphere*, Habermas makes what may well strike contemporary readers as a surprising claim: "I do think that I have been a reformist all my life, and maybe I have become a bit more so in recent years. Nevertheless, I mostly feel I am the last Marxist."[9] This claim seems especially surprising in light of the growing lament in recent years that Habermas, as well as, following him, much work in contemporary critical theory, has given up entirely on the Marxist project of critiquing capitalism.[10] There is a widespread sense that Habermas has long since moved so far away from the political radicalism that marked his early work that his position has now passed reformism—let alone radical reformism[11]—and settled into resignation.[12] But if Habermas has in fact largely given up on the project of critiquing capitalism, having resigned himself to the lack of viable alternatives, then in what sense could he take himself to be the last Marxist?

The context for this claim helps to reveal the answer to this question. Habermas makes this claim in response to a question from Nancy Fraser about the contrast between the emancipatory vision outlined at the end of *The Structural Transformation of the Public Sphere*, which called, among other things, for a democratization of the economic sphere, and the less critical stance toward capitalism laid out in his work of the late 1980s, which held that capitalist markets and state bureaucracies are necessary features of social life in complex societies, and that the best we can hope for is a critical public sphere that serves as a check on their growth and influence.[13] Fraser asks Habermas whether capitalism is in fact compatible with the idea of a genuinely nonexclusionary and democratic public sphere. In response, Habermas effectively accuses Fraser of being a utopian socialist,[14] rejecting her implicit appeal to the possibility of a wholesale revolutionary overthrow of capitalism as naïve and romantic. Habermas's inheritance of Marx is, in his view, tied to his reformism; like Marx, who was also critical of the utopian socialists of his own time,[15] Habermas understands the critical task not as that of proposing an ideal vision for society but rather as one of diagnosing and building upon existing historical possibilities.[16]

In other words, Habermas's response highlights the specific sense in which he considers himself to be the last Marxist, and it has less to do with the critique of capitalism than it does with his appropriation of Marx's historical methodology, that is to say, with what Habermas once called the reconstruction of historical materialism.[17] In this context, reconstruction refers to a theoretical project that aims at "taking a theory apart and putting it back together again in a new form in order to attain more fully the goal it has set for itself" (CES, 95).[18] Habermas's work from the 1950s through the 1970s was devoted largely to the reconstructive task of taking Marx's theory of historical materialism apart and putting it back together so that it could more fully attain its own goals. Through the 1970s, this took the form of the development of a theory of social evolution. As I shall argue, Habermas can still be understood as faithful to the legacy of Marx in this specific sense,[19] even though the role that his reconstruction of historical materialism plays in his work after the 1970s—and, in particular, in relationship to his theory of communicative action and his discourse ethics—remains to be clarified. I will address these issues in the next two sections of this chapter.

Before turning to that task, in this section, I discuss Habermas's early attempts to reconstruct historical materialism in his work of the 1970s. Only once we have spelled out this aspect of Habermas's work will we be in a position to understand the role that ideas of historical progress—specifically, notions of learning processes, social evolution, and modernization—play in his overall project.

Two aspects of Habermas's early attempt to develop what McCarthy calls an "empirical philosophy of history with practical (political) intent" (CES, ix) are worth highlighting at the outset. The first is its empirical—as opposed to metaphysical—character. An *empirical* philosophy of history rejects the assumption of an ahistorical, hence metaphysical, goal that serves as a transcendent standard or benchmark against which claims of historical development or progress could be measured. The second is its practical, political intent. A *practically oriented* philosophy of history views the meaning or goal of history—its projected future—not as "a product of contemplation or of scientific prediction but of a situationally engaged practical reason" (CES, x). Notice that these two features correspond to what I called in the previous chapter progress as a "fact"—albeit one that is grounded empirically rather than metaphysically—and progress as an imperative.

These two features help to explain why Habermas initially turns to Marx rather than to Hegel for his understanding of history. To be sure, as Habermas acknowledges, it was Hegel who first articulated the historicity of philosophical reason, and hence, it was Hegel who first articulated the deep, internal connection between philosophy and history. But Habermas finds Hegel's account of the relationship between the philosophy of history and politics to be inconsistent. On the one hand, Hegel's official position, articulated in the preface to the *Philosophy of Right*, is that "philosophy cannot instruct the world about what it ought to be; it is solely reality which is reflected in its concepts, reality as it is. It cannot direct itself critically against this, but only against the abstractions which push themselves between reason become objective and our subjective consciousness" (TP, 178–179). And yet, on the other hand, in his political writings, Hegel often seemed to be instructing the world about what it ought to be. "The mere fact," Habermas writes, "that Hegel wrote political polemics throws a particular light on the relation of his theory to praxis. For how can the intention of changing reality . . . be reconciled with a theory which must reject as vain any such claim?" (TP, 177).

Moreover, on Habermas's reading, Hegel's official position has the conservative aim of reconciling us with existing social and political reality, as opposed to transforming it through practical-political means. In this way, Hegel remains overly bound to his own time and context: "Hegel, too, in spite of his own claims, continues a particularism to which German philosophy owes its estrangement from the Western spirit. To overcome this was necessarily easier for a Rhenish Jew in exile in London, than for a Tübingen seminarian and Prussian official in Restoration Berlin" (TP, 194).

Marx's philosophy of history not only overcomes the particularism that plagues Hegel's political philosophy, thereby preserving its critical, political edge, but also resists the Hegelian urge to understand history as a totality that can be philosophically comprehended from the point of view of the Absolute. As Habermas puts it, "The philosophy of history only divests itself of this absolute point of view, from which history is reflected philosophically as a totality, with the transformation of its dialectic into a materialistic one" (TP, 247). Marxist philosophy of history is both retrospective and prospective, that is, both backward- and forward-looking, but, for Marx, the forward-looking dimension has a specifically practical character: "The meaning of history as a whole is revealed theoretically to the degree to which mankind practically undertakes to make with will and consciousness that history which it has always made anyhow. *In so doing, critique must comprehend itself as a moment within the situation which it is seeking to supercede*" (TP, 248).[20] In other words, critique that takes on board this Marxist understanding of history must be thoroughly immanent; it cannot set itself outside of its own historical situation.

As Habermas reads it, Marx's philosophy of history nevertheless shares two presuppositions with classical philosophy of history: that the history of the world is a unified story and that history can be made by human beings. Both of these assumptions are grounded in what Habermas calls the "objective tendencies" of European historical development in the eighteenth and nineteenth centuries (TP, 250). The idea of global unity arose in the eighteenth century as European thinkers reflected upon their experiences of colonization, empire building, and the so-called civilizing religious mission.[21] The idea that history can be made by human beings arose out of the ideas of rationality and autonomy that were central to the European Enlightenment.[22] Hence, these two presuppositions of the philosophy of history have their origins in what Habermas characterizes as the objective historical tendencies of European bourgeois society of the eighteenth and nineteenth centuries; in this sense, the emergence of the second, historicist Enlightenment can be understood as bourgeois European society "attaining consciousness of itself" (TP, 250).

Moreover, Habermas argues, these objective historical tendencies only grew stronger through the first half of the twentieth century. Given the global social, economic, and political interconnectedness and interdependence brought about by "industrial society and its technically mediated commerce" (TP, 250)—what would now be placed under the heading of globalization—"particular histories have coalesced into the history of *one* world" (TP, 251). And the Cold War arms race confronted its contemporaries with the irony that we are capable of making our own history even as we remain incapable of asserting control over it: "Thus the immanent presuppositions of the philosophy of history have not by any means become invalid; on the contrary, it is only today that they have become true. That is why all the counterideologies, which allege that the way the philosophy of history poses the question is now outdated, must arouse a suspicion of escapism" (TP, 251).

At the same time, these objective historical tendencies enable us to call into question an assumption that classical philosophy of history takes over from theology: namely, the very idea of history as a totality. If global unity and the capacity to make history are themselves historical developments that have emerged relatively recently, then they cannot be made the premises of an understanding of history *as a whole*: "Especially the materialistic philosophy of history should comprehend its presuppositions in terms of the context of the epoch in which it emerged historically. It should incorporate critically into its self-consciousness the fact that the two categories—the unity of the world, and that history can be made—have only acquired their truth in history at a specific phase" (TP, 251). Although Marx himself never explicitly posed the epistemological question of the conditions of possibility of an empirical philosophy of history with practical-political intent, through a reconstruction of Marx's historical materialism, Habermas claims to be able to offer "an explanation of social evolution which is so comprehensive that it embraces the interrelationships of the theory's own origins and application" (TP, 1). The theory accomplishes this by specifying the historical conditions under which reflection upon history became possible for us and came to be thought of as central to the project of critical theory. In this way, Habermas strives to situate his historically self-conscious critical theory historically, that is, in its own historical situation.

Habermas's defense of the continued historical relevance of Marx's theory of historical materialism notwithstanding, he identifies three major shortcomings in Marx's account: its overly narrow conception of historical development, its objectivism, and its lack of a clear normative foundation (CES, 96–98). Habermas proposes to overcome these shortcomings in part by drawing on the insights of the theory of communicative action that he was at that time beginning to develop.

Habermas finds Marx's account overly narrow insofar as it conceives of historical development solely in the dimension of the development of productive forces, spurred by an increase in technical-scientific knowledge. Habermas thus proposes to broaden Marx's understanding of historical development with the inclusion of an additional dimension: moral-practical development (see CES, 148). Hence, Habermas distinguishes between rationalization at the purposive-rational or strategic level, which is akin to the development of productive forces that Marx identified as the motor of historical progress, and rationalization in the domain of communicative action, which Habermas considers to be equally if not more important for explaining social evolution (CES, 118).[23] Moral-practical development consists in part in a progressive decentration of worldviews and heightening of reflexivity: "In both dimensions [that is, individual ego development and social evolution], development apparently leads to a growing decentration of interpretive systems and to an ever-clearer categorical demarcation of the subjectivity of internal nature from the objectivity of external nature, as well as from the normativity of social reality and the intersubjectivity of linguistic reality" (CES, 106). The progressive decentration of worldviews at both the individual and the social level is necessary for the demanding form of communicative interaction that

Habermas calls discourse. Rationalization in the domain of communicative action also consists in

> extirpating those relations of force that are inconspicuously set in the very structures of communication and that prevent conscious settlement of conflicts, and consensual regulation of conflicts, by means of intrapsychic as well as interpersonal communicative barriers. Rationalization means overcoming such systematically distorted communication in which the action-supporting consensus concerning the reciprocally raised validity claims . . . can be sustained in appearance only, that is, counter-factually. . . . [Progress in this domain] cannot be measured against the choice of correct strategies, but rather against the intersubjectivity of understanding achieved without force, that is, against the expansion of the domain of consensual action together with the re-establishment of undistorted communication. (CES, 119–120)

In other words, moral-practical rationalization in the domain of communicative action consists in progressively working free of the power or force relations that distort communication—at both the intra- and intersubjective levels—and working toward the kind of undistorted communication that characterizes what Habermas would later call the idealizing presuppositions of discourse.

Regarding the charge of objectivism, Habermas notes that Marx's philosophy of history shares a number of problematic presuppositions with the traditional or classical philosophy of history that he attempts to move beyond. These include objectivistic assumptions about the "*unilinear, necessary, uninterrupted, and progressive development of a macrosubject*" of world history (CES, 139). Habermas proposes a weaker version of the philosophy of history that jettisons these objectivistic assumptions. In Habermas's reconstruction, the macrosubject of world history is replaced by the idea that "the bearers of evolution are rather societies and the acting subjects integrated into them; social evolution can be discerned in those structures that are replaced by more comprehensive structures in accord with a pattern that is to be rationally reconstructed" (CES, 140). While Habermas acknowledges that social systems can, in a sense, "solve" problems that threaten their existence, they can only do this by "drawing on the learning capacities of social subjects" (CES, 154). Hence, "the evolutionary learning process of societies is dependent on the competences of the individuals that belong to them" (CES, 154).

With regard to objectivistic assumptions about the necessity, unilinearity, and uninterruptibility of historical development, Habermas attempts to address these problems by distinguishing between the logic and the dynamics of historical development.[24] As he explains: "If we separate the logic from the dynamics of development—that is, the rationally reconstructible *pattern* of a hierarchy of more and more comprehensive structures from the *processes* through which the empirical substrates develop—then we need require of history neither unilinearity nor necessity, neither continuity nor irreversibility" (CES, 140). In other words, although Habermas maintains that we can rationally reconstruct a universal and invariant logic of developmental stages through which the process of social evolution moves, whether or not any individual society actually moves through those stages and, to a certain extent, just how particular societies undergo this process are historically contingent matters left up to the dynamics of historical change. Hence, whether and at what time or pace individual societies will move through the various stages of historical development depend on *contingent* processes that can be investigated empirically; there are multiple paths that can lead to the same developmental stage such that the dynamics of development are *multilinear* rather than unilinear;[25] and, far from being uninterruptible or irreversible, regressions in social evolution at the level of historical dynamics are always possible (German fascism serving as a prime example) (CES, 140–141).

The problem of normative foundations is closely related to ideas of historical progress or teleology. Habermas acknowledges that this is "the most controversial point," and yet he maintains that "when we speak of evolution, we do in fact mean cumulative processes that exhibit a direction" (CES, 141). How, then, is the direction of historical progress to be determined? By means of what criterion do we judge a historical change to be progressive or regressive?

Lacking clear normative foundations, Marx was unable to answer such questions. Habermas, by contrast, argues that progress is measured in each of the two dimensions of historical development that he has specified—the development of productive forces and technical-scientific knowledge, on the one hand, and the development of moral-practical knowledge, on the other hand—and in each case it is measured against the criterion of a universal validity claim—the truth of propositions, in the first case, and the rightness of norms, in the second case. "I would like, therefore," Habermas writes, "to defend the thesis that the criteria of social progress singled out by historical materialism as the development of productive forces and the maturity of forms of social intercourse can be systematically justified" (CES, 142).

But how exactly does this systematic justification go? Habermas sketches his answer by claiming that the theoretician of social evolution is already implicitly committed to certain presuppositions:

> The presupposition, for instance, that true propositions are preferable to false ones, and that right (i.e., justifiable) norms are preferable to wrong ones. For a living being that maintains itself in the structures of ordinary language communication, the validity basis of speech has the binding force of universal and unavoidable—in this sense transcendental—presuppositions. . . . If we are not free then to reject or to accept the validity claims bound up with the cognitive potential of the human species, it is senseless to want to "decide" for or against reason, for or against the expansion of the potential of reasoned action. For these reasons I do not regard the choice of the historical-materialist criterion of progress as arbitrary. The development of productive forces, in conjunction with the maturity of the forms of social integration, means progress of learning ability in both dimensions: progress in objectivating knowledge and in moral-practical insight. (CES, 177)

The reference to the universal and unavoidable presuppositions of the validity basis of speech is to Habermas's theory of universal pragmatics. This theory was introduced in the mid-1970s (see CES, 1–68) and later formed a key component of the argument of *The*

Theory of Communicative Action (see TCA1, chap. 3). It continues to play a central role in Habermas's more recent work, since his discourse ethics can be understood as a systematic attempt to clarify the presuppositions involved in one of the three forms of discourse that are analyzed by universal pragmatics, namely, moral-practical discourse.[26] The passage just quoted seems to suggest that universal pragmatics provides the justification or the criterion for the general claims about historical progress made in the theory of social evolution; this, in turn, suggests that Habermas's formal-pragmatic analysis of moral-practical discourses, which culminates in his discourse ethics, provides the justificatory basis for judgments of progress in the moral-practical realm. However, a closer examination of Habermas's theory of universal pragmatics and the role that it plays in his overall social theory, offered in the next section, reveals the situation to be much more complicated than this.

Before I get to that, however, allow me to recap a few important points. First, even though Habermas acknowledges that European colonialism, imperialism, and the so-called civilizing mission serve as objective historical tendencies for the development of Marx's philosophy of history, he does not see this as reason to question the possible Eurocentric biases of that theory. From the point of view of post- or decolonial theory, this seems like a rather large lacuna in Habermas's otherwise subtly historicized reading of Marx's theory of history. Second, even as Habermas jettisons the metaphysical trappings of the traditional philosophy of history—its objectivistic assumptions about the necessity, unilinearity, and uninterruptibility of historical progress—he retains what is arguably its most controversial core: namely, the idea of historical progress itself and the assumption that European modernity can and should be understood as the result of a process of progressive historical development. These moves open him up to the frequently leveled charge of Eurocentrism. Third, and finally, although Habermas adopts certain formal features of Marx's philosophy of history, particularly its practical, political character, he nonetheless views Marx's historical materialism as normatively deficient, in two senses. Marx not only lacks a clear delineation between technical-scientific and moral-practical progress; he also lacks a clear normative grounding for judgments of the latter sort. As I have already indicated, addressing this normative deficit is a central aim of *The Theory of Communicative Action*.

MODERNITY AND NORMATIVITY IN *THE THEORY OF COMMUNICATIVE ACTION*

The question of the relationship between formal-universal pragmatics and the theory of modernity is central to Habermas's *Theory of Communicative Action*, specifically, to whether and if so how that text accomplishes its stated aim of producing a critical theory that validates its own critical standards. In order to illuminate this question, I devote the bulk of this section to the difficult and complex task of reconstructing the overall argument of volume 1 of *The Theory of Communicative Action*, since this volume grounds the normative perspective of the critical theory that is then fleshed out in volume 2. But the basic problem can already be sketched out rather simply. At first glance, as we saw at the end of the previous section, Habermas's theory of universal pragmatics looks as if it serves to ground his normative position. As Habermas states in his initial formulation of universal pragmatics, the theory aspires to "identify and reconstruct universal conditions of possible understanding" (CES, 1). It asserts that there is a universal core to communicative competence, and that this core involves the differentiation of three distinct validity claims—claims to truth, to normative rightness/appropriateness, and to sincerity—and of three distinct world-relations—to the objective, intersubjective, and subjective worlds, respectively. Every utterance raises at least one of the three validity claims; in fact, most utterances will raise all three claims simultaneously, and communicative competence further consists in the ability to thematize the specific validity claims raised in a particular utterance and, when necessary, to defend those validity claims with reasons. For Habermas, understanding an utterance requires understanding and taking a yes-no position on the reasons that might be adduced to support the validity claims that are implicitly raised therein; hence, there is an unavoidable validity basis to communicative speech. On one reading of Habermas's project, this internal connection between understanding and validity is the source of normativity for Habermas. The link between understanding an utterance and coming to an understanding using language serves as the basis for his account of communicative rationality as a process of adjudicating the validity of claims to truth or normative rightness.[27]

Habermas himself suggests this way of understanding his project when he claims, in the conclusion to *The Theory of Communicative Action*, that this theory offers an analysis that "*to begin with*, proceeds reconstructively, that is, unhistorically. It describes structures of action and structures of mutual understanding that are found in the intuitive knowledge of competent members of modern societies" (TCA2, 383).[28]

However, this way of understanding Habermas's project overlooks the simple fact that the methodology of rational reconstruction proceeds by way of a systematic reconstruction of the intuitive knowledge of a very specific group of people, namely, "competent members of modern societies," where "competent" means adult subjects who have learned to differentiate the three validity claims and have mastered the three-world structure of communication. As Habermas himself puts this point: "Our formal-pragmatic description of the general structure of speech acts has to draw on the pretheoretical knowledge of speakers who belong to a modern and—in a sense still to be explained more precisely—rationalized lifeworld" (TCA2, 77). As Titus Stahl points out, the normative potentials that are unearthed by this type of reconstructive analysis "are neither historically invariant nor transcendentally given."[29] In what sense, then, can they be taken to be universal? The answer is that they represent the implicit telos toward which language universally aims, insofar as it functions as a medium of communication. In this way, the normative potentials built into the communicative use of language should be understood as universal in a specifically Hegelian sense: they are first not in the order of existence but rather in the order of explanation.[30] But this assumption raises two related questions: First, why are these particular capabilities taken to be the telos at which communication aims, as opposed to, say, a historically contingent set of linguistic practices? Second, why are only those speakers who have mastered these communicative functions taken to be competent? If universal pragmatics were to offer an independent, strongly transcendental account of the normative potentials that are necessarily and unavoidably built into communication, such that something would not count as an instance of communication unless it conformed to the rules uncovered by universal pragmatics, then it could serve to justify these claims. But since universal pragmatics itself rests on the prior assumption that modern, posttraditional structures of communication and postconventional forms of identity are superior to premodern, traditional ones, that is, that they more fully realize the inherent telos of language as a medium of communication, the theory cannot play this justificatory role. As McCarthy notes, the problem of ethno- or Eurocentrism already emerges here, since Habermas is implicitly working with "a conception of the end point of the history of reason" that privileges a Western point of view.[31]

To state the problem even more succinctly, the central aim of Habermas's work is to put critical theory on a secure normative footing. His account of formal or universal pragmatics—insofar as it picks out the normative potentials inherent in the communicative use of language—might be taken to provide the necessary normative grounding by providing the criteria on the basis of which different worldviews or lifeworld structures can be evaluated.[32] And yet, insofar as universal pragmatics reconstructs the intuitive, pretheoretical knowledge of subjects who are deemed competent insofar as they have mastered the specific use of language required by modernity, it already *presupposes* a certain conception of social evolution or historical progress. The question is, what serves as the basis for this presupposition? Formal pragmatics cannot play this role since this would beg the question of why the norms embedded in modern lifeworlds deserve to be followed. If formal pragmatics does not provide the justificatory basis for the theory of social evolution, then could the latter provide the justificatory basis for the former? Or are the two theories supposed to be mutually reinforcing?

These are questions that go right to the heart of the argument of *The Theory of Communicative Action*. As mentioned above, the stated aim of that work is to produce a critical theory that validates its own critical standards. And yet the structure of the argument that is supposed to accomplish this is difficult to discern. What is most striking about the structure of the book is the way that Habermas toggles back and forth between formal-pragmatic and empirical-historical considerations. Habermas begins with a preliminary specification of the concept of rationality. Central to this concept are the ideas of susceptibility to criticism and grounding with reasons: "The rationality inherent in [communicative] practice is seen in the fact that a communicatively achieved agreement must be based *in the end* on reasons. And the rationality of those who participate in this communicative practice is determined by whether, if necessary, they could, *under suitable circumstances*, provide reasons for their expressions" (TCA1, 17). This leads Habermas to sketch out a theory of argumentation, since argumentation serves as a "court of appeal" that allows us to continue communicative action in cases of disagreement over the reasons for actors' utterances, by shifting to the more demanding level of discourse—theoretical discourse for the adjudication of truth claims, practical discourse for the adjudication of normative claims.[33] In this context, Habermas notes that his controversial proposal of the ideal speech situation "may be unsatisfactory in its details" but that he is still committed to its central aim, namely

> to reconstruct the general symmetry conditions that every competent speaker must presuppose are sufficiently satisfied insofar as he intends to enter into argumentation at all. Participants in argumentation have to presuppose in general that the structure of their communication, by virtue of features that can be described in purely formal terms, excludes all force—whether it arises from within the process of reaching understanding itself or influences it from the outside—except the force of the better argument (and thus that it also excludes, on their part, all motives except that of a cooperative search for the truth). From this perspective argumentation can be conceived as *a reflective continuation, with different means, of action oriented to reaching understanding.* (TCA1, 25)

After sketching out this conception of communicative rationality as a process of asking for and giving reasons in defense of the validity claims that are unavoidably raised in communicative utterances, Habermas admits that this preliminary specification is grounded in a particular point of view, inasmuch as it reflects the preunderstanding of a modern subject. Claiming universality for this conception of rationality thus involves claiming universality for our modern, Occidental understanding of the world (TCA1, 44), which in turn raises the question of how such a claim can be justified. In an effort to answer this question, Habermas draws his infamous contrast between the mythical and the modern understandings of the world. The point of this contrast is, first, to "clarify the sense in which the modern understanding of the world can claim universality" and, second, to "indicate the evolutionary perspective we can adopt if we want, with Max Weber, to posit a world-historical process of rationalization of worldviews" (TCA1, 45). Mythical worldviews are distinct from modern ones in two ways: first, they fail to differentiate the objective, social, and subjective worlds (and hence they also fail to differentiate claims to truth, normative validity, and sincerity); and, second, they do not identify themselves *as* worldviews, as cultural traditions, that is, they lack reflexivity about their own status (TCA1, 52).

Of course, this contrast does not yet justify the claim that the differentiation of validity claims and heightened reflexivity that are constitutive of modern worldviews can be considered universal. In an attempt to justify this claim, Habermas reviews the arguments for and against a universalistic conception of rationality that emerged in the so-called rationality debates among anthropologists and philosophers of the 1960s and 1970s.[34] Without going into the details of the arguments, we can at least summarize the main lessons that Habermas draws from this debate. First, Habermas insists that social-scientific interpreters have no choice but to take up a yes-no position on the validity claims implicitly raised by the social actors that they are studying. For example, cultural anthropologists studying the rituals of "primitive" tribes, such as the Azande of Central Africa, have no choice but to take up a yes-no position on their validity claims, such as those raised by the Azande's belief in witchcraft. Second, one can be hermeneutically charitable toward forms of life that are radically different from one's own without thereby embracing relativism. For example, the Azande's belief in witchcraft can be reconstructed in such a way that it is understood as coherent and logical and yet still be judged inferior from a modern, scientific point of view (TCA1, 55–56). Habermas acknowledges that such a judgment raises the worry that we are judging one worldview (that of the Azande) by the standards of another (modern, scientific rationality) and thus assuming precisely what we are trying to prove, namely, the superiority of the modern worldview over the mythical. Nevertheless, he suggests two criteria that might serve to justify such judgments: cognitive adequacy and the degree of openness in worldviews. Cognitive adequacy refers not to the truth or falsity of worldviews as a whole—since worldviews as a whole do not admit of truth or falsity—but rather to the number and kind of true statements that they make possible; if modern, scientific worldviews make possible more and better true statements than the Azande worldview does, then they are more cognitively adequate. The degree of openness refers to the openness to criticism and the readiness to learn embedded in worldviews. To be sure, both of these criteria could be viewed as hypostatizations of certain features of modern, Western scientific rationality—which is marked by an emphasis on cognitive-instrumental truth and which could never have arisen without the basic attitudes of openness to criticism and readiness to learn—but, for Habermas, this is not because the criteria themselves are inappropriate but rather because they have been understood too narrowly, in the context of a merely cognitive-instrumental conception of rationality, as opposed to the broader conception of rationality that Habermas endorses.

Indeed, and somewhat curiously, this is precisely the main lesson that Habermas draws from his review of the rationality/relativism debate: namely, that what is distinctive of the modern West is not scientific rationality per se but rather the hypostatization thereof. As he puts it, "The rationality debate carried on in England suggests that the modern understanding of the world is indeed based on general structures of rationality but that modern Western societies promote a distorted understanding of rationality that is fixed on cognitive-instrumental aspects and is to that extent particularistic" (TCA1, 66). But Habermas hasn't really established, through his review of this debate, that the modern understanding of the world per se is based on structures of rationality that we can regard as general or universal. We could agree with Habermas that the equation of the modern worldview with the perspective of modern scientific rationality is overly narrow, but this by itself doesn't establish the rational superiority of the modern worldview. At most he has showed that one aspect of the modern worldview—modern scientific rationality—"belongs to a complex of cognitive-instrumental rationality that can certainly claim validity beyond the context of particular cultures" (TCAI, 65). Even if we grant him this claim, it doesn't license the conclusion that the rationality of worldviews in general or their moral-practical validity spheres in particular can also be judged impartially in terms of a criterion of openness/closedness.

And yet this is precisely Habermas's conclusion (TCA1, 66). If worldviews can be judged in terms of their rationality, then changes from one worldview to another can be understood not as discontinuous transformations but rather in terms of "an internally reconstructible growth in knowledge," that is, a process of increasing rationalization, or a learning process (TCA1, 66). Recalling his earlier distinction between the logics and the dynamics of historical development, Habermas insists that such learning processes are neither continuous nor linear (TCA1, 67). Nevertheless, in these learning processes, the superseded stage is categorically devalued, that is, certain kinds of reasons are no longer convincing: "These *devaluative shifts* appear to be connected with socio-evolutionary transitions to new levels of learning, with which the conditions of possible learning processes in the dimensions of objectivating thought, moral-practical insight, and aesthetic-expressive capacity are altered" (TCA1, 68).

However, Habermas does not seem satisfied with this account of the superiority of the modern worldview, since in a subsequent chapter he raises once again the question of how we can know that the conception of rationality that he has been sketching out is in fact universal. At this point, he argues that if we assume that some normative concept of rationality is necessarily presupposed in all social theory, then metatheoretical and methodological considerations compel us to posit a universal conception of rationality. From a metatheoretical perspective, without a universalist conception of rationality, our social theory will be "limited from the start to a particular, culturally or historically bound perspective"; from a methodological perspective, sociology's claim to objectivity is dependent upon the positing of "general and encompassing structures of rationality" (TCA1, 137). There are four core components to Habermas's conception of rationality: first, the three formal world concepts (objective, intersubjective, and subjective); second, the corresponding validity claims (truth, normative rightness, and sincerity); third, the concept of a rationally motivated agreement; and fourth, the concept of reaching understanding through speech.[35] "If the requirement of objectivity is to be satisfied," Habermas notes, "this structure would have to be shown to be *universally valid* in a specific sense. This is a very strong requirement for someone who is operating without metaphysical support and is also no longer confident that a rigorous transcendental-pragmatic program, claiming to provide ultimate grounds, can be carried out" (TCA1, 137).

Habermas thus admits that he takes on a sizable burden of proof in claiming universal validity for his concept of rationality while eschewing metaphysical or transcendental-pragmatic support. He offers three possible ways that this burden of proof could be met. First, it could be met through the development of the theory of formal or universal pragmatics. However, Habermas emphasizes the limited role that this theory can play in justifying the claim to universality for Habermas's conception of communicative rationality: "This program holds out no prospect of an equivalent for a transcendental deduction of the communicative universals described" (TCA1, 138). At most the hypothetical reconstructions of the intuitive knowledge of speakers can be rendered plausible by checking against the intuitions of competent speakers; the universalistic claims of formal pragmatics cannot be "conclusively redeemed (in the sense of transcendental philosophy)" (TCA1, 138). The second way the burden of proof could be met is by assessing the empirical usefulness of the account of communicative rationality, for example, through an analysis of communicative pathologies, evolutionary accounts of social life, and developmental psychology. Although

Habermas is hopeful that his account of communicative rationality will prove empirically fruitful, he admits that this approach would require a great deal of effort. The third and "somewhat less demanding" way of meeting the burden of proof is "to work up the sociological approaches to a theory of social rationalization" (TCA1, 139). This path is easier because it allows us to link up with a well-developed tradition in social theory, and this is the path that Habermas follows in the remainder of *The Theory of Communicative Action*.

In other words, the structure of the argument in *The Theory of Communicative Action* is such that the theory of formal pragmatics is quite clearly *not* used to justify the theory of social evolution as a process of rationalization. Formal pragmatics is presented as an empirical research program awaiting empirical confirmation, not as a foundational plank in a normative argument. Moreover, insofar as this research program already presupposes the superiority of the modern conception of rationality—by equating the intuitive knowledge of competent members of modern societies with the universal presuppositions of communicative action—it cannot serve as the basis for the claim to its superiority without begging the question. Although Habermas does return to the theory of formal pragmatics at key points in volume 1 of *The Theory of Communicative Action*—especially chapter 3—he does so to further *elucidate* the conception of rationality that gets its preliminary specification in the opening pages of the book, not to *justify* or *ground* that conception. Habermas's stated argument for the universality of his conception of communicative rationality is altogether different, and it turns on his reading of the history of social theory and his claim that the problems that arise within that history can best be solved through the development of a theory of communicative action.

Habermas's reading of the history of social theory, from Weber to Lukács to Mead and Durkheim and back to Weber again, forms the basis of the structure of the rest of *The Theory of Communicative Action*. This reading makes it clear that although Habermas offers the theory of communicative action as an alternative to the objectivist, Marxist philosophy of history, he nevertheless remains committed to the theory of social evolution that he developed in the 1970s (see TCA2, 382–383). Reading Durkheim through Mead,

Habermas articulates in volume 2 of *The Theory of Communicative Action* an account of the emergence of modernity as a "development toward rationality" (TCA2, 91). The central notion here is the communicative rationalization of the lifeworld, which consists in the differentiation of structural components of the lifeworld (culture, society, and personality), the replacement of sacred knowledge with knowledge based on the rational adjudication of validity claims, the separation of law from morality and the universalization of both, and heightened individual autonomy and reflexivity (see TCA2, 107). Drawing on his distinction between a developmental logic and the dynamics of historical change, Habermas discerns a developmental logic in the rationalization of the lifeworld, that is, a directional learning process that brings with it an increase in rationality. Habermas fills out this idea as follows: "The further the structural components of the lifeworld and the processes that contribute to maintaining them get differentiated, the more interaction contexts come under conditions of rationally motivated mutual understanding, that is, of consensus formation that rests *in the end* on the authority of the better argument" (TCA2, 145). The ideal toward which this developmental learning process aims is characterized as a situation of "universal discourse," that is, "an idealized lifeworld reproduced through processes of mutual understanding that have been largely detached from normative contexts and transferred over to rationally motivated yes/no positions" (TCA2, 145).

Counter-Enlightenment critics have, on Habermas's view, correctly discerned distinctively pathological tendencies in modernity, but they have mistakenly attributed those tendencies to the rationalization of lifeworld itself. Habermas, by contrast, offers a broader conception of society that encompasses not only lifeworld but also systems perspectives and that enables him to locate the pathologies of modernity in the relationship between lifeworld and system (TCA2, 148ff.). Accordingly, Habermas also offers a broader conception of social evolution in volume 2 of *The Theory of Communicative Action*, according to which social evolution is "a second-order process of differentiation: system and lifeworld are differentiated in the sense that the complexity of the one and the rationality of the other grow" (TCA2, 153). Social evolution consists not only in the increasing rationalization and internal differentiation of the lifeworld and the increasing complexity and internal differentiation of social systems;[36] it also consists in a decoupling of system from lifeworld. This decoupling leads to an "irresistible irony of the world-historical process of enlightenment": "the rationalization of the lifeworld makes possible a heightening of systemic complexity, which becomes so hypertrophied that it unleashes system imperatives that burst the capacity of the lifeworld they instrumentalize" (TCA2, 155). Hence, Habermas transforms Weber's paradox of rationalization into a conflict between the rationalization of the lifeworld and the colonization of the lifeworld by system imperatives. "The rationalization of the lifeworld makes possible the emergence and growth of subsystems whose independent imperatives turn back destructively upon the lifeworld itself" (TCA2, 186). Previous social theories have been unable to see this because they have focused narrowly either on the lifeworld perspective or on the system perspective, without being able to illuminate social evolution as a two-track process of increasing social integration—in the form of a "harmonizing of action orientations"—and system integration—in the form of the "functional intermeshing of action consequences" (TCA2, 202). Habermas understands the history of social theory since Marx "as the unmixing of two paradigms that could no longer be integrated into a two-level concept of society connecting system and lifeworld" and suggests that his theory of communicative action offers a "sufficiently complex metatheoretical framework" for making sense of the complexities of modernization (TCA2, 202).

In sum, at least as far as the argument of *The Theory of Communicative Action* goes, formal pragmatics does not serve to justify Habermas's conception of rationality or his closely related account of normativity. Nor does formal pragmatics stand on its own, independent of the theory of social evolution. Rather, the claim to universality of Habermas's concept of communicative rationality rests on his reading of the history of social theory and on the ability of the theory of communicative action to solve problems generated within that history that could not be solved in its own terms. I would like to emphasize two points about this strategy. First, as

I discussed in the previous chapter, drawing on the work of historical sociologist Gurminder Bhambra, the social theory whose history Habermas reconstructs largely converges in its shared commitment to the developmental superiority of modernity, even as it remains cognizant of modernity's downsides. In that sense, the theory of modernity does quite a bit of largely implicit justificatory work in the argument of *The Theory of Communicative Action*. Second, Habermas does not consider the possibility that, as Bhambra argues, the belief in the developmental superiority of modernity does not itself have an evidentiary basis but rather rests on a questionable normative decisionism. As such, Habermas does not acknowledge what Bhambra calls the disciplinary "legitimation crises" that emerge for sociology as a result of calling into question the relationship between modernity and Eurocentrism.[37] Habermas's recent embrace of the multiple modernities paradigm, discussed in more detail below, constitutes a significant but, in my view, ultimately unsatisfactory attempt to respond to this worry.

FROM HEGEL TO KANT AND BACK AGAIN: HABERMAS'S DISCOURSE ETHICS

Before turning to a discussion of multiple modernities in Habermas, in this section I consider an alternative interpretation of Habermas's strategy for grounding normativity. As James Gordon Finlayson has recently argued,[38] a prominent line of interpretation holds that it is Habermas's discourse ethics, articulated in the 1980s just on the heels of his theory of communicative action, that serves to ground the normativity of his approach to critical theory. The central idea of Habermas's discourse ethics is the reformulation of Kant's categorical imperative into a discursive procedure for moral argumentation (D). Habermas states this reformulated categorical imperative in his original version of discourse ethics as follows: "Only those norms can claim to be valid that meet (or could meet) with the approval of all affected in their capacity *as participants in a practical discourse*" (DE, 66). From this basic principle of discourse ethics (D) combined with an account of the normative preconditions of argumentation in general, Habermas claims to be able to derive his basic moral principle, the principle of universalization (U) (see BFN, 109; IO, 43). (U) states that a moral norm is valid if and only if "all affected can accept the consequences and the side effects its general observance can be anticipated to have for the satisfaction of everyone's interests" (DE, 65).[39] According to this proposed reading, Habermas's neo-Kantian discourse ethics offers an independent justification of (D), which provides a procedure for determining the validity of norms generally, and a derivation of (U), which provides a procedure for determining the validity of specifically moral norms; together, these two principles then serve to justify the normative claims of critical theory, including its claims about historical progress and social evolution.

However, as Finlayson has argued, discourse ethics alone cannot play this justificatory role. Two of the reasons that Finlayson offers for this claim are particularly germane for this discussion.[40] First, to read Habermas as a Kantian constructivist is to say that discourse ethics gives us a basic moral and political norm (D) that is derived in a constructivist way from the demands of practical reason and that can in turn serve to justify a universal moral norm (U), which provides a standard against which particular normative claims can be measured. But this is to turn discourse ethics into a version of political philosophy as applied ethics, thus sacrificing the methodological distinctiveness of critical theory. As Finlayson puts it: "Critical social theory, in Habermas's eyes, is not applied ethics, and cannot derive its normative resources from an antecedently worked out moral theory."[41] If critical theory is to avoid collapsing into applied ethics, it must draw its normative content from within the existing social world, not from an account of practical reason as such.[42] Second, Finlayson points out that Habermas's basic moral principle—(U), the principle of universalization—is not a transhistorical moral principle; rather, it is reconstructed from an analysis of modern forms of communicative practice. This is so because discourse ethics is "very closely entwined with the theory of communicative action in as much as it consists in a rational reconstruction of moral discourse: essentially what it does is to provide a more fine-grained account of what it is for a communicative agent to discursively redeem (or make good) a validity-claim to rightness."[43] And since, as I argued above, the rational reconstruction of communicative rationality consists in the reconstruction of the intuitive knowledge of competent members of modern societies, the same goes for discourse ethics. Thus, it can't be "antecedently worked out" at all.

In other words, as Finlayson puts the point elsewhere, "Habermas's conception of *morality* has been hand in glove with a conception of *modernity* and with a theory of *modernization*."[44] Even if this wasn't totally explicit in his earliest formulations of the discourse ethics project, Habermas himself has clearly conceded this point in his more recent writings on this topic. The justification of both (D) and (U) relies on the premises of modernization theory. As Habermas says of (D): "The discourse principle provides an answer to the predicament in which the members of any moral community find themselves when, in making the transition to a modern, pluralistic society, they find themselves faced with the dilemma that though they still argue with reasons about moral judgments and beliefs, their substantive background consensus on the underlying moral norms has been shattered" (IO, 39). In that sense, the discourse principle already presupposes the "transition to a posttraditional morality" (IO, 40). Similarly, with respect to his "justification strategy" for (U), Habermas notes that this strategy "must be supplemented with genealogical arguments drawing on premises of modernization theory, if (U) is to be rendered plausible. With (U) we reassure ourselves in a reflexive manner of a residual normative substance which is preserved in posttraditional societies by the formal features of argumentation and action oriented to reaching a shared understanding" (IO, 45).[45] Inasmuch as the justification strategy for both (D) and (U) rests on Habermas's theory of modernity, discourse ethics quite obviously can't serve as the normative foundation for that theory.[46]

Although Finlayson is at pains to establish the connection between Habermas's justification of discourse ethics and his theory of modernity, he also maintains that at one time Habermas attempted to offer an independent justification for his moral theory. In that sense, Finlayson sees Habermas as having at one time attempted to offer a Kantian constructivist account of morality, only to revert in the end back to his Hegelian theory of modernity, first laid out in *The Theory of Communicative Action*. Unlike Finlayson, I'm not convinced that Habermas ever intended to offer a Kantian constructivist defense of discourse ethics. For even in his original formulation of the discourse ethics program, Habermas's defense of discourse ethics against the moral skeptic bottomed out in a claim about the ethical substance of a communicatively structured form of life.[47] The moral skeptic, Habermas argues in "Discourse Ethics," cannot deny the validity of the basic presuppositions of discourse, on which (D) and (U) are based, without falling into a performative contradiction. Hence, in the end, the skeptic's only option, says Habermas, is to opt out of communication altogether. However, in so doing,

> The skeptic voluntarily terminates his membership in the community of beings who argue—no less and no more. By refusing to argue, for instance, he cannot, even indirectly, deny that he moves in a shared sociocultural form of life, that he grew up in a web of communicative action, and that he reproduces his life in that web. In a word, the skeptic may reject morality, but he cannot reject the ethical substance (*Sittlichkeit*) of the life circumstances in which he spends his waking hours, not unless he is willing to take refuge in suicide or serious mental illness. (DE, 100)

Moreover, even if we were to accept that the Kantian constructivist interpretation of the justification strategy for discourse ethics is a plausible reading of some of Habermas's texts, this reading does not fit easily into his overall theoretical system, and he quite clearly rejects it in his most recent discussions of this issue. This means that Habermas can't be a straightforward Kantian constructivist,[48] and that discourse ethics cannot serve as the normative foundation for his theory of modernity because its plausibility rests, at least in part, on that theory.

As Finlayson sees it, the moral of the story is that Habermas should "abandon the forlorn task of convincing the moral skeptic" and stick to the more feasible task of explicating and elucidating "the self-understanding of agents who already recognize the normative meaning of moral utterances and the validity of moral norms; the self-understanding, that is, of modern moral agents."[49] Habermas's protestations to the contrary notwithstanding (see IO, 43), Finlayson maintains that since the moral skeptic will always be able to claim that the theory of modernity is "merely an *ethnocentric prejudice*," she will also always be able to claim the same of (D).[50] Understanding his project as the internal elucidation of the modern normative point of view would have the advantage of sidestepping worries about how that point of view itself is to be justified, but it would come at a rather high price for Habermas, who continually resists the kind of contextualist account of normativity that such an interpretation presupposes. For example, in *Between Facts and Norms*, Habermas maintains that although contextualism is "an understandable response to the failures of the philosophy of history and philosophical anthropology, it never gets beyond the defiant appeal to the normative force of the factual" (BFN, 2).[51] Similarly, in his recent work on religion, Habermas associates contextualism with those magical-mythical worldviews that never made the great cognitive advance characteristic of the Axial Age: the construction of the extramundane standpoint of the divine, the vantage point from which the world could be understood as a whole. Hence, Habermas now describes contextualism as a form of neopaganism (see RR1, 159; BNR, 246).[52] Habermas articulates the problem with contextualism as follows:

> The historicism of paradigms and world-pictures, now rife, is a second-level empiricism which undermines the serious task confronting a subject who takes up a positive or negative stance towards validity-claims. Such claims are always raised here and now, in a local context—but they also transcend all merely provincial yardsticks. When one paradigm or world picture is worth as much as the next, when different discourses encode everything that can be true or false, good or evil, in different ways, then this closes down the normative dimension which enables us to identify the traits of an unhappy and distorted life. (RR1, 134)

The central problem with contextualist positions, then, is that they "imply the rejection of the universalistic significance of unconditioned validity claims" (RR1, 159). In other words, Habermas assumes that contextualism at the metanormative level undermines universalism at the level of first-order, substantive norms; he assumes, that is, that metanormative contextualism entails first-order moral and political relativism. In chapter 6, I argue against this assumption and develop an account of normativity that combines metanormative contextualism about normative justification with first-order universalism. My reflections in this chapter suggest that such an approach should be congenial to Habermas, since his own normative position seems to end up in some variety of contextualism, his protestations to the contrary notwithstanding.

Habermas seems to have two choices here. He can either bite the bullet and accept that his moral project entails an internal elucidation of the modern moral point of view. Or he can argue that the theory of modernity and discourse ethics support each other in a coherentist fashion. This way of understanding his project quite clearly raises worries about circularity: the rational reconstruction of communicative competence presupposes the superiority of modernity, while the theory of modernity presupposes the superiority of a rationalized lifeworld. Of course, one could always accept that at this most basic level, the theory is circular, but argue that this circularity isn't vicious. Still, it is telling that the two most prominent post-Habermasian German critical theorists have rejected this kind of coherentist strategy, and have instead picked up either the Kantian-constructivist or the Hegelian-historicist aspects of Habermas's work and developed those further.

Moreover, with respect to the problem of Eurocentrism in Habermas's work, the crucial point is that however the question of the structure of Habermas's normative theory gets settled—whether we read him as offering an internal, contextualist elucidation of the modern moral point of view or as adopting a coherentist picture in which discourse ethics and the theory of modernity provide justificatory support for each other—it is clear that the theory of modernity plays a crucial role in grounding the normative perspective of Habermas's critical theory. Whether Habermas is a neo-Hegelian reconstructivist or a quasi-Hegelian, quasi-Kantian coherentist about normativity, the theory of modernity is doing important metanormative work for him. This means that giving up that theory would require substantial changes in his account of normativity.

EUROCENTRISM, MULTIPLE MODERNITIES, AND HISTORICAL PROGRESS

If, as I argued above, Habermas is best understood not as a constructivist but rather as either a reconstructivist or a coherentist about the sources of normativity, then this goes a long way toward explaining his ongoing and staunch defense of the ideals of the Enlightenment (see, most notably, PDM). For, as we have seen, on either of these interpretations of his project, the thought that the normative resources of the Enlightenment or of European modernity are the result of a process of sociocultural learning and rationalization plays a central role in grounding the normativity of critical theory for Habermas. But perhaps no other aspect of Habermas's work has generated as much criticism as this idea. To date, much of this criticism has focused on his dismissive and tendentious readings of poststructuralist and psychoanalytic thinkers.[53] And yet, the grounding of normativity in the achievements of European modernity clearly leaves Habermas open to critique from a post- or decolonial perspective as well. Enrique Dussel puts the point well when he notes that Habermas's defense of modernity as an exclusively European phenomenon occludes the non-European periphery in relation to which Europe constituted itself. "The occlusion of this periphery," Dussel continues, "leads the major contemporary thinkers of the 'center' [such as Habermas] into a Eurocentric fallacy in their understanding of modernity."[54] Thus, Habermas's reconstruction of the philosophical discourse of modernity follows Hegel in taking the decisive events in the formation of modernity to be the Reformation, the Enlightenment, and the French Revolution; conspicuously absent from this list is the conquest of the Americas.[55] More recently, Habermas himself has acknowledged this problem: "The Enlightenment remained ignorant of the barbaric reverse side of its own mirror for too long. Its universal claims made it easy to overlook the particularistic kernel of its European origin. This immobilized, rigidified rationalism has been transformed into the stifling power of a capitalistic world civilization, which assimilates alien cultures and abandons its own traditions to oblivion" (RR1, 130). Facing up to the barbarism at the heart of European colonialism and its postcolonial, neoliberal, capitalist legacy rightly has the effect of undermining an overly confident self-understanding of modernity (EFK, 39).

And yet, in his recent work, Habermas continues to endorse the idea that the rationalized lifeworld of European modernity represents the outcome of a historical learning process—even going so far as to use the term "civilizing" to characterize Europe in relation to the rest of the world (see DW, 16)—and to defend his view against the charge of Eurocentrism that this endorsement invites. His response involves appealing to the *necessity* and *unavoidability* of the universalizable norms central to the legacy of the European Enlightenment. For example, with respect to the central principle of discourse ethics, (U), Habermas argues that it is grounded in the unavoidable presuppositions of a communicative form of life to which there is no coherent alternative, to which the only possible alternatives are "the monadic isolation of strategic action, or schizophrenia and suicide" (DE, 102). Hence, (U) is, as Habermas puts it, an "inescapable presupposition of [an] irreplaceable discourse and in that sense universal" (DE, 84).[56] Similarly, with respect to political modernity, Habermas maintains that there is no viable alternative, since no purely premodern societies remain in our globalized world (EFK, 28). And in his recent work on religion, even as Habermas acknowledges the rootedness of the normative ideals of the Enlightenment in the Jewish and Christian religious traditions, he nevertheless defends their necessity and unavoidability. "Universalistic egalitarianism, from which sprang the ideals of freedom and a collective life in solidarity, the autonomous conduct of life and emancipation, the individual morality of conscience, human rights and democracy, is the direct legacy of the Judaic ethic of justice and the Christian ethic of love" (RR1, 149). And yet, Habermas continues, "This legacy, substantially unchanged, has been the object of a continual critical reappropriation and reinterpretation. *Up to this very day there is no alternative to it.* And in light of the current challenges of a postnational constellation, we must draw sustenance now, as in the past, from this substance. Everything else is idle postmodern talk" (RR1, 149, emphasis added).

As I mentioned above, Habermas is well aware of the ways in which Enlightenment ideals, particularly ideals of progress, modernization, and development, have been entangled with the so-called civilizing mission of the West. Nevertheless, as he makes clear in his discussion of Kant's philosophy of history, he believes that these ideals can be disentangled from their ideological roots. Although Habermas's own philosophy of history shares with Kant's the "heuristic aim" of lending the "idea of the cosmopolitan condition empirical probability and plausibility" (DW, 145), Habermas insists that, in taking up Kant's philosophical-historical project, we must "look beyond the prejudices associated with [Kant's] historical horizon" (DW, 145). These prejudices include an insensitivity to cultural differences, a blindness to the explosive force of nationalism, a "'humanist' conviction of the superiority of European civilization and the white race" (DW, 146), and a lack of awareness of the fact that "European international law" was "embedded in a common Christian culture" (DW, 146). However, Habermas insists:

> The provinciality of our historical consciousness vis-à-vis the future is not an objection to the universalistic program of Kantian moral and legal theory. Its blind spots betray a historically understandable selectivity in the *application* of the cognitive procedure of universalization and mutual perspective-taking which Kant associates with practical reason and which underlies the cosmopolitan transformation of international law. (DW, 146)

In other words, the problem, in Habermas's view, does not lie at the level of the normative justification of the Kantian moral and political project of cosmopolitanism, only at the level of its selective and inappropriate application.

Moreover, through his engagement with the literature on multiple modernities,[57] Habermas attempts to distance himself from the Eurocentrism of earlier theories of modernization (see esp. EFK). After noting that classical social theory from Saint-Simon to Parsons based its understanding of modernity on a theory of social evolution that took Western civilization as paradigmatic, Habermas asks whether "the global society can still be grasped in terms of categories of social evolution read off from the Western model" (EFK, 20). Rejecting functionalist accounts of modernization that view the emerging world society solely as the result of the spread of functional subsystems—in commerce, science and technology, communication, education, and so forth—across national boundaries and culturalist accounts that view civilizations as self-enclosed cultures and associate "modernity" with the project of Western culture alone, Habermas draws on the multiple modernities paradigm to offer a two-track analysis of modernization. The functionalist perspective captures an important truth, namely, that functionally integrated systems—most importantly, the global economy, but also global systems of scientific research, communication, athletic contest, and so on—place significant constraints on all members of the emerging world society. In that sense, all members of the emerging world society share the same globalized infrastructure. However, what the functionalist perspective misses is the fact that "*different* cultures assimilate and adapt these processes emanating from Western culture *in their own ways*. . . . Other civilizations respond to the pressures from the West to modernize their societies as *challenges* to which they seek answers that draw upon their own cultural resources" (EFK, 24). In other words, the spread of a globalized infrastructure isn't the end of the story about modernization; that shared infrastructure is compatible with a high degree of cultural hybridity. This is the truth that the culturalist perspective points to, though it goes too far in this direction by equating modernization with Westernization.[58] In light of these considerations, Habermas offers the following "reflexive concept of 'modernity'": "Based on *the same* globalized social infrastructure (whose primary feature is the stubborn orientation to the scientific-technological control of nature and the world, the bureaucratic exercise of power, and the capitalist production of wealth), 'modernity' today represents something like the shared arena in which *different civilizations* encounter one another as they modify this infrastructure in more or less culture-specific ways" (EFK, 25).

However, it is far from clear that the shift to the multiple modernities paradigm actually resolves the problem of Eurocentrism. For one thing, Habermas's version of the multiple modernities paradigm assumes that the functional infrastructure of modernity includes both capitalist markets and bureaucratic, positive law, and that these two functional systems develop together. On this assumption, the emergence of positive law and the democratic legal systems that serve to guarantee bourgeois rights become something like a consolation prize, a beneficial side effect of the inevitable, inexorable rise of modern capitalism. However, as Samir Amin argues in his classic study *Eurocentrism*, this connection between capitalism and bureaucratic positive law holds only in the center of the capitalist world system and not in the periphery. While Amin agrees with Habermas on the basic distinction between functional and cultural dimensions of modernization and on the claim that capitalist economic systems can be instantiated in a variety of different cultural forms and inflections, he also maintains that the global spread of capitalism is not only compatible with the continuation of so-called premodern forms of domination;[59] it also *requires* a persistent, ineliminable gap between a (democratic) center and a subaltern periphery that in turn provides fertile ground for antidemocratic movements in the periphery.[60] Amin's analysis thus throws cold water on the Habermasian idea that although the global spread of capitalism may be problematic, at least it brings positive law and, eventually, democratic rights in its train. To assume this is, as Amin's work reminds us, to indulge in a Eurocentric "refusal to grant imperialism all of the decisive importance that it has in really existing capitalism,"[61] a refusal that is, Amin contends, unfortunately characteristic of much Western Marxism. This refusal is related to a failure to see that "the contradiction between the centers and the peripheries constitutes the fundamental contradiction of the modern world."[62]

Furthermore, as Gurminder Bhambra argues, the theory of multiple modernities, and in particular the distinction between a shared process of functional or systemic modernization tempered by particular cultural instantiations of that process, seeks "to contain challenges to the dominant theoretical framework of sociology by not allowing 'difference' *to make a difference* to the original categories of modernity."[63] In that sense, the multiple modernities paradigm "does nothing to address the fundamental problems with the conceptualization of modernity itself."[64] Bhambra's claim is made plausible by the fact that Habermas's embrace of the multiple modernities paradigm does not compel him to let go of the version of the story about the developmental superiority of European modernity that he has defended since he first offered his theory of social evolution. For example, Habermas continues to associate heightened reflexivity with an irreversible moral-political learning process and claims that "we can indeed trace the, for now, last socially relevant push in the reflexivity of consciousness to Western modernity" (PWS, 2). This push in reflexivity is evidenced by a number of developments, including the instrumental attitude of state bureaucracy toward political power that emerges in early European modernity, the self-reflexivity of modern positive law and rational morality, and the historical consciousness that emerges in nineteenth-century European thought. The heightened reflexivity and increased decentration of individual and group perspectives that result from these developments constitute, for Habermas, irreversible social-cognitive learning processes and "indubitable" instances of historical progress (PWS, 2). Moreover, these pushes further a set of transformations that Habermas, in his recent work on religion, traces back to the emergence of the Axial Age:[65] "In European modernity, we observe a further cognitive push in the *same* dimensions. We observe a sharpening of the consciousness of contingency and an extension of futural anticipation; egalitarian universalism becomes more pointed in law and morality; and there is progressive individualization. In any case, we still draw our normative self-understanding from this (disregarding short-winded, fashionable denials)" (PWS, 8).

So, even in the face of the charge of Eurocentrism, Habermas remains committed to a progressive view of history according to which European modernity represents a moral-political advance over premodern forms of life. And even as he recognizes the need to rethink the central assumptions of modernization theory, he insists that we shouldn't throw the baby out with the bathwater by rejecting the idea of European modernity as a privileged example of sociocultural learning processes in an effort to avoid Eurocentrism. Indeed, this stance shouldn't be at all surprising since the main outlines of this very same understanding of social evolution as a process of moral-political learning that is characterized by greater degrees of reflexivity and decentration of worldviews go all the way back to Habermas's work on social evolution from the 1970s.[66]

The difficulty, for our purposes, is that the assumption of the developmental superiority and unavoidability of certain features of European modernity—however much that assumption is attenuated by Habermas's acknowledgment of the contingency of historical developments and the tendency to regression or by his more recent talk of multiple modernities—does not sit well with Habermas's own stated goal for the structure of ongoing debate within the global public sphere, in which "the West is one participant among others, and all participants must be willing to be enlightened by others about their respective blind spots" (PWS, 1). That is to say, Habermas's philosophical commitment to understanding European modernity as the outcome of a process of social evolution and moral-political learning, insofar as it positions the European or Euro-American participant as developmentally superior to members of traditional or "nonmodern" cultures, is at odds with his professed desire for an intercultural dialogue in the global public sphere in which we are open to being enlightened by others about our own blind spots. As Habermas recognizes in the context of his recent work on religion, to position others as anachronistic holdovers from an earlier stage of development is "to fail to take [them] seriously as modern contemporaries," a failure that is "as incompatible with the requirement of reciprocal recognition as it is with the willingness to adopt the perspectives of others in the give and take of arguments and positions" (R, 372). However, Habermas has yet to work through the implications that this postsecular insight has for his reliance on the theories of social evolution and modernity; as a result, these theories form the Eurocentric kernel at the center of his critical theory and constitute a serious obstacle to the project of decolonizing Habermasian critical theory.

Habermas attempts to respond to this kind of worry by distinguishing between a philosophical (or metaphilosophical) reconstruction of the nature of postmetaphysical thinking, on the one hand, and the actual intercultural dialogue, on the other. His own reconstruction of postmetaphysical thinking—understood as a form of thought that is highly reflexive, decentered, historically conscious, attuned to the fact of pluralism, and secular without being secularistic—is offered as "a meta-philosophical proposal that is to apply, not only to Western thought, but to contemporary thought in general" (PWS, 7). This proposal, like all such proposals, is open to critical discussion by other philosophers. When it comes to actual intercultural dialogue about some specific political or cultural issue, by contrast, we are to comport ourselves not as philosophers but rather "as second persons to participants from other cultural backgrounds. . . . In this *performative* role, we may be able to learn of the need to correct our possible Western biases in the reconstruction of postmetaphysical thinking. For fallibilist consciousness naturally belongs to postmetaphysical thinking" (PWS, 7).

Hence, the Habermasian participant in an intercultural dialogue in a transnational or global public sphere is supposed to be able to toggle back and forth between two different points of view. At a philosophical level, she draws her own normative perspective and orientation from an understanding of European modernity as the outcome of a historical learning process; hence, at a metanormative level, she views her own postmetaphysical and postsecular point of view as developmentally superior to traditional or religious points of view. And yet, as a participant in intercultural dialogue with those who do not share this postmetaphysical orientation, she is supposed to be open to learning from these others and in particular open to learning from them about her own Western biases. It is as if Habermas would have us say something like the following: "We believe that our modern European point of view represents a developmental advance over premodern or traditional forms of life, including your own. But, since we are fallibilists, we know that we could be wrong, so we'd like to engage in an open dialogue with you, who are not the beneficiaries of this historical legacy, to find out what we might learn from you."

Such a stance, however, arguably places insuperable cognitive obstacles on Western participants in intercultural dialogue.[67] A

Western participant who views, at a metanormative level, her own form of life as the outcome of a historical developmental learning process can be as open-minded and fallibilist as she likes; in the process of dialogue with non-Western others, she can never be sure whether she is disagreeing with the content of their views for good reasons or dismissing them out of hand because she views their adherents as developmentally inferior, as not yet having learned something that she now knows. This is not a matter of good or bad will on the part of the Western participant; it is simply a function of the logic of her own developmentalist metanormative position. Such a developmentalist account inevitably invites the temptation to view those who are designated as nonmodern as what Dipesh Chakrabarty calls "human embodiments of the principle of anachronism."[68] The crucial point is this: viewing one's dialogue partners in this way is not conducive to adopting a stance of dialogical openness and inclusion.

So what sort of metanormative position does facilitate such a stance? Chakrabarty argues that in order to be truly open, an intercultural dialogue must be open-ended and nonteleological. As Chakrabarty puts it:

> A dialogue can be genuinely open only under one condition: that no party puts itself in a position where it can unilaterally decide the final outcomes of the conversation. This never happens between the modern and the nonmodern because, however noncoercive the conversation between the transcendent academic observer and the subaltern who enters into a historical dialogue with him, this dialogue takes place within a field of possibilities that is already structured from the beginning in favor of certain outcomes.[69]

A genuinely open dialogue between the modern and the subaltern requires, for Chakrabarty, "an openness so radical that I can express it only in Heideggerian terms: the capacity to hear that which one does not already understand."[70] This kind of openness requires moderns to be "open to the possibility of our thought systems . . . being rendered finite by the presence of the other."[71] But this requires a stance of humility about the grounding of our normative commitments at the metanormative level, at the level of the thought systems and forms of understanding that undergird our normative principles.

Saba Mahmood captures this stance well in her reflections on her relationship as a feminist to the members of the Egyptian women's piety movement that she studied for her anthropological fieldwork:

> Do my political visions ever run up against the responsibility that I incur for the destruction of life forms so that "unenlightened" women may be taught to live more freely? Do I even fully comprehend the forms of life that I want so passionately to remake? Would an intimate knowledge of lifeworlds distinct from mine ever lead me to question my own certainty about what I prescribe as a superior way of life for others?[72]

The end point of this line of questioning, for Mahmood, is the adoption of a stance of humility toward one's own normative and political commitments, a humility that is rooted in an awareness of the limits and contingencies of the ways in which those commitments are grounded. This awareness, in turn, facilitates a willingness to have one's own commitments destabilized in the encounter with other forms of life.[73] For Mahmood, this mode of encountering the Other requires a particular epistemic (or what I would call metanormative) stance; this stance, in turn, is characterized by the epistemic virtue of humility, which demands the acceptance and acknowledgment of the finitude and contingency of my own form of life, and the suspension of the assumption that my form of life is superior to those of the cultural Others with whom I am in dialogue. Contra Habermas (TCA1, 107–120), Mahmood suggests not only that understanding another culture or form of life does not require that I take a yes-no position on the validity of its fundamental beliefs and practices, but that such a judgmental stance actively *impedes* understanding. Contra McCarthy, she contends that we are not compelled to regard any worldview that has not yet undergone the historicist enlightenment as inferior to ours in that respect. What we are compelled to do is to apply the insights of the historicist enlightenment more fully and self-reflexively to our own view, to accept its finitude and contingencies by adopting a stance of humility toward it. This is the epistemic or metanormative stance required for the sort of genuine openness to subaltern others that is required if we are to decolonize critical theory. As I will argue in more detail in chapter 5, Adorno and Foucault offer important resources for further developing this notion of epistemic or metanormative humility.

The central puzzle of Habermas's work is how he actually accomplishes his aim of putting critical theory on a secure normative footing. In this chapter, I have argued that his theory of social evolution and the closely related theory of modernity, far from being outdated relics of Habermas's early work, are crucial for solving this puzzle. No straightforward Kantian constructivist, Habermas maintains, in a neo-Hegelian fashion, that the norms embedded in our practices of communication and our modern, posttraditional form of life deserve our support insofar as they are the outcome of a sociocultural learning process. They are universal in a peculiar, and peculiarly Hegelian, sense: first not in the order of existence but rather in the order of explanation, inasmuch as they represent the inherent telos of the communicative use of language. Hence the form of life in which they are embedded and to which there is no viable alternative is understood as a cognitive advance over premodern, traditional forms of life.

In answer to the question posed in the introduction to this chapter—is communicative ethics a theory of justice, a theory of universalist morality, or a metatheory of normative justification?—my answer is: all of the above. Primarily, Habermas's theory is a metanormative theory of justification, that is, a metaethical theory of moral epistemology. That theory of justification, in turn, grounds his universalist moral theory. What is less clear is how exactly Habermas understands the relationship between the metanormative and normative parts of his project. This chapter has presented three possible ways of understanding this relationship. First, the universalistic accounts of language, communicative rationality, and discourse ethics could serve to ground the rest of the normative theory, including the theory of modernity. As I have argued, this is not, as is sometimes supposed, Habermas's position, though it does roughly capture the structure of Rainer Forst's avowedly Kantian constructivist view, which I discuss in more detail in chapter 4. As noted above and explored in more detail in chapter 4, a problem with this position is that it risks giving up on one of the central commitments of critical theory, its resolution to draw its normative perspective from *within* the existing social world. Taking up Habermas's project in this neo-Kantian direction thus threatens to transform critical theory into a version of political philosophy as applied ethics. Second, the theory of modernity could play the role of justifying normativity; on this alternative, formal pragmatics and discourse ethics would be construed in a much weaker sense, as elucidations of the linguistic or moral understanding of modern agents, that is, as an internal immanent reconstruction of aspects of a modern, rationalized lifeworld.[74] This strategy, which is basically the strategy adopted by Axel Honneth, as I will argue in the next chapter, has the advantage of hewing more closely to the methodology of critical theory as immanent critique, but it has the disadvantage of entailing a much more contextualist metanormative position than Habermas wants to have. The third alternative, which is the one that I have defended in this chapter, views formal pragmatics and the theory of modernity as providing mutual support for each other. This strategy not only also leads to worries about contextualism, since the methodology of rational reconstruction has to presuppose the superiority of the point of view of modernity and hence Habermas can give no independent justification of that standpoint; it also raises concerns about circularity. I suspect that this is why the most prominent post-Habermasian German Frankfurt School theorists have abandoned this strategy and instead chosen either a more straightforwardly Kantian (in the case of Forst) or more straightforwardly Hegelian (in the case of Honneth) path.

I will return to some of these conceptual and epistemological worries about contextualism in the final chapter. The important point for now is that once we see the crucial role that the theories of social evolution and modernity are playing in Habermas's attempt to ground the normative perspective of critical theory, it becomes clearer why he is so unwilling to give up his commitment to claims about the superiority of certain aspects of European modernity. It is not that he just so happens to be a big fan of the Enlightenment; rather, the idea that the Enlightenment represents a developmental advance over previous forms of life is doing a fair amount of justificatory, metanormative work for him. Hence he can't really give up this commitment without rethinking his approach to grounding normativity. As I discussed above, one of the goals of Habermas's theory of social evolution was to specify the historical conditions under which reflection on history became possible for us. As Habermas has acknowledged in some of his recent work, colonialism and the so-called civilizing mission of the West are important features of those historical conditions. But Habermas does not push this crucial insight far enough. Situating our historically self-conscious philosophy within our own time requires something more than what Habermas supposed in the 1970s. It requires problematizing the historical story that positions European modernity as the outcome of a developmental learning process, inasmuch as this story necessarily positions non- or premodern Others as cognitively and normatively inferior to "us." It requires rethinking the relationship between our metanormative justificatory strategy and the stance that we take toward those we deem to be non- or premodern in intercultural dialogues that aim toward openness and inclusion. It may even require refraining from designating Others as non- or premodern in the first place, inasmuch as, as Chakrabarty reminds us, such designations may be nothing more than gestures of the powerful.[75] If critical theory is to undertake the difficult work of decolonizing itself, it will need to scrutinize much more carefully the (post)colonial power investments of its own strategies for grounding normativity.

3

The Ineliminability of Progress?

HONNETH'S HEGELIAN CONTEXTUALISM

Like Habermas, Axel Honneth has long been concerned with the problem of grounding the normative perspective of critical theory. Although both theorists share the general ambition of grounding critical theory's normative perspective immanently, from within existing social reality, Honneth has criticized Habermas's theory of communicative action for anchoring its normative perspective in an account of societal rationalization processes that take place behind the backs and above the heads of the individuals involved (CP, chap. 9).[1] Such an approach fails to give critical theory a pretheoretical foothold in actual social life. By contrast, Honneth locates the source of innerworldly or intramundane transcendence in what he calls "pre-theoretical praxis," that is, in the empirical experiences and attitudes of social actors, particularly their experiences of injustice (SDD, 64). With this shift in focus, the anchor for critical theory becomes the feeling of moral disrespect that accompanies experiences of misrecognition, and the normative core of critical theory shifts from the Habermasian idea of communication free from domination to that idea's intersubjective and sociological preconditions: namely, relations of social recognition.

Over the last twenty-five years, Honneth has developed his theory of recognition into a rich, productive, and comprehensive paradigm for critical theory. His systematic presentation of three distinct yet interrelated spheres of recognition—the family, legal rights, and social esteem—each with its distinctive role to play in the development of key aspects of individual autonomy—self-confidence, self-respect, and self-esteem—has enabled Honneth to make contributions to a wide range of contemporary debates, ranging from theories of the self and the relevance of psychoanalysis for critical theory to the best way to critique contemporary capitalism and the conditions under which democracy can flourish. And yet, as with Habermas, Honneth's strategy for grounding the normativity of his theory of recognition is not entirely clear and is open to competing interpretations. In a perspicacious essay on Honneth's early work, Christopher Zurn noted this unclarity. Honneth's normative theory is grounded in a sociological analysis of experiences of injustice and struggles for recognition; on the basis of this analysis, Honneth then offers an abstract formal conception of ethical life that attempts to spell out the necessary conditions for full ethical self-realization that can, in turn, serve as the normative standard for social critique. This "formal conception of ethical life" spells out "the entirety of intersubjective conditions that can be shown to serve as necessary preconditions for individual self-realization" (SR, 173). And yet, Zurn asks, "how is it possible for Honneth to defend his implicit claim that uncoerced, full self-realization can serve as *the* critical yardstick for the social conditions of the good life *just because* it can be abstracted as a structurally necessary telos immanent in social relations of recognition?"[2] How, in other words, do we know that the normative perspective that we reconstruct through a sociological analysis of struggles for recognition is itself valid and deserving of our support?

Zurn articulates three possible strategies that Honneth might adopt for responding to this question: the first is a constructivist strategy that links the formal conception of ethical life to the background conditions for Habermasian-style discourse ethics; the second is a historical, reconstructivist strategy that presents the formal conception of ethical life as the result of a directed process of historical development; and the third is a philosophical-anthropological strategy that grounds the formal conception of ethical life in a universal conception of human nature.[3] In his recent work, Honneth has made it quite clear that he has no interest in pursuing the first strategy.[4] However, as Zurn has suggested more recently, Honneth "has not yet settled decisively between the second and third options, but is still actively grappling with the problem."[5]

In what follows, I shall argue that Honneth's main strategy for grounding normativity in his recent work is Zurn's second option, that of historical, normative reconstruction though, as we will see, his philosophical anthropology does still play a role, if a somewhat problematic one. This historically reconstructivist strategy for grounding normativity leads Honneth to make strong claims about the centrality of the backward-looking idea of historical progress—what I have been calling progress as a "fact"—for critical theory. For example, in a recent programmatic essay, Honneth claims that critical theory offers a version of ethical perfectionism in which "the normative goal of societies should consist in the reciprocal enabling of self-realization, although what favors this goal is grasped as the grounded result of a certain analysis of the process of human development" (CT, 795). In other words, what favors the normative goal that animates critical theory—"the reciprocal enabling of self-realization"—is that it is understood as the result of a developmental process. In this way, Honneth clearly roots the forward looking idea of progress as an imperative in a backward looking story about the process of historical progress or development that has led up to "us." In his recent work, Honneth not only argues that the project of critical theory cannot be renewed today without the idea of historical progress; he also maintains that this idea is ineliminable for anyone who takes a stand on political issues or events in their own time.[6] In other words, the idea of historical progress is not only a normative necessity for critical theory if it is to avoid collapsing into relativism or conventionalism; it is also a practical-transcendental necessity—an unavoidable commitment—whenever we take a certain stance with respect to political struggles in our own time.[7] This strategy and these claims raise deep and difficult questions about the relationship between the normativity of critical theory and the idea of historical progress, questions that I shall attempt to address in this chapter. As I see it, Honneth's claim that the idea of historical progress is necessary for critical theory is not only plagued by conceptual problems; it also leaves him vulnerable to the kinds of post- and decolonial objections that I discussed in chapters 1 and 2. To be clear: Honneth does not explicitly make any claims about the superiority of Western, industrialized, wealthy European and American democracies vis-à-vis non-Western societies. Nonetheless, it is a plausible inference from his progressive reading of the central practices and institutions of modern, Western societies to the claim that such societies are developmentally superior not only to the premodern, feudal European societies from which they emerged but also to other actually existing "premodern" or "nonmodern" societies.[8] At the very least, and especially in light of Honneth's stated aim of reanimating Hegel's intertwining of theory and history, which was itself deeply marked by colonial commitments and logics, Honneth owes us an explanation for why he is not committed to such a claim. And, as we will see below, Honneth can escape such criticisms only at considerable cost to his own theory.

After laying out Honneth's conception of historical progress and clarifying the role that this conception plays in his understanding of the methodology and aims of critical theory, I critically assess his arguments for the ineliminability of progress. I argue that Honneth fails to make the case for his practical-transcendental claim that critical theory requires a robust conception of historical progress. Moreover, drawing on the insights of queer postcolonial theory, I argue that it's a good thing, too, since critical theorists ought to be skeptical of such a robust conception of progress and of the role that such a conception plays in undergirding the normativity of Honneth's critical theory. Finally, I consider Honneth's options for responding to the charge of Eurocentrism, each of which I find problematic. A far better way for critical theory to decolonize itself, as I shall argue in chapter 5, is through a thoroughgoing problematization of the idea of historical progress.

PROGRESS AND CRITICAL THEORY

Honneth's defense of the ineliminability of the idea of historical progress for critical theory is laid out clearly and succinctly in his essay titled "The Irreducibility [*Unhintergebarkeit*] of Progress:

Kant's Account of the Relationship Between Morality and History." In that essay, Honneth offers an original reading and defense of what he calls Kant's unofficial or implicit philosophy of history and argues, following on this reading of Kant, that the acceptance of a certain understanding of progress is unavoidable for any theory that aims to be critical. Distinguishing between "system-conforming" and "system-bursting" aspects of Kant's philosophy of history, Honneth identifies two aspects of the system-bursting or unofficial conception of history found in Kant's work. The first aspect concerns Kant's normative justification for the idea of historical progress, that is to say, his account of why we have a right to this idea. The second aspect concerns his descriptive account of history as a progressive development. Only by drawing on both of these aspects of Kant's system-bursting account of progress, Honneth argues, can his philosophy of history become relevant for us today. Together, these two system-bursting aspects of Kant's account present an understanding of progress as a cumulative but contingent and conflict-ridden learning process that, as Honneth says, "necessarily shapes the historical self-understanding of the supporters of the Enlightenment" (IP, 18). In other words, all those who side with the political achievements and normative self-understandings of the Enlightenment must understand themselves as heirs to this learning process, a process that they also aim to advance through their own actions in their own time.

Kant famously held that we have a right to assume, as a regulative principle, that human history is characterized by the progressive development of humankind's rational potential. Although Kant maintained that we cannot know the direction of history as a whole, since this lies beyond the bounds of our possible experience, he nevertheless is typically taken to have offered two different sorts of reasons for the claim that we have a right to assume or to posit a progressive understanding of human history. The first, theoretical, reason appeals to our cognitive interest in unifying our experience of the world, including the disordered events of the past.[9] As a unifying a priori principle, Kant proposes the purposiveness of nature, which allows us to comprehend history "as a system" through which Nature uses evil to produce good, rather than as "a planless conglomeration of human actions."[10] The second, practical, reason appeals to the role that the idea of historical progress plays in orienting our efforts to promote the highest good, which is our moral duty.[11]

Kant's theoretical and practical arguments are complicated, and they rely on controversial premises from his critical philosophy—I take it that this is what Honneth means by calling them "system-conforming," meaning that they conform to Kant's critical system. I won't go into the details of either argument here, however, since Honneth introduces them only by way of a contrast with a third—unofficial, implicit, and largely unrecognized—justificatory argument for the idea of historical progress to be found in Kant's writings. This unofficial, "system-bursting" argument does not rely on problematic presuppositions about the purposiveness of nature or about the possibility of uncovering synthetic a priori principles of pure practical reason, and in that sense it bursts the boundaries of Kant's own critical system in a distinctly Hegelian fashion.[12] Honneth labels this third model "hermeneutic-explicative." With this third model, Honneth writes:

> Kant attempts to make intelligible or to explicate which concept of history someone who understands their own writerly activity as a contribution to a process of enlightenment would necessarily have to commit themselves to. A subject with such a self-understanding, so Kant wants to demonstrate, *has no alternative* than to understand the developmental process that precedes him as the gradual achievement of something better, and conversely to construe the time that still lies before him as an opportunity for further improvement. For the normative standards according to which this subject measures the moral quality of his current circumstances in his practical engagements demand from him that he judge the conditions of the past as inferior and the potential circumstances of the future as superior. (IP, 8)

Unlike Kant's other two arguments justifying the idea of historical progress, which are addressed to interpreters or observers of history, this hermeneutic-explicative argument is addressed to members of an enlightened public who are participants in a process of moral-political progress. Moreover, Honneth maintains, only with this third argument does Kant attempt to demonstrate, by means of a transcendental argument, the ineliminability of the idea of progress. In other words, whereas Kant's other two arguments merely contend that we have a *right* to understand history in terms of progress, this argument purports to establish that simply by taking an affirmative or a negative stance toward some event in their historical present, individuals thereby *necessarily* and *unavoidably* commit themselves to viewing that event, first, as better than what came before it and, second, as potentially not as good as what will come after. When Kant's contemporaries affirm the French Revolution, for example, "the standpoint of their historical consciousness shifts in the moment of affirmation because now they must unify all historically prior occurrences and circumstances in light of the most recent developments into a directed process in which the moral achievements of the present mark a successful intermediary stage" (IP, 10).

To be sure, for Kant, even this hermeneutic-explicative model of progress is still ultimately dependent upon his moral philosophy, for it is his moral philosophy that allows him to claim the moral legitimacy of the French Revolution. Nevertheless, Honneth maintains that, with this third model, Kant engages in a "moderate de-transcendentalization" of practical reason, that is to say, he situates practical reason historically, in that he understands "the hypothesis of progress as the product of a perspectival shift of the historical subject him or herself" (IP, 11). In so doing, Kant moves closer to Hegel's account of the historical realization of practical reason,[13] but without accepting Hegel's own philosophy of history, which, on Honneth's reading, is plagued by a commitment to an objective teleology.[14] In that sense, Hegel's philosophy of history is, according to Honneth, much more in step with Kant's system-conforming understanding of history, the one based on his philosophy of nature. The core of this idea, and what protects this third Kantian argument from ending up in Hegel's philosophy of history, is what Honneth calls the "hermeneutic thought that the chaotic multiplicity of history must appear as a directed process of progress *only to those individuals who must historically situate themselves in their present context in the interests of politico-moral improvement*" (IP, 11, emphasis added).

Turning now to Kant's descriptive account of historical progress, Honneth acknowledges Kant's rather unfortunate tendency to produce a speculative philosophy of history in which even the most objectionable and repugnant aspects of our history can be seen as fulfilling Nature's secret intention to secure our moral progress. And yet, he maintains, implicit in Kant's writings is a second, system-bursting descriptive account, analogous to his hermeneutic-explicative argument for the necessity of the idea of historical progress for those subjects who are committed to progressive social change. This alternative descriptive account construes progress not in terms of natural teleology but rather as a historical learning process. The idea of a historical learning process presupposes that a certain aptitude for learning exists at the level of the species, and that each generation has the ability not only to repeat but also to enrich and build upon the heritage that it inherits from previous generations. On this model, knowledge is built cumulatively through the efforts of successive generations. "Once such a mechanism of learning spanning the generations is presupposed," Honneth writes, "human history, taken as a whole, could therefore be understood as a cognitive process of progress: indeed, as the unfolding of moral rationalization" (IP, 14–15).

Moreover, Kant's account of this learning process is not an overly idealized one. He concedes that this process of moral rationalization faces formidable obstacles, in the form of what Honneth calls "counterforces" that serve as obstacles to historical learning. One of these counterforces, perhaps the most relevant for our discussion, is the human tendency to conform to conventional modes of thinking. Kant's essay "What Is Enlightenment?" memorably opens with the claim that this tendency is exploited by powerful people who use their power to prevent their subordinates from making free and undistorted use of their own faculty of intelligence. "After the guardians have first made their domestic cattle dumb and have made sure that these placid creatures will not dare take a single step without the harness of the cart by which they are confined," Kant writes, "the guardians then show them the danger which threatens if they try to go alone."[15] In other words, dominant groups employ techniques designed to prevent their subordinates from types of learning that would undermine the legitimacy of the existing system of dominance and subordination. Hence, relations of social and cultural domination are obstacles to historical learning processes, and the ubiquity of such power relations makes the historical realization of reason a "deeply discontinuous process" (IP, 16). There is, however, in Honneth's view, an antidote to this counterforce, because

> moral attainments with universalistic validity necessarily leave traces in social memory. This is because events of such magnitude, which affectively touch on the "interests of humanity," can no longer fall into oblivion with respect to the species' learning capacity. The result is that, like stages or degrees, they mark a progress in the process of a future emancipation of humanity that is irreducible.
>
> (IP, 17)

In other words, once achieved, certain stages of progress cannot be abandoned at will; they are irreversible not in the sense that they cannot be undone but rather in the sense that any deviation from those achievements must necessarily be viewed as a regression.

Moreover, progress is understood as a process of expanding social rationalization, whereby existing relations of power and domination and other pathological deformations of reason are progressively overcome. As was the case for Habermas, progress is thus understood as a process of historical development whereby a socially instantiated reason is progressively purified of power relations.[16] Honneth maintains, further, that critical theory *must* be grounded in some notion of a basic interest in a progressive realization of socially instantiated reason, through which reason gradually becomes less pathological by disentangling itself from power relations. "Without a realistic concept of 'emancipatory interest' that puts at its center the idea of an indestructible core of rational responsiveness on the part of subjects," Honneth writes, "the critical project will have no future" (SPR, 41–42). Like Kant, Honneth believes that this realization of reason is possible only at the social—rather than the individual—level.[17] Hence, critical theory, in Honneth's view, "relies on the possibility of viewing history with reason as its guiding thread" (SPR, 20).

In his unofficial, system-bursting philosophy of history, Honneth argues, Kant provides us with a way of viewing history with reason as its guiding thread by motivating a belief in "a process towards the better, one that takes the shape of [a] learning process that is repeatedly violently interrupted, but that can never really be fully halted" (IP, 17). Kant offers a teleological account of directed historical progress, but, unlike Hegel's, his teleology is not an objective teleology governed by the unfolding of spirit over the heads and behind the backs of actors. Rather, it is "a construction that subjects acting in the sense of enlightenment must achieve in order to gain a clear consciousness of the historical place of their own projects" (IP, 17). Moreover, Honneth maintains that this idea of a teleological, directed learning process "*necessarily* shapes the historical self-understanding of the supporters of the Enlightenment" (IP, 18, emphasis added). Following Kant's transcendental argument, Honneth maintains that "all those who actively side with the moral achievements of the Enlightenment are thus forced to see the history preceding them as a conflict-ridden learning process, which, as heirs of this process, they have to continue in their own time" (IP, 18).

In other words, just as Kant's contemporaries who cheered on the French Revolution were thereby compelled to see that event as an intermediary stage in a directed process of moral-political development, those of us who today affirm the expansion of marriage rights for gays and lesbians (*if* we do so affirm them) are similarly compelled to view this development as an intermediary stage in a directed historical process of moral-political progress. I will return to a more detailed discussion of this issue below, but for now please note that I phrase this point hypothetically because I do not want to overlook the importance of the queer-left critique of gay marriage on the grounds that it fails to challenge the deep structures of heteronormativity and thereby institutes a homonormativity that contributes to the marginalization of those sexual minorities who do not approximate the heterosexual norm.[18] This is an important critique that must be reckoned with by anyone who wishes to hold up the expansion of marriage rights as evidence of moral or political progress, even if we restrict our notion of progress to the historically and contextually limited notion of progress in history that I outlined in chapter 1. My aim, however, is not to settle that debate but rather to focus on a different but, as it will turn out, not unrelated question: Supposing that we do wish to affirm the expansion of marriage rights to gays and lesbians, to what, if any, conception of progress are we thereby committed? Are we thereby committed to a robust notion of *historical* progress, that is, to a backward-looking claim about progress as a historical "fact," a claim that regards our form of ethical life as being in some way superior to those that preceded it? This is the question that Honneth's work poses and, as I will discuss below, the queer-left critique of gay marriage offers good reasons for critical theorists to be wary of Honneth's contention that such an affirmation would commit us to this robust conception of historical progress.

SOCIAL FREEDOM AS PROGRESS

Before returning to the issue of gay marriage in the next section, I first want to examine Honneth's turn to Hegel to put some social-theoretical meat on the bones of Kant's system-bursting, unofficial philosophy of history. This turn, articulated in Honneth's recently published magnum opus, *Freedom's Right*, is motivated in part by his diagnosis of what he regards as a major weakness of contemporary political philosophy, namely, its focus on abstract normative rules or principles, divorced from an understanding of the norms that prevail in given practices and institutions. In other words, even as his methodological approach to the philosophy of history draws more on Kant than on Hegel, Honneth is sharply critical of the Kantian nature of much recent work in political philosophy, which strives to stipulate freestanding normative principles that can then be used as standards to judge the normative legitimacy of existing social orders. Like Raymond Geuss and Bernard Williams, though for somewhat different reasons and with different effects, Honneth rejects this applied ethics approach to political theory.[19] Convinced by Hegel's "impotence of the mere ought" objection to

Kant, Honneth argues that rather than positing abstract normative ideals, critical theory must seek to build on the normativity inherent in existing social reality.[20] Hence, it must be anchored in a fine-grained, historically sensitive, social-theoretical analysis of that social reality. Honneth's recent work thus attempts to revive and update Hegel's ethical-political project of unifying normative and empirical-social projects "by demonstrating the largely rational character of the institutional reality of his time, while conversely showing moral rationality to have already been realized in core modern institutions" (FR, 2).

There are four fundamental methodological premises in *Freedom's Right*: first, the reproduction of society hinges on shared fundamental normative ideals and values; second, the theory of justice draws its normativity from those values and ideals; third, the methodology of the theory of justice is therefore that of normative reconstruction; but, fourth, this does not amount to solely an apology for the status quo because there is always room for criticism of the ways in which values and ideals that are universally shared (within a particular society) are imperfectly realized (FR, 3–10). The first two methodological premises are indicative of Honneth's commitment to the project of immanent critique, insofar as they show that he locates the normative resources on which his critical theory depends in the shared fundamental norms and values that are instantiated in existing social institutions. In other words, unlike neo-Kantians such as his Frankfurt colleague Rainer Forst, whose work I will discuss in more detail in the next chapter, Honneth refuses to base his normative project on a constructivist justification of abstract, "transcendent" normative principles. Moreover, Honneth insists that such a constructivist justification of norms "becomes superfluous once we can prove that the prevailing values are normatively superior to historically antecedent social ideals or 'ultimate values.'" "Of course," Honneth continues, "such an immanent procedure ultimately entails an element of historical-teleological thinking, but this type of historical teleology is ultimately inevitable" (FR, 5). Here, Honneth makes clear that he not only believes that some sort of commitment to historical teleology is inevitable for critical theory, but also thinks that historical teleological thinking plays a role in securing the validity of the normative principles and commitments that we find in our existing social world, for such thinking renders constructivist attempts to ground normativity "superfluous." In other words, the idea of historical teleology or progress plays a key role in Honneth's metanormative position. I will return to this issue in the next section.

Guided by this understanding of the relationship between normativity and historical progress, Honneth's methodological approach in *Freedom's Right* is one of normative reconstruction. Note that this methodology is distinct from, though not wholly unrelated to, the method of rational reconstruction employed by Habermas, discussed in chapter 2. Whereas Habermasian rational reconstruction aims to reconstruct the implicit know-how of competent communicative actors to yield putatively universal features of the pragmatic use of language, Honneth's normative reconstruction starts with values and norms that have been immanently justified through historical learning processes—that is, with the values that are embodied in our enduring social institutions and practices—and then, in turn, analyzes existing institutions and practices in light of the degree to which they embody and realize values that have been socially legitimated through those historical learning processes.[21] The central argument of *Freedom's Right* is that the one value that has been the most important for structuring the social order of Western modernity is the idea of freedom understood as autonomy. As Honneth explains: "No social ethic and no social critique seems capable of transcending the horizon opened up two centuries ago by linking the conception of justice to the idea of autonomy" (FR, 16). Freedom thus serves as the normative foundation for all particular conceptions of justice and this realization "represents the outcome of a centuries-long learning process" (FR, 17). Honneth continues:

> This fusion between conceptions of justice and the idea of autonomy represents an achievement of modernity that can only be reversed at the price of cognitive barbarism. . . . This teleological perspective, an inevitable element of modernity's self-understanding, strips the above-described fact [that is, the fact of the tight connection

> between justice and freedom] of its contingent historical character. For reasons that claim universal validity, we can now regard the idea of individual self-determination as the normative point of reference for all modern conceptions of justice. (FR, 17–18)

In other words, the teleological understanding of history, which is itself a feature of modernity's own self-understanding, allows Honneth to argue not only that justice and freedom *are* linked in modernity but that they *ought* to be, precisely because this link represents progress over premodern normative political self-understandings, and the reversal of this link would signal a return to cognitive barbarism.

The first part of Honneth's book traces the historical unfolding of the idea of freedom, from incomplete understandings of negative freedom and reflexive freedom, to the culmination of this unfolding in the idea of social freedom. Basically this is the story of the historical development of the idea of freedom from Hobbes and Locke through Rousseau and Kant to Hegel. In good Hegelian fashion, the idea of social freedom incorporates and builds upon negative and reflexive freedom, while avoiding the one-sidedness of each conception. Social freedom refers to a situation in which individual intentions are not only negatively free of external influence (as required by negative freedom) and autonomously and reflexively determined (as required by reflexive freedom), but also mirrored in and supported by existing social reality. Hegel initially introduces the idea of social freedom for reasons rooted in his logic; hence, he argues that the idea of negative freedom is incomplete because it leaves out subjectivity, that is, the subject's capacity for self-determination, and the idea of reflexive freedom is incomplete because it leaves out objectivity, that is, the objective social conditions needed to realize freedom. Although Honneth endorses this argument, he also maintains that the case for social freedom does not stand or fall with it. That is to say, considerations of Hegelian logic aside, Honneth maintains that Hegel "is right that we cannot experience ourselves as free as long as the preconditions for the implementation of our autonomous aims cannot be found in external reality" (FR, 47).[22]

Like Hegel's *Philosophy of Right*, then, Honneth's *Freedom's Right* reconstructs not our ethical or moral ideals or principles but rather our form of ethical life (*Sittlichkeit*), the social conditions in which our normative conception of freedom can be realized. The bulk of the book offers a historical and social-theoretical reconstruction of the ways in which freedom has been progressively realized and institutionalized in the major institutions of modern European society, including the family, the market, and the state. To be sure, Honneth acknowledges, we can no longer share Hegel's supreme confidence that the historical process by means of which rational freedom is gradually and progressively realized is necessary and inevitable. Hegel's confidence about this was, on Honneth's view, grounded in his objective teleology, and it was this confidence that assured him that by reconstructing our modern form of ethical life, he was reconstructing something of value, something that carries normative weight. This is the kind of optimism about historical progress that Honneth thinks we can no longer share. Nevertheless, he maintains, we can still share enough of Hegel's confidence about our judgments about the direction of historical progress to underwrite our normative projects, even after we strip his normative reconstruction of its metaphysical foundations and objective teleology. Indeed, not only *can* we share some of Hegel's confidence about progress, we *must* do so insofar as we find ourselves committed to the validity of our core social institutions. Once again, Honneth offers a transcendental argument for the necessity of a belief in historical progress, though here the argument is slightly different from the one articulated in the previous section. According to this slightly different version of the argument, the fact that subjects "actively preserve and reproduce free institutions" gives us "theoretical evidence of their historical value" insofar as through their very allegiance to and preservation of those institutions, subjects indicate that they view them as worthy of their allegiance, because they are the outcome of a process of historical progress (FR, 59). In other words, Honneth draws on the Hegelian notion of objective spirit, insofar as he assumes that what explains the continued existence of the core institutions of modernity is the fact that subjects "can view them as justified in principle" (FR, 184).

Although he leaves open the question of whether or not Hegel's view allowed for the possibility of revolutionary change in the form of ethical life, Honneth acknowledges that the predominant tendency in Hegel's work is to view the historical process of realizing freedom as having been completed and to understand the social institutions of his own time as representing the "culmination of the moral history of humanity" (FR, 62). In other words, Honneth identifies in Hegel's work a tendency toward a problematic status quo bias. Recall that the fourth methodological premise of *Freedom's Right* holds that normative reconstruction is not biased toward the status quo insofar as it offers room for criticism of the imperfect realization of ideals and values. With respect to Hegel's assumption that the institutions of his own time represent the culmination of the moral history of humanity, Honneth wryly observes, "Of course, in attempting to pick up Hegel's project again after two hundred years, we know better" (FR, 62). Hence, Honneth's goal is not to attempt to reconstruct the elements of social freedom per se or for all time, but rather to identify the elements of a culture of freedom "for the brief moment of a historical epoch," something like the epoch of late, Western modernity (FR, 64). That is the goal of *Freedom's Right*, which proceeds through a historical and sociological reconstruction of the emergence and institutionalization of negative legal freedoms and reflexive moral freedom, both of which enable but do not fully realize freedom, to the idea of social freedom, which refers to the full realization of freedom in the major institutions of society (the family, the market, and the state).

Honneth's empirically rich and substantive historical and sociological reconstruction of the major institutions of modern society takes up the majority of this substantial book. Although there is much in that reconstruction that is worthy of discussion, and although I discuss Honneth's treatment of the expansion of marriage rights in the institution of the family below, for the most part, I restrict my focus to an assessment of Honneth's methodology of normative reconstruction, and leave aside the details of his picture of the core institutions of modern society. Hence, in the next section, I focus my critical attention on Honneth's transcendental argument(s) for the idea of historical progress and on the resulting status quo bias in his methodology.

THE INELIMINABILITY OF PROGRESS?

As we have already seen, Honneth actually offers two slightly different transcendental arguments for the claim that a belief in progress is ineliminable, though he doesn't explicitly mark the difference between the two. In the first and weaker version of the argument, which appears in his essay on Kant's philosophy of history, Honneth maintains that those who explicitly endorse the moral or political developments of their own time—that is, those who are not merely historical observers or interpreters but rather participants in and supporters of a process of enlightenment—are necessarily committed to the idea of historical progress, and, in particular, they are committed to seeing the events in their own time as intermediate stages in a conflict-ridden and discontinuous but unstoppable historical learning process. Presumably Honneth believes that critical theorists count as participants in and supporters of the Enlightenment in this sense; hence, this argument should be taken to imply that critical theorists are so committed. In the second version, which appears in *Freedom's Right*, Honneth makes the substantially stronger claim that all those who actively take part in the reproduction of the core social institutions of modernity thereby can be assumed to view them as justified and thus (for the same reasons cited above) as the outcome of a historical learning process.

With respect to Honneth's first argument, I'm not convinced that it is in fact the case that by siding with a current historical event, we thereby commit ourselves to a robust conception of historical progress. Certainly we commit ourselves to the view that we regard the event in question as the best of the available alternatives. But even if we are thereby committed to the claim that choosing this alternative would constitute progress in a forward-looking sense—that is, that it would be better than the present state of affairs, the status quo—this does not necessarily commit us to a backward-looking story according to which the present state of affairs is an intermediary stage in a directed process of sociocultural learning. All that we are committed to is the thought that the event in question is better than available alternatives. Indeed, such a commitment need not even entail any commitment to a forward-looking notion of progress. It may well be that we regard all of the available alternatives as bad or problematic in some sense, even when compared to the status quo, and that the one that we favor is merely the least bad or least problematic option among those alternatives.[23] To be sure, in making judgments about which of the available alternatives are better and which are worse, we are appealing, implicitly or explicitly, to some normative standard or value that justifies such a judgment. In that sense, we may well be committed implicitly to the *possibility* of progress as a forward-looking moral or political imperative, that is, to the very idea that things *could* be better than they presently are. But from this it does not follow that we are committed to holding that whichever option we favor among the available alternatives would *in fact* constitute progress over the status quo; nor does it follow that we are committed to a backward-looking claim about how the present state of affairs is normatively superior to historically antecedent ideals or values.

So, to return to the example mentioned above, *if* I side with the expansion of marriage rights for gays and lesbians, I am thereby committed to the claim that legally recognized gay marriage is better than certain alternatives that are currently on the table, where those alternatives might range from the abolition of marriage altogether to a separate but equal system of civil unions to the criminalization of homosexuality. I am also, implicitly or explicitly, appealing to some normative principle or value—say, the value of formal equality or equal protection under the law or even the expansion of the institutionalization of social freedom or of prevailing structures of social and legal recognition—that I take to justify that claim. This may very well mean that I am committed to some understanding of the *possibility* of moral or political progress, that is, to the idea that an expansion of marriage rights would constitute a further realization of a certain conception of equality and that this would be a good or desirable thing. But why should I think that by appealing to this normative principle and to the expansion of marriage rights as a further realization of it that I am thereby committed to the much stronger claim that the historical form of life that gave rise to such a principle and its expansion and realization is the result of a cumulative, directed, transhistorical, sociocultural learning process? Such a commitment does not seem to be at all necessary in order to justify my stance on gay marriage. On the contrary, a commitment such as this is doing a different kind of normative work, namely, the work of justifying my normative principles themselves. I will discuss this point in more detail in the next section.

Before I get to that, however, I want to extend some of my arguments from chapter 1, and argue that any theory that purports to be critical should be extremely wary of such robust claims to progress as a historical "fact," that is, to backward-looking conceptions of progress that understand history as a learning process that has led up to "us." In order to see why this is the case, let's examine the issue of gay marriage in more detail. This example plays an important role in Honneth's normative reconstruction of the realization of social freedom in (European) modernity, particularly in his discussion of intimate relationships. In that context, Honneth cites the cultural and legal recognition of homosexual relationships and the push for the expansion of marriage rights to homosexuals as the culmination of a progressive "democratization" of romantic love that has taken place over the last two centuries (FR, 144). In recent years, in the wake of the so-called sexual revolution that began in the 1960s—characterized by the legalization of birth control, increasing toleration for homosexuality, the integration of women into the work force, flexible divorce laws, and the lifting of taboos on pre- and extramarital sex—the traditional nuclear family has been deinstitutionalized and intimate relationships have been rendered more autonomous (FR, 145). As a result, Honneth contends, "in contemporary Western societies, intimate relationships of limited duration now represent for all mature subjects, regardless of their sexual orientation, a possibility of personal attachment in its own right. We are both legally and culturally free to attach ourselves to men or women to whom we are sexually and emotionally attracted" (FR, 145).

However, such intimate relationships come, in Honneth's view, with certain normative obligations that are designed to "guarantee the identity of these relationships beyond the immediate moment" (FR, 145). Because individuals who enter into intimate relationships expect to be loved for who they are, and because who they are changes over time, intimate relationships have a future-oriented character: they involve a commitment to love the person that one's partner will become, and an expectation to be loved by one's partner for the person that one will become. This commitment must ultimately be grounded in a shared history as a couple; hence, intimate love relationships "represent a pact to form a community of memory [*Erinnerungsgemeinschaft*] in which looking back on a commonly shared history should be so encouraging and motivating as to last longer than the changes in both partners' personalities" (FR, 146–147).

In Honneth's view, both homosexual and heterosexual couples can fulfill these norms governing intimate relationships, but homosexual couples, despite being culturally and legally tolerated, are still at a "decisive disadvantage compared to heterosexual couples" inasmuch as "they still are not able to legally marry, and thus have no legal opportunity to commit to the economic security of the partner who does not earn an income" (FR, 149). Although such couples are capable of experiencing social freedom in their intimate partnerships—by finding themselves fully at home in another, in particular by having their physical and emotional needs and integrity protected by their partner—they receive no protection from the state in the event that their relationship dissolves. However, Honneth optimistically maintains that the historical trend is such that the "source of the reasons used to justify excluding homosexual couples from the legal privileges of officially sanctioned marriage will dry up" (FR, 150), and the only options that will remain will be either abolishing marriage altogether or extending marriage rights to all intimate life partnerships.[24]

By emphasizing the normative obligations, shared past, and future-oriented character of intimate relationships, Honneth's discussion clearly takes committed, monogamous, long-term relationships as the paradigm cases for intimate relationships. Moreover, he maintains that such relationships play a crucial social role inasmuch as they protect the natural neediness of individuals and thus provide "a specific experience of mutual recognition from which they derive elementary self-confidence" (FR, 154; cf. SR, 95–107); in this way, they serve as the foundation of our modern form of ethical life and its expression of social freedom. As a result of these claims, Honneth seems vulnerable to the queer-left criticism that his defense of gay marriage as a further step in the democratization of romantic love is both heteronormative—in that it implicitly privileges a bourgeois-romantic conception of heterosexual marriage—and homonormative—in that it implicitly privileges those queer relationships that most closely approximate this heterosexual norm.[25]

However, I want to focus on a different problem here, a problem that emerges implicitly when we consider Honneth's account of gay marriage in light of his claims about progress as a historical "fact." If, as Honneth argues in his essay on Kant's philosophy of history, by cheering on the expansion of marriage rights to gays and lesbians in our own time we are thereby necessarily committed to viewing this shift as an intermediate stage in a directed sociocultural learning process and if this learning process is understood as historical progress in a robust sense, then it seems to me that Honneth is implicitly committed to claiming that the expansion of marriage rights within European and American contexts not only constitutes progress for us, by our lights, but also serves as evidence that "our" late modern, European-American form of ethical life is superior to those forms of life that do not tolerate or accept gay marriage. I want to emphasize that this is a claim about what Honneth is implicitly committed to as a result of the structure of his argument; I'm not saying that he actually argues for this point. As a matter of fact, his whole analysis of intimate relationships and of social freedom in *Freedom's Right* is confined to the European and American context. However, read in light of his claim that a commitment to a robust conception of historical progress is ineliminable for critical theory and is invoked whenever we support a social or political development in our own time, Honneth's analysis of intimate relationships suggests that he views the expansion of marriage rights and the cultural recognition of (certain forms of) homosexual partnerships as indications of the stage of development or learning of a form of ethical life. In other words, it suggests that he thinks that societies that recognize (certain kinds of) homosexual relationships have progressed further and learned more than those that have not.[26]

But, you might be wondering, what's wrong with that? After all, it is not at all uncommon for people to respond to skepticism about the notion of historical progress by saying something like: "Of course there is historical progress! Look at the situation of women, or gays and lesbians. Are you saying that the liberation of women and the cultural recognition of gays and lesbians *don't* count as instances of historical progress? How could someone who calls herself a progressive or a feminist possibly say such a thing?" In order to get a grip on why we should be hesitant to understand the legal and cultural recognition of homosexual relationships, for example, as evidence for a robust conception of historical progress, we have to think about the ways that heteronormativity and nationalism have intertwined over the last twenty years to form what Jasbir Puar calls homonationalism. As Puar argues, homonationalism takes several forms, but one of those forms is what she calls an American and European "sexual exceptionalism."[27] If "exceptionalism" denotes the "process whereby a national population comes to believe in its own superiority and its own singularity,"[28] then sexual exceptionalism is the process whereby greater cultural and legal recognition for homosexuality is taken as an implicit justification of American and European cultural—historical—superiority.[29] The central claim of Puar's critique of homonationalism is this: "The historical and contemporaneous production of an emergent normativity, homonormativity, ties the recognition of homosexual subjects, both legally and representationally, to the national and transnational political agendas of US imperialism."[30] Homonormativity refers to a sexual politics that does not challenge but rather embraces dominant heteronormative cultural forms, including domesticity, consumption, and reproduction.[31] The intertwining of homonormativity and cultural (not to mention political) imperialism means that the attribution of a cultural or moral backwardness—that is, a lack of sociocultural learning or development—to those cultures or societies that do not legally recognize homosexual subjects is central to homonationalism. Puar's aim is not to determine whether or not the

Western cultures are indeed exceptional—though one gets the distinct sense that she rather doubts it—but rather to illustrate the ways in which such claims to exceptionalism intertwine with unexamined assumptions about race, nationality, religious identity, and class. In the European context, for example, she argues that

> gay marriage . . . has become a steep but necessary insurance premium, . . . whereby an otherwise ambivalent if not hostile populace can guarantee that extra bit of security that is bought by yet another marker in the distance between barbarism and civilization, one that justifies further targeting of a perversely sexualized and racialized Muslim population . . . who refuse to properly assimilate, in contrast to the upright homosexuals engaged in sanctioned kinship norms.[32]

Homonationalism in both the United States and Europe is thus characterized by a double movement: certain homonormative forms of homosexuality are embraced, to the exclusion of other sexual minorities, especially racially or ethnically marked or working-class queers; and this inclusion is then used as a justification for our cultural superiority to those racialized cultural or religious others who do not accept or even tolerate homosexuality. Homonationalism not only underwrites the judgment that these other cultures are backward, thus reinforcing informal imperialism; it also serves to disavow homophobia in the United States and Europe by projecting it onto other spaces.[33]

In other words, summing up Puar's critique, viewing the legalization of gay marriage as evidence of our own position in a directed, progressive historical learning process seems to implicate us in a culturally imperialist logic according to which our support for gay marriage is evidence of our superiority over those "backward" forms of ethical life that don't recognize or tolerate gay marriage. Not only does this logic split queers by conferring recognition only on those who most closely approximate the heterosexual norm, it also amounts to an attempt to take a stand against one form of domination—the subordination of gays and lesbians—by enacting another—informal or cultural imperialism. Hence, not only does this perspective seem to presuppose a hegemonic, straight, heteronormative point of view (from which gay marriage looks like progress), it also represents a failure to think intersectionally about domination and subordination in a transnational frame. To be clear: I am not claiming that this is a reason to be opposed to gay marriage. In this sense I would not go as far as Puar, who views gay marriage as a "conservative victor[y] at best, if at all."[34] I don't want to take a position on this debate here. All I am saying is that *if* one is in favor of the expansion of marriage rights for gays and lesbians then that need not—indeed, should not, for the reasons elaborated by Puar—commit one to a belief in a robust, backward-looking conception of historical progress, that is, to a conception of progress as a historical "fact." In other words, what I am suggesting is that the intersection of pro–gay marriage arguments and cultural imperialism gives us a reason to resist Honneth's claim that being in favor of gay marriage requires me to view it as evidence that the United States and Europe, for example, are at an intermediary stage in a directed historical learning process, since this implies that those societies that do not allow gay marriage are backward or inferior to us, at least in this respect, and this is a judgment that evinces an imperialist sensibility. Just to be clear: this does not mean that we should not say, for example, that we think that societies that criminalize homosexuality are *wrong*. As I suggested in my discussion of Habermas in chapter 2, there's an important difference between disagreeing with someone and judging them to be backward. To disagree with someone is to treat them as a moral contemporary; to judge them to be backward or developmentally inferior is not.[35]

With respect to Honneth's second version of the transcendental argument, the one that asserts that the fact that the core institutions of society are reproduced indicates that they are viewed as legitimate, and that viewing them as legitimate entails a commitment to historical progress, this version seems to turn on a highly questionable assumption about how much can be read into the reproduction and maintenance of existing social institutions. Of course, we could agree that, as Bernard Williams has put the point, "any human group living in a moderately stable social order under peace shares some set of ethical understandings, some rules and concepts that govern their relations."[36] But how far does this get us?

After all, can't individuals reproduce and maintain existing social institutions for all sorts of reasons, even while retaining a belief in the illegitimacy of those very institutions? Can't they even reproduce and maintain existing institutions unreflectively, for no particular reason at all other than that this is just the way things are or what one does?[37] Here the case of gay marriage is once again illustrative. If, as Judith Butler has argued, subjects who do not comply with a heteronormative conception of how sex, gender, sexual desire, and sexual practices are supposed to coincide (with males performing masculinity and desiring and having sex with females who perform femininity, and vice versa) are thereby rendered unintelligible and unrecognizable, then individuals may well uphold heterosexual marriage simply because to do otherwise is to risk a kind of social death.[38] Moreover, and more pragmatically, it is entirely possible for individuals, whether gay or straight, to decide to marry in order to obtain health insurance or tax benefits, to secure parental or adoption rights or other pragmatic social goods, all the while believing that marriage is a deeply problematic and even illegitimate social institution. I've even attended weddings where couples have engaged in a lengthy critique of the institution of marriage during their exchange of vows, as a form of public protest against the institution in which they are at that moment reproducing. (Admittedly, these were the weddings of academics. Still.) But if this is the case, then it follows that a belief in the legitimacy of social institutions cannot be read off of their maintenance and reproduction in any straightforward manner.

Furthermore, the maintenance and reproduction of institutions and practices that embody certain normative commitments can also be viewed, as Honneth well knows, in Foucaultian terms as a function of the internalization and inculcation of disciplinary power relations.[39] As Williams puts this point, articulating what he calls "the critical theory principle": "Acceptance of a justification does not count if the acceptance itself is produced by the coercive power which is supposedly being justified."[40] Indeed, the idea that there is often a significant gap between de facto and genuine acceptance of the legitimacy of existing social institutions has long been seen as central to the very idea of a critical theory.[41] In his discussion of the modern democratic, constitutional state, Honneth acknowledges this Foucaultian point about the maintenance and reproduction of social institutions, but ultimately rejects it on normative grounds. Following Habermas, Honneth understands the democratic constitutional state not as an idealized moral concept that outstrips social reality, but rather as "merely the historical outcome of a conception that has been accepted within Western Europe ever since the days of the French Revolution" (FR, 306). Honneth admits that it is possible to view the democratic constitutional state in a different way, as "a large organization concerned solely with the expansion of its own power" (FR, 307). Following Habermas, Honneth considers this to be taking up a radically external perspective on the state, as opposed to an internal, reconstructive perspective. Although such an external perspective has the advantage of "being immune to any illusions," it nevertheless deprives us of the possibility of taking up a normative perspective on the state (FR, 307). Why should this be the case? The answer, for Honneth, is that normativity can be found only within the existing social world. As such, it can be accessed only via an internal reconstruction—that is, a reconstruction from the first-person point of view of a participant in a normatively structured social reality—of the ideals and values that are embodied in the existing institutions and practices that are central to one's society. In other words, only by taking up an internally, first-person or participant-oriented, normative perspective on the state can we understand one-sided exercises of force on the part of democratic states as illegitimate abuses of state authority in the first place. An abuse of state power counts as an abuse, says Honneth, only if we accept the idea that the democratic state requires legitimation. "If we give up the foundation of such a concept of the constitutional state, as does Foucault in his theory of power or in 'realist' historiography," Honneth writes, "then both the 'selectivities' of the modern state and its extra-legal violence can only be viewed as entirely normal applications of state power" (FR, 308).

In response to this argument, I want to make two related points. First, analyzing the role that power plays in reproducing and maintaining existing social institutions and practices does not necessarily undermine the possibility of taking up a normative perspective with respect to those practices. The assumption that it does depends on a problematic splitting, familiar within second-, third-, and fourth-generation Frankfurt School critical theory, of the first-person participant and third-person observer points of view. The familiar version of this split holds that the normativity of the social world is accessible only from the internal, first-person, reconstructive point of view of a participant in a normative social order, whereas the analysis of power relations necessarily refers us to the third-person, objectivating, external point of view of the neutral social-scientific observer.[42] Although a complete social theory will, on this view, need to encompass both points of view—both the normative and the empirical—it also must endeavor to keep them apart from each other, so that normativity and reason can remain pure of power relations at the conceptual level.[43] Foucault's work challenges this central assumption of contemporary Frankfurt School critical theory by asserting that rationality or normativity and power are always and necessarily entangled with each other, and that it is precisely this spiral that critical thought must ceaselessly interrogate (SKP, 357–358). This leads Foucault to adopt a genealogical method that is best understood not as taking up an external, objectivating, third-person perspective on our social world but rather on the model of an anthropological participant-observer, conducting an internal ethnology of his own culture. I will return to this point in chapters 5 and 6.

This also leads to my second, and related, point: relegating power to the empirical, third-person point of view not only preserves the pernicious fiction of a power-free normative lifeworld that Honneth himself argued against in his critique of Habermas (see CP, 299–303); it also downplays the role that power plays in social relations and thereby blunts the critical force of Honneth's critical theory. To be sure, in other writings, Honneth admits that his normatively reconstructive approach to critical theory must have a genealogical moment built into it. This is the lesson that the first generation of the Frankfurt School drew from the horrors of fascism, which distorted the original meaning of the normative horizon of the Enlightenment into its barbaric opposite. However, Honneth has a limited conception of genealogy as purely subversive, and he allows genealogy to play an overly circumscribed role within his critical theory; it serves only as a "metacritical standpoint" that enables critical theorists to study "the real context of application of moral norms" that have been derived and justified through the methodology of normative reconstruction (RSC, 52). In other words, for Honneth, as for McCarthy, genealogy can enlighten us only about the ways in which the normative principles that we reconstruct from within the first-person point of view can go astray in practice, but it has nothing to say about the norms themselves. But this is precisely to miss the radical point of genealogy, which has to do with the entanglement of reasons and normativity with power relations.

In sum, Honneth's transcendental arguments for the ineliminability of a robust conception of historical progress are unconvincing. He hasn't succeeded in showing that we—where the "we" refers either to critical theorists or to participants in modern social orders—are compelled to endorse the strong, backward-looking idea of progress as a historical "fact" that he spells out. And, I also want to argue, it's a good thing, too, since, as the discussion of gay marriage in this section shows, Honneth's robust conception of historical progress seems to implicate us in a homonormative and culturally imperialist logic that is deeply problematic from the perspective of queer postcolonial theory. I will return to this point momentarily, but before I do that, I want to explore in more detail the role that the notion of historical progress plays in underwriting Honneth's conception of normativity. This will serve to show how much is at stake for Honneth's normative framework and, hence, for his conception of critical theory in this discussion of historical progress.

HISTORICAL PROGRESS AND NORMATIVITY

Recall from our discussion of *Freedom's Right* that Honneth not only offers a transcendental argument for the ineliminability of a robust notion of historical progress for critical theory, but also connects his conception of historical progress to the normative grounding of critical social theory as a form of immanent critique. In this regard, consider once again the passage from *Freedom's Right* that I quoted above, in which Honneth criticizes constructivist approaches to normativity:

> We should follow Hegel in abstaining from presenting a free-standing, constructive justification of norms of justice prior to immanent analysis; such an additional justification becomes superfluous once we can prove that the prevailing values are normatively superior to historically antecedent social ideals or "ultimate values." Of course, such an immanent procedure ultimately entails an element of historical-teleological thinking, but this is ultimately inevitable. (FR, 5)

Here, Honneth goes so far as to claim not only that we can "prove" that our norms are superior to previous ones, but that such a proof serves to underwrite the validity of our normative commitments. This follows from Honneth's contention that the claim that "our" normative principles—the principles that inhere in our existing social institutions—are normatively superior to historically antecedent principles takes the place of a constructivist justification of norms, rendering such a justification "superfluous." This suggests, and this point is absolutely crucial, that in Honneth's work it is the idea of historical progress that ultimately answers the question of why the normative principles that we find within our existing social world deserve our support. Unlike constructivist approaches, which seek to ground their normative claims procedurally, Honneth's reconstructivist approach rests on the idea that the norms that are embedded in our practices and institutions deserve our allegiance not because or to the extent that they conform to certain abstract procedural requirements—the demands of public reason, or discourse ethics, or the right to justification—but because we can, indeed, must, understand them as the outcome of a historical learning process.[44]

Honneth makes this point even more explicit in another recent essay, titled "Reconstructive Social Criticism with a Genealogical Proviso." There he argues that every reconstructive conception of social critique faces the problem that "it cannot really justify what makes the ideals from its own culture chosen to be a reference point normatively defensible or desirable in the first place" (RSC, 50). For

Honneth, what distinguishes critical theory's particular version of reconstructive social criticism from other versions is that it seeks to address this problem by appealing to the following left-Hegelian premises: first, that "social reproduction occurs through forms of social practice in which the rational achievements of human beings are incorporated" (RSC, 50); and, second, that "these rational achievements unfold according to progress that is realized through the learning process in connection with social action" (RSC, 50). Putting these two premises together, critical theory's left-Hegelian variety of reconstructive social criticism thus holds that "at each new level of social reproduction, human rationality . . . takes on a more highly developed form, so that the whole of human history can be spoken of as a process of the realization of reason" (RSC, 50). In this way, critical theory combines an immanent reconstructive normative procedure with a context-transcending conception of rationality understood in terms of a directed, historical learning process. "The critique of society," Honneth writes, "can be based on ideals within the given social order that at the same time can justifiedly be shown to be the expression of progress in the process of social rationalization. To this extent, the critical model of the Frankfurt School presupposes if not precisely a philosophy of history then a concept of the directed development of human rationality" (RSC, 51). Moreover, it is only by appealing to this notion of the directed development of human rationality that critical theory is able to break out of the problem of conventionalism that threatens all reconstructive forms of social critique.

Honneth has further detailed his understanding of the relationship between normativity and historical progress in a more recent paper titled "The Normativity of Ethical Life." This paper opens with a discussion of what Honneth calls, following Terry Pinkard, the paradox of Kantian normativity. This paradox consists in the fact that a Kantian account of moral normativity necessarily relies on a view of freedom understood as autonomous self-determination that already has normativity built into it. Hence, the validity of certain normative principles must already be presupposed in an account that attempts to construct normativity out of a conception of practical self-determination. Note that my discussion of Habermas in the previous chapter suggests that Habermas himself is aware of this paradox and seeks to avoid it. This is why he acknowledges that the discourse principle cannot be grounded in a purely constructivist manner, but instead must be understood as at least partially dependent upon the theory of modernity inasmuch as formal pragmatics reconstructs the communicative competence of a peculiarly modern subject: a postconventional member of a posttraditional society. Hence, the paradox of Kantian normativity leads Honneth, like Habermas before him, back to Hegel and to a Hegelian historicism about normativity.[45] But this strategy comes with dangers of its own, not least of which is the charge of conventionalism. In "The Normativity of Ethical Life," Honneth seeks to exonerate a Hegelian-contextualist account of moral normativity from the charge of conventionalism by arguing that such an account can provide immanent criteria for distinguishing between genuinely valid and merely accepted norms; crucially, these criteria allow for such distinctions not only within a particular form of ethical life but also across the historical breaks that separate one form of ethical life from another.[46]

Honneth starts with the idea that Hegel's notion of ethical life consists not in a straightforward rejection of Kantian morality but rather in an embedding of Kantian morality—especially the principle of universalization—within past and present social practices and institutions. Hence, for Hegel, "a practice deserves the label 'ethical' only if a group of persons, which may vary in size, follows a norm to which each among them may in principle appeal to evaluate the actions of one of the other participants" (NEL, 819). That is to say, the term "ethical" refers not to whatever social practices happen to be accepted but rather to forms of reciprocal recognition that intertwine with structures of self-determination. The "act of reciprocal recognition" underlies "shared obligations" and this involves each according to the others a particular kind of freedom (NEL, 820). Hegel's transformation of Kantian morality also consists in showing that within a form of ethical life, duty and inclination are never separated in the way that Kant tended to suppose. A norm is only really socially embedded when it manifests itself in an interdependent relationship between our duties and inclinations (NEL, 820). In other words, "Hegel insists that whenever the members of a social group have subjected themselves to some moral norm by reciprocally according each other the relevant kind of authority, the norm itself must be reflective of some ethical value that expresses the inclinations and intentions of each of the agents" or else it could not be viewed as an expression of their freedom (NEL, 820). Hence, Hegel views moral norms as conceptually inseparable from values because without such "substantive ethical content" the norms would not be capable of generating collective processes of "reciprocal self-constraint" (NEL, 821).

These considerations give rise to two immanent criteria for the normative validity of forms of ethical life, that is, for distinguishing between norms that are objectively valid and those that are merely de facto accepted; the former are distinguished from the latter "both by the fact that they are appealed to as principles for the reciprocal evaluation of actions within a group and by the fact that they express values affirmed by the members of the group" (NEL, 821). Note, however, that these two criteria do not yet fully address the charge of conventionalism, since they do not fully capture the moral universalism of the Kantian account of morality that Hegel seeks to embed within the reality of social practices and institutions. Why is this so? Because the criteria delimited thus far remain *internal* to a particular form of ethical life, whereas "applying the Categorical Imperative is meant to curtail our self-love not just in relation to the members of our particular group but rather in relation to all human beings, and to thereby ensure that we respect them in the way morality requires" (NEL, 822). Hegel's own answer to this challenge is to appeal to his philosophy of history, the final stage of which is the ethical equivalent of Kantian universal morality. As we have already seen, however, Honneth assumes that this philosophy of history with its objective teleology is no longer plausible. And yet, he asks once again whether we can "conceive of this sort of progress even without presupposing an objectivist philosophy of history" (NEL, 822). By the terms of his own argument, the charge of conventionalism or cultural relativism cannot really be answered without this robust account of progress as a historical "fact," since without it the Hegelian approach to morality isn't genuinely universal, thus it doesn't succeed in its task of embedding

Kantian universalist morality within social practices and institutions and forms of life.

Honneth attempts to construct a nonobjectivist philosophy of history by showing that these two immanent criteria of normativity by themselves generate a certain conception of history. The fact that a form of ethical life entails, as Honneth has argued, the reciprocal recognition of the evaluative authority of other members of a group opens up a certain historical dynamic whereby "each member of the collectivity may criticize the actions of the other or others and may call on them to act in a more adequate way" (NEL, 822). This means that forms of ethical life are necessarily open to internal contestation and historical revision. Moreover, since each form of ethical life depends upon the ethical resonance of norms—that is, that the norms accurately express the collective self-understanding of members—and since individual inclinations and self-understandings change over time, it is possible for ethical norms to lose their motivational power over time. This leads to a different kind of openness of forms of ethical life, by means of which norms may lose their objective validity over time, and thus stop being integral to that form of ethical life. In other words, internal to Hegel's concept of ethical life are certain elements of historical change that, according to Honneth, may provide us with clues to how to reconstruct the idea of historical progress in a nonobjectivist manner. Honneth's strategy is to use the formal structure provided by Kant's philosophy of history to fill in details of Hegel's theory of ethical life; hence, the *form* of Honneth's account is Kantian in the sense that it employs a hypothetically intended rather than an objective conception of progress, but the *content* of this account is provided by Hegel's theory of mutual recognition. As we have seen, Honneth prefers Kant's account in large part because it is a modal account, that is, because it refers us to the *possibility* of historical progress rather than to its necessity as understood through an objective teleology.

How, then, does Honneth propose to make sense of progress? He starts with the idea that the internal contestation and criticism of norms from within a form of ethical life yield new insights that build up over time:

> The various innovations in the practice of a given ethical norm, which in essence amount either to an increasing generalization or an increasing differentiation of that norm, are not lost from one generation to the next but gradually add up to yield thresholds that all future arguments offered by the members of the group must be able to cross. So conceived, the history of an ethical sphere is an unplanned learning process kept in motion by a struggle for recognition. (NEL, 823–824)

Note that this conception of progress becomes much less plausible if we assume that the social world is structured by relations of domination, for attentiveness to this feature of social life should make us suspicious that those innovations that "add up" and are passed down from one generation to the next may well be those that are all too complicit with the powers that be.[47] Be that as it may, even if we accept the conception of progress outlined here, inasmuch as these are struggles within an ethical sphere or form of ethical life over the correct application of a particular norm, this conception accounts only for what I have called progress in history, that is, for the progressive realization of the particular norms that are embedded in a particular form of ethical life. As I argued above, Honneth believes that he needs a more robust account of historical progress as a "fact," an account of the changes that lead one form of life to wither away and another to take its place, in order to address the charge of conventionalism.

This more robust conception of historical progress takes the form of an account of how we might explain historical breaks between different forms of ethical life in terms of a process of learning. In order to explain such breaks, Honneth offers an analogy between struggles within a particular ethical sphere that lead individuals to develop a new conception of ethical life and the often conflict-ridden process through which an adolescent grows into an adult. Both processes appeal to a socializing feedback effect by means of which the struggle within a particular form of life (or subjectivity) leads the society (or the individual) to develop a new form of life (or subjectivity) so different from the first as to be almost unrecognizable. In such cases, "in the course of a protracted conflict over the adequate realization of a given ethical principle the motives of the parties to this conflict are transformed to a point where they no longer consider the relevant norm to be desirable at all" (NEL, 824). Here we no longer have a conflict over the correct application of an existing norm but rather over the justification or validity of a normative principle itself. This account offers "an explanation of why over time certain ethical norms lose their collective acceptability and are gradually replaced by others that are more open and more universalizable" (NEL, 824). As the (in my view inadvisable) analogy with the adolescent suggests, Honneth is committed to a strong claim about the cognitive superiority of European modernity. But he is also committed to claims about its moral superiority, as he makes clear in the following passage from his debate with Nancy Fraser: "Like all internally situated social theorists who proceed from the legitimacy of the modern social order—be it Hegel, Marx, or Durkheim—I had to first presume *the moral superiority of modernity* by assuming that its normative constitution is the result of past directed development" (RR2, 184, emphasis added). Moreover, Honneth admits that this assumption is necessary for grounding his own normative perspective, for, he continues, "only on the assumption that the new order involves a morally superior form of social integration can its internal principles be considered a legitimate, justified starting part for outlining a political ethic" (RR2, 184).

Honneth's account of a socially effective reason that develops through historical learning processes can thus be understood as an instance of what postcolonial theorists, following Said, have called historicism. Historicism, as Chakrabarty explains, "tells us that in order to understand the nature of anything in this world we must see it as an historically developing entity, that is, first, as an individual and unique whole—as some kind of unity at least in potentia—and, second, as something that develops over time."[48] Moreover, Honneth's is a particular version of historicism whereby European modernity seems to occupy a unique and superior place in the historical development of social, political, and ethical orders. As Chakrabarty understands it, historicism can accommodate complexities and unevenness in the process of development, and it need not entail strong claims to an objective teleology in history; what is central to historicism are the ideas of historical development and of the cognitive and moral superiority of European modernity. Moreover, Chakrabarty argues, it is historicism that provided the justification for consigning "Indians, Africans, and other 'rude' nations to an imaginary waiting room of history. In doing so, it converted history itself into a version of this waiting room. . . . That was what historicist consciousness was: a recommendation to the colonized to wait."[49]

In response to this criticism, it seems to me that Honneth has two options. First, he could attempt to restrict the scope of his claims about historical progress. He could insist that he is claiming moral and cognitive superiority for the form of ethical life of European modernity only vis-à-vis its own historical antecedents, and that such a claim does not entail any negative judgments regarding the developmental status of the forms of ethical life found in other societies,[50] or that it entails such judgments only to the extent that other societies share certain features of our own socially institutionalized recognition order (R2, 46). This would be to draw a clear distinction between his own version of historical-teleological thinking and the Kantian and Hegelian philosophies of history from which it draws inspiration, a distinction that Honneth has so far failed to make explicit. Such a move, if it could be carried out consistently, would insulate Honneth from the kind of postcolonial critique that I have been pressing. But it would come at a high cost for Honneth, since it would greatly circumscribe the significance of his critical theory, effectively conceding that his approach is "unable to give voice to the moral concerns of large portions of the world's population" (R2, 46) and in that sense is ill-equipped to contribute to the task of constructing a critical theory of world society.[51] Moreover, for reasons explored in chapter 1, it isn't at all clear that this move could be carried out consistently. To claim that the idea that European modernity represents the outcome of a process of progressive historical development is only a claim about *Europe's* history, and doesn't entail any judgments about the rest of the world, is to presuppose that the idea and the history of European modernity can be disentangled from colonialism and from the relationship to Latin American and Orientalized others on which both the idea and the material reality of European modernity were founded. To say this would be to presuppose a closed and insular understanding of European history and of European discourses of historical progress that seems, in light of recent historical scholarship, highly implausible.

Honneth's second option is to bite the bullet and reply that it is true that we—that is, critical theorists—may be, on his view, compelled to view European modernity as morally superior to pre- or nonmodern or traditional forms of life or social orders, but that this need not be viewed as problematic inasmuch as such a perspective does not in any way license the further claim that we are justified in forcing our form of life on them. Especially given that the normative core of our form of life is, for Honneth, freedom, there is something deeply contradictory and self-undermining about trying to force people to be free. In order truly to realize freedom, members of pre- or nonmodern social orders would have to freely come to realize the value of freedom on their own, and presumably they would do so through the same sort of social struggles for recognition and learning processes that have marked European history, on Honneth's account. Hence, Honneth could claim that his robust account of historical progress may entail a certain judgment of cognitive and even moral superiority vis-à-vis "nonmodern" or traditional forms of life, but it does not justify political, much less military, interventions in traditional societies whose aim is to force their targets to adopt "modern" ways of life, whether those be cashed out in terms of democracy, capitalism, or the liberation of women and the protection of gay rights.

However, this response fails to acknowledge the extent to which the conceptual judgment of the inferiority of pre- or nonmodern peoples is always already bound up with actually existing informal and cultural imperialism. As I discussed in chapter 1, not only has the claim of moral and cognitive superiority repeatedly been used as a justification for imperialism and colonialism—and here I think critical theorists should be given serious pause by the very fact that their conception of historical progress overlaps with the neoconservative political worldview to such a degree that spelling out the differences between the two becomes necessary in the first place—but this claim to superiority and the developmentalist conception of history used to support it are themselves gestures of the powerful. In other words, as the post- and decolonial critiques discussed in chapter 1 show, the political and epistemological dimensions of the discourse of progress are intertwined. Inasmuch as it is the task of critical theory to reflect on the power-laden social and historical conditions of its own theoretical enterprise, this intertwining generates an imperative to interrogate the assumptions and judgments about historical progress that have been an integral part of critical theory's left-Hegelian heritage inasmuch as these have been and continue to be entangled with relations of informal imperialism.[52]

Even if this pressing post- or decolonial objection to Honneth's defense of historical progress could be adequately addressed, however, there is a serious conceptual objection lurking in the background. Here the question is whether Honneth's strategy for grounding his normative perspective in a robust conception of historical progress can possibly work. This question becomes especially pressing when we consider that what seems to differentiate Hegel from the historicists by whom he was influenced (but with whom he disagreed) is the positing of the point of view of Absolute knowing that serves as the suprahistorical criterion for assessing historically existing forms of life.[53] Insofar as Honneth seems to eschew this idea, with its appeal to a wholly transcendent and therefore non-socially situated normative criterion, and this metaphysical way of reading Hegel, (how) can he avoid collapsing into historicism?

One possible response would be for Honneth to appeal here to his philosophical anthropology to provide some criteria for judging which transformations between forms of ethical life should count as progress and which should not. Honneth's philosophical anthropology, which is developed out of his reading of psychoanalysis, postulates a universal and anthropologically basic drive for recognition and inclusion that is rooted in human psychology. Two central assumptions of this philosophical anthropology are that individuals cannot be indifferent to the limitation of their own rational capacities inasmuch as such limitation causes them to suffer and that such suffering impels such individuals to strive for emancipation (CT, 805–806). In Honneth's critical-theoretical paradigm, these two deep-seated anthropological characteristics provide the impetus for ongoing social struggles for recognition that seek to expand existing structures of individualization and inclusion. Transitions between forms of life could then be judged as progressive or regressive on the basis of whether or not they expand structures of individualization and inclusion (see RR2, 184–185).

Honneth's philosophical anthropology has been criticized for being overly optimistic, insufficiently attentive to the fundamental ambivalence that structures human psychic life.[54] I'm sympathetic with such criticisms, but would like to focus here on a different question, namely, what is the status of the normative criteria that are provided by this account of philosophical anthropology? Are they contextually grounded within a specific form of ethical life? In which case, how can they serve as the criteria by means of which we make sense of breaks between forms and justify the normative point of view of modernity itself? Or are they context-independent and universal? In which case, doesn't this appeal violate Honneth's aspiration to offer a contextualist account of normativity that finds its normative criteria within the social world? If the criteria of inclusiveness and individualization are taken to be universal, then Honneth's account of normativity isn't ultimately a contextualist one, since it is grounded in a metanormative philosophical anthropology that is not contextual but rather universal (or at least aspires to be).[55] But this move not only seems to violate Honneth's aspiration to offer a contextualist account of normativity; it also threatens to run aground on the paradox of Kantian normativity that Honneth had turned to Hegelian contextualism in an attempt to avoid. After all, it could easily be argued that Honneth's philosophical anthropology already presupposes the very normative content—namely, the *value* of inclusiveness and individualization—for which it is supposed to provide a justification. On the other hand, if these criteria are themselves contextually and historically rooted and emerge out of an internal reconstruction of the background convictions of members of modern social orders, then the attempt to use these criteria to justify the normative superiority of modernity seems circular. This circularity comes out rather clearly in Honneth's initial presentation of these two criteria for moral progress in the context of his debate with Nancy Fraser, since he begins with the presumption of the "moral superiority of modernity" (RR2, 184), which in turn, via a reflection on their implicit background convictions, yields "two criteria that together can justify talk of progress in the relations of recognition," namely, individualization and inclusion (RR2, 184), which then are invoked as justification for understanding the "breakthrough to the modern, liberal-capitalist social order as moral progress, since the differentiation of the three recognition spheres of love, legal equality, and the achievement principle went along with an increase in the social possibilities for individualization as well as a rise in social inclusion" (RR2, 185).

In other words, Honneth is caught in a double bind here:[56] he thinks that he needs a robust conception of historical progress as a "fact" to avoid the charges of conventionalism and relativism, but he can't make this account of historical progress work without violating his attempt to give a Hegelian, immanent, contextualist account of normativity and hence running afoul of his own critique of the paradox of Kantian normativity.

In conclusion, it is worth reviewing how Honneth ends up in this position: he wants to avoid abstract Kantianism, which strives to avoid the charge of conventionalism by offering an independent, universal normative standard against which existing institutions and practices can be measured. Honneth thinks that such approaches are vulnerable to the impotence of the mere ought objection and also that they inevitably face feasibility worries (that is, worries that they are overly utopian). So instead his strategy is to ground his normative ideals with a thoroughly immanent strategy, while attempting to avoid the collapse into conventionalism or relativism. The notion of the historical-developmental superiority of our own form of ethical life thus steps in to allow Honneth to split this difference between abstract Kantianism and relativism.

However, as I have just argued, it isn't clear that this strategy can really work, since it seems to be able to avoid collapsing back into the contextualist relativism or conventionalism that Honneth strives to resist only by retreating to a noncontextualist philosophical anthropology. If this is correct, then it seems that perhaps the best, most consistent way of interpreting Honneth's claims about progress is to reformulate them in the following, rather less robust way: we have to regard our existing institutions and progressive political developments as instances of historical progress for us, by our own lights, according to our own, internally derived normative criteria. This would be a third alternative, between what I have called the robust conception of historical progress as a "fact" and the more local, contingent, and contextually grounded conception of progress in history. Such a medium-strength account would still be committed to the idea of progress as a historical "fact" but it would view that idea as being justified by certain normative principles that are internal to our form of life—for example, because we value social freedom, we regard the institutions of European modernity to be an advance over pre- or nonmodern forms of life. However, it should be fairly obvious that if we think about progress in this less robust way, then it cannot really do the metanormative work of justifying our normative principles that Honneth wants it to do. Also it is still problematic for the political reason that being committed to the moral superiority of our modern (European or Euro-American) form of life seems also to commit us to viewing pre- or nonmodern or traditional forms of life as morally and cognitively inferior. This commitment leaves Honneth vulnerable to postcolonial objections that can be avoided, if at all, only by circumscribing the normative scope of Honneth's theory so much and offering such a narrow and implausible reading of European history as to make his theory seem positively parochial. In other words, he can avoid a "postcolonial" critique of his own theory only by ceding his ability to offer a critical theory of the postcolonial condition. Honneth's commitment to the ineliminability of historical progress, even if recast in a less robust way, and his understanding of the relationship between progress as a forward-looking, moral-political imperative and progress as a backward-looking historical "fact" thus make it difficult to see how Honneth's work could help us to accomplish the kind of decolonization of critical theory that is an especially pressing task if critical theory aims to be truly critical, that is, to clarify the struggles and wishes of our postcolonial, globalized age.

The robust notion of historical progress that Honneth advocates is not only extremely difficult to work out conceptually but also carries dangerous and problematic political implications. I submit that critical theorists would be better off without it. I also disagree with Honneth's contention that we need a robust account of historical progress to secure the normativity of critical theory. To the contrary, as I will argue for in more detail in the concluding chapter, I think that we can make do with a thoroughgoing metanormative contextualism, and that this doesn't have to collapse into relativism at the first-order, substantive normative level. Moreover, even if we reformulate (or interpret) progress in a more modest form—as historical progress "for us"—such an idea still stands in the way of an openness to postcolonial difference and an inclusiveness of postcolonial others. In order to have this openness and inclusiveness, that is, in order to realize fully the normative legacy of the Enlightenment, we need a different sort of relationship to our history, one that is neither subversive nor vindicatory, but rather problematizing. I shall argue in chapter 5 that valuable resources for this project of critical genealogical problematization can be found in the work of Adorno and Foucault.

4

From Hegelian Reconstructivism to Kantian Constructivism

FORST'S THEORY OF JUSTIFICATION

My discussion of Habermas in chapter 2 suggested two possible strategies for critical theorists working in a post-Habermasian vein for thinking about the relationship between history and normativity. The first strategy is to work out a more consistently Hegelian, contextualist strategy for grounding normativity, while attempting to avoid a collapse into conventionalism or historicism. As we saw in the preceding chapter, Axel Honneth adopts this strategy, but in the end he finds himself caught on the horns of a dilemma: either he either must appeal to an ahistorical philosophical anthropology in order to justify the robust account of historical progress that undergirds his normative project, thus running afoul of his own critique of the paradox of Kantian normativity, or he must accept the considerably less robust notion of progress that follows from contextualism. The second strategy is to avoid the apparent dangers of historical and normative contextualism by taking a more consistently Kantian constructivist route for grounding normativity. This is the strategy found in the work of Rainer Forst. As I will discuss in this chapter, this alternative strategy for grounding normativity avoids the problematic reliance on a theory of modernity that plagues Habermas and Honneth, but it runs into problems of its own, and as such it, too, stands in need of decolonization.

Forst's return to Kant is motivated, at least in part, by what he sees as the dangers of a Hegelian strategy for grounding normativity. These dangers are clearly articulated in his discussion of Rawls in his first book, *Contexts of Justice*. Against those who read Rawls as a contextualist about normativity, Forst reads him as a constructivist. The motivation for this reading is captured in the following question: "Can. . . . a culturally and historically anchored argument raise a claim to universality only if it is based on a Hegelian philosophy of history in the form of the thesis that American (or 'Western') political culture represents the normative endpoint of political developments?" (CJ, 173). Forst's answer to this question is an unequivocal "no." As he puts it: "That we can reconstruct the right from familiar conceptions does not mean that it is right because it corresponds to 'our' familiar conceptions" (CJ, 175). Similarly, even in his most historically grounded work, *Toleration in Conflict*, Forst makes it clear that the normative perspective that informs his critical history of the concept of toleration does not rest on a "teleological developmental perspective," and in raising this point he explicitly distinguishes his strategy for grounding normativity from that of Axel Honneth (TC, 27n31). The concept of toleration is a normatively dependent concept, for Forst, which is to say that it relies for its normative force on some more fundamental principles or values, and in order to play the foundational role of grounding normatively dependent concepts such as toleration, these principles must themselves be normatively freestanding (TC, 33). At the conclusion of his exhaustive historical survey of the discourse of toleration in the West, Forst makes the following methodological observation: "The critical historical perspective teaches us which of the justifications of toleration is superior to the others. Nevertheless, this is not a historical truth in the sense that 'history gives rise to' this form of respect; even as historical, it remains primarily a truth of practical reason" (TC, 445). Hence, it is clear that normativity, for Forst, is not grounded in a (pragmatic, empirical, de-transcendentalized) philosophy of history—in a "historical truth"—but rather, as we shall see in this chapter, in a neo-Kantian conception of practical reason that is designed to provide the freestanding foundation for normatively dependent concepts such as toleration.

Forst's distinctive strategy for grounding normativity has implications for his thinking about historical progress, and, conversely, his reflections on progress help to further elucidate his motivations for adopting this strategy. Specifically, Forst maintains that his normative strategy not only allows him to articulate a freestanding criterion or standard for judgments about what constitutes historical progress—thus avoiding the kinds of circularity worries that plague Habermas's and Honneth's accounts—but also allows him to respond to the kinds of post- and decolonial critiques of progress discussed in previous chapters. In other words, whereas for Habermas and Honneth, the notion of historical progress serves, at least in part, to justify the normativity of the principles that we find in our social world, for Forst, the normativity of the principle of justification, which is not grounded historically but rather in the demands of practical reason itself, provides the standard by means of which judgments of historical progress (or regress) can be made. Forst maintains, however, that his theory of justificatory justice is sensitive to the specific contexts in which normative questions are discussed and debated by agents and that his conception of practical reason is nonmetaphysical and anti-foundationalist; as such, he contends that his account of justice can avoid the charges of abstract formalism and implicit ethnocentrism that postcolonial critics have typically leveled against Kantian normative projects. After discussing these aspects of Forst's view, I turn to Forst's constructivist strategy for grounding normativity and its relation to contextualism and his closely related account of practical reason. Throughout this discussion, I consider to what (ultimately rather limited) extent Forst's theory can be considered contextualist and the related question of whether he can in fact avoid the charges of abstract formalism and implicit ethnocentrism.

While granting that Forst's approach avoids some of the problems that plague Habermas's and Honneth's accounts, I argue that these advantages come at a rather high cost. Specifically, I raise two further challenges to Forst's neo-Kantian account of normativity. First, this approach leads him to give an unsatisfactory analysis of power because power is now theorized entirely from the point of view of reason and so becomes noumenal. This highly cognitivist conception of power is inadequate for a critical theory that aims to put, as Forst says, first things first, by starting with a critique of power relations. Second, and relatedly, I argue that his way of understanding the relationship between reason and power tends, as Honneth also suggests, toward a methodology of political philosophy as applied ethics that sacrifices the methodological distinctiveness of critical theory. Moreover, and perhaps more importantly, this approach obscures some of the very power relations that critical theory aims to critique, including the kinds of informally imperialist and neocolonial power relations highlighted by post- and decolonial critiques of progress.

PROGRESS TOWARD JUSTICE

Forst's short essay "On the Concept of Progress" opens with an acknowledgment of the specific—and highly problematic—historical context for the development of the concept of progress in the Western tradition. Colonialism was a—if not the—decisive feature of this context, such that the flipside of "progress" in modernity has been "economic exploitation, political oppression, and cultural dominance" of the rest by the West (ZBF, 42, translation mine). Thus, Forst contends, the intertwining of the discourse of progress with the legacy of colonialism is "decisive for the way in which we relate ourselves to the concept of progress" (ZBF, 42). However, even as we acknowledge and take up a critical stance toward the relationship between progress and colonialism, Forst insists, in much the same spirit as Honneth, that "from the participant's perspective . . . it is very difficult for human beings not to see themselves as progressive beings" (ZBF, 43). Ultimately, in his view, all critiques of progress—including the postcolonial critique of the coloniality of power—are also based on the idea of a "striving toward progression," where "progression" is understood in terms of overcoming social obstacles and striving for individual and collective improvement (ZBF, 43).

In other words, in Forst's view, we must be attuned to the *dialectic* of progress in modernity, in which every critique of progress necessarily relies, at least implicitly, on the concept of progress to formulate its critique. No society or form of social criticism, according to Forst, can entirely foreswear progress as a moral-political imperative, for the concept of progress expresses a deeply social-normative impulse that is generated from within societies that are stratified or riven with relations of dominance and subordination: progress is “a demand that comes from those who have been oppressed . . . or whose lives are characterized by injustice” (ZBF, 43). But the flipside of this dialectic is that the discourse of progress must always go hand in hand with the critique of progress that has accompanied it throughout the history of modernity. Thus, for example, we should not accept current discourses of moral-political progress or economic development uncritically; rather, we should be attentive to the ways in which they are bound up with neocolonial and informally imperialist power relations. Framed in this way, for example, the discourses of progress and development employed by powerful states and international financial institutions should be interrogated for their power effects, at the same time that resistance to this agenda on the part of less powerful states or individual actors within them should be understood as being fueled by an emancipatory desire for progress (ZBF, 46–48).

Thus the crucial issue, for Forst, is not whether we are for or against progress, since, on his view, we can only be against it by being for it. Interestingly, however, the converse doesn’t hold in quite the same way, though Forst does not note the asymmetry here: one *can* be for progress without also being against it, as ill-advised as such a stance may be, and it is precisely this feature of the discourse of progress that has linked it to ideological forms of self-congratulation and thus given it such a bad name. In other words, the claim that one can only be against progress by being for it is backed by a transcendental argument—in any attempt to critique progress we necessarily appeal explicitly or implicitly to the very idea that we critique. The converse claim is backed not by a transcendental argument, but rather by the weaker claim that in light of the past and present entanglements of discourses of progress with relations of colonialism and imperialism, whenever one is for progress one ought not to take such a stance uncritically. But note also that Forst’s transcendental argument only goes through if the two different aspects of progress that I distinguished in chapter 1 are conflated. Once we distinguish between progress as a moral and political imperative and progress as a historical "fact," the options become more varied and complex: one *can* be against progress as a "fact," as a backward-looking claim about what has led up to "us," while still being for progress as a forward-looking moral and political imperative. As we'll see in the next chapter, this is basically Adorno's position.

However, as I just said, the crucial issue for Forst is not whether we are for or against progress, but rather who determines what counts as progress, and "correctly understood," Forst writes, "this is the question of justice" (ZBF, 48). Hence, like toleration, progress is, according to Forst, a normatively dependent concept. It derives its normative force from a concept of justice that is understood in political terms as democratic self-determination.[1] For Forst, as we will see below, this notion of political justice is ultimately based on his fundamental normative concept of the basic human right to justification. This right requires that no one shall be subjected to rules or institutions that cannot be justified to him or her as a free and equal member of society. In the context of discourses of progress, this requirement means that no one can determine for anyone else what progress means or whether or not a particular social, political, economic, or cultural transformation constitutes progress. In other words, the basic right to justification, which is translated in the political arena into a right to political self-determination, serves as the criterion by means of which we assess what counts as progress.

I will discuss the difficult question of how Forst seeks to ground this normatively independent concept of justice understood as the basic human right to justification below. With respect to the dialectic of progress, Forst considers the possible objection that the claim that progress is a normatively dependent concept returns us to the postcolonial critique of progress as a mechanism of colonialism and Western cultural imperialism, since progress has now been defined in terms of putatively Western normative concepts such as justice, democracy, and political autonomy or self-determination. In response to this worry, Forst again insists that the critique of oppressive or colonizing notions of progress itself presumes that self-determination is normatively desirable. He also suggests that the apparent dilemma posed by the dialectic of progress can be resolved by seeing progress as a reflexive concept which demands that "each process of progress must be constantly questioned as to whether it, rightly understood, lies in the social interests of those who are a part of these processes" (ZBF, 50). The reflexive principle of progress holds that none other than those affected by whatever is proposed as an instance of progress may determine whether such instances count as genuinely progressive.

However, Forst also makes clear that "if the language of human rights, self-determination, and justice should be the language of progress, this is not primarily a historical or sociological insight or claim. It results rather from the moral imperative of the critique of false conceptions of progress themselves" (ZBF, 51). In other words, even if it is true that we can reconstruct a notion of justice from "our" familiar understanding of political self-determination or democracy, this does not mean that this notion of justice is right because it is ours. The claim that progress understood as an expansion of political self-determination is to be valued rests not on any historical or social-evolutionary claim about the cognitive or developmental superiority of the modern, posttraditional form of life that gave rise to the discourse of progress. Rather, it rests on a moral insight into the imperative of self-determination, which in turn rests on what Forst calls the basic human right to justification. This basic right has been, on Forst's view, progressively though by no means uniformly or consistently realized through human history, but its normativity is not historically indexed or situated. In other words, the right to justification rests not on a reconstructivist reading of historical progress and social evolution but rather on a constructivist account of the demands of practical reason.

CONSTRUCTIVISM VS. RECONSTRUCTIVISM, UNIVERSALISM VS. CONTEXTUALISM: THE BASIC RIGHT TO JUSTIFICATION

Although Forst insists that his project is non-foundationalist (see, for example, JJ, 182) insofar as he rejects the possibility of an "ultimate" foundation or ground for normativity (RJ, 81), the structure of his account of normativity is clearly and even avowedly foundationalist, inasmuch as he grounds his account of social and political justice in a fundamental moral right, which is also a human right. This is the right to justification. In this sense, there is a distinctively Platonic aspect to Forst's project, insofar as it seeks to ground all normative phenomenon in a "*single* root" that forms the "normative core" of talk of justice in all social and political contexts, "the one basic human *right to justification*" (RJ, vii). This is the core normative principle that serves as the basis for such normatively dependent concepts as toleration and progress. This right rests, in turn, on a conception of practical reason that will be discussed in more detail below.

If, however, there is no ultimate foundation or ground for normativity, then what accounts for the validity of our moral and political norms, in particular, the fundamental principle of or right to justification? In response to this metaethical question, Forst offers a constructivist response.[2] Morality rests upon its own validity; it does not draw its normativity or validity from God or any other source. In this sense, morality is autonomous. And yet moral norms are capable of being genuinely valid.[3] Their validity is a function of their having survived an idealized procedure of practical deliberation, what Forst calls a justification procedure. Forst formulates the core insight of constructivism as follows: "There is no objective, or in any other sense valid, order of values that takes priority over the justification procedure. Only those norms that can successfully withstand this procedure count as valid" (RJ, 48).

On Forst's particular version of constructivism, the justification procedure centers on two criteria: reciprocity and generality. The reciprocity criterion concerns both the content of justificatory claims—one may not raise specific claims while rejecting similar claims raised by others—and the reasons offered for them—one may not simply assume that one's own convictions, beliefs, needs, interests, or perspectives will be shared by others such that one can claim to speak for them or in the name of their "true" interests (RJ, 49). The generality criterion holds that one may not disregard the objections of any person who is affected by a proposed norm and that the reasons offered in favor of the norm's legitimacy must be capable of being shared by all (RJ, 49). For Forst, the world of moral normativity is constructed by means of a principle of reciprocal and general justification; the binding force of norms rests on the fact that no good reasons can be offered against them (RJ, 50). The relevant sense of "no good reasons" refers to the Scanlonian idea of "reasonable rejection." Hence, Forst writes, "Normativity is generated by a discursive justification procedure that equips norms with reasons that cannot be [reasonably] rejected. These reasons are the ground on which the normativity of autonomous morality rests" (RJ, 51). But what it means to say that a norm can't be reasonably rejected is just that it meets the criteria of reciprocity and generality.

And yet, as Forst realizes, there is a limit to the work that constructivism can do. This limit is expressed in the following question: What is the source of the normativity of the justification procedure—the principle of justification—itself, on the basis of which moral and political norms are to be constructed? Whereas Habermas or Honneth might appeal to the idea that modernity is the outcome of a social-evolutionary or developmental learning process as a way of addressing the question of why the conception of morality that we inherit from the Enlightenment deserves our support, Forst's answer to this question is to assert that the moral ought "brings its own reasons with it so that there can be no question of other reasons" and that recognizing this just is what it means to become a moral subject (RJ, 99). Hence, he claims, "The moral law does not need any further justifying reasons over and above the practical knowledge that one is a 'justifying being' with a fundamental duty to provide justifications and . . . [that] 'being human,' insofar as it necessarily implies being a 'fellow human,' already has a normative character that entails the duty to provide justifications in moral contexts" (RJ, 100). So the ultimate foundation of Forst's moral and political constructivism is a certain conception of what it means to be human, a conception that is essentially equated with an account of practical reason.[4] Forst is quite explicit that this account cannot itself be constructed, though it can be reconstructed through an internal analysis of the features of our normative world (RJ, 5).

A common criticism of constructivism is that it must either bottom out in some foundation that is not itself constructed but instead forms a realist ground or end up being circular.[5] Forst explicitly denies that his constructivism ultimately rests on a moral realist ground;[6] this is the basis for his repeated insistence that there is no "ultimate" foundation for morality. Rather, he adopts the strategy of admitting to a kind of circularity in the way in which the construction procedure itself is grounded, while insisting that this circularity is virtuous and reflexive rather than vicious and question begging—hence, he calls it "recursive" rather than "circular." The notion of reconstruction plays a crucial role here; for Forst, even the principle of justification itself "must be 'recursively' reconstructed" (RJ, 81). What does "reconstruction" mean for Forst? Although Forst indicates that he does not wish to take on board the whole of Habermas's "comprehensive theory of truth and argumentation" (RJ, 271n29), his usage of the term closely tracks Habermas's notion of rational reconstruction. As we have seen, for Habermas, rational reconstruction refers to the reflective articulation, refinement, and elaboration of the intuitive pretheoretical knowledge of competent social actors. Thus, for example, Habermas's rational reconstruction of communicative competence draws on work in the empirical sciences to generate a quasi-transcendental account of the rational-normative potentials built into linguistic communication (see CES and TCA1). Similarly, Forst's reconstructive approach to the moral point of view starts with a pragmatic analysis of moral validity claims and inquires "into the conditions of justification of such claims" (RJ, 48–49). This recursive, reconstructive analysis generates the criteria of generality and reciprocity, in the sense that, by means of a reflexive articulation of what we are implicitly committed to as moral agents, it uncovers that what it means for a competent moral actor to redeem a moral validity claim is just for him or her to be able to defend that claim in a reciprocal and general way, in a way that no one can reasonably reject.[7]

As Forst acknowledges in his earlier work, this reconstruction of practical reason "can be nothing more than a *self-reconstruction* of reason and as such cannot claim absolute or 'ultimately grounded' authority, but it does claim 'recursive,' best justified authority with respect to its subject matter: the 'reasonable' validity of norms" (CJ, 199, emphasis added). As such, Forst's recursive approach "steers a path between realism and relativism, without abandoning the claim to validity of universalist moral principles" (CJ, 199). So, the ultimate, as it were, non-foundationalist foundation of Forst's approach is the reconstructive analysis of what we are implicitly committed to as practically reasoning moral agents.

A standard worry about discursive, proceduralist conceptions of normativity such as this one is that they are overly abstract and as such too divorced from the concrete contexts in which actual agents debate and discuss normative questions and concerns to be of much use for thinking about politics. This complaint about neo-Kantian conceptions of normativity has been raised from a variety of different perspectives, including Hegelian and communitarian thinkers, but, as I'll discuss below, it also figures prominently in postcolonial critique. One of the distinctive features of Forst's approach is that it aims to do justice to a substantial number of contextualist commitments, but without sacrificing the moral and political universalism of the Kantian tradition. As Forst explains in the introduction to *Contexts of Justice*, his aim is to offer a conception of justice that "avoids both the criticism of context blindness and a contextualism that fails to recognize the universalist core of the call for 'justice'" (CJ, xii). In *Contexts of Justice*, Forst differentiates four conceptually and analytically distinct—if always overlapping in practice—contexts of justice: the ethical, the legal, the political, and the moral. On Forst's account, justice requires doing justice to persons across all four of these dimensions. His theory of justice is grounded in an account of justification, where validity must always be claimed and redeemed in particular—ethical, legal, political, or moral—intersubjective justificatory contexts. Hence, Forst's "*theory* of justice is at the same time context-bound and context-transcending insofar as it takes these normative dimensions into consideration, without absolutizing any particular one" (CJ, 5). As will become clearer in the next two chapters, I share Forst's overall interest in combining the insights of universalism and contextualism, but have a different understanding of the best way to do this. Hence it is worth taking some time to clarify how

Forst attempts to do this and in what precise—and ultimately rather limited—sense his constructivist view can also be considered a contextualist one.

For Forst, the distinct contexts of justice and of justification—the ethical, legal, political, and moral—overlap and intersect in practice, and yet there is a structure and a hierarchy to their interrelation.[8] For example, ethical values raise a distinctive kind of validity claim; "they are valid only for individuals who can identify with these values, that is, who can affirm them as part of their identities in view of their life histories (as histories within communities and particular contexts)" (CJ, 28). In other words, ethical claims necessarily refer to persons insofar as they are members of particular communities with particular values and conceptions of the good. Legal norms, by contrast, refer to all members of a legal community, and as such they must be justified in more general terms, according to an abstract notion of a legal person whose basic legal-political rights provide for the protection of individuals as ethical persons (CJ, 82). In this way, legal norms provide a framework within which individuals can pursue their own ethically rooted conceptions of the good. Legal norms, in turn, derive their validity from moral norms that are reciprocally and generally justified; these moral norms, when translated into legal-political contexts, yield a system of basic human rights that has a moral basis (CJ, 82).[9]

Hence, morality is, for Forst, a kind of limit concept; ethical, legal, and political norms may be justified with respect to the context of distinct ethical, legal, and political communities, but they cannot violate or contravene the dictates of morality. As Forst puts the point with respect to legal norms: "Basic rights do indeed have a concrete legal content, but they require moral justification: they form the core of the protection of the person, and, for moral reasons, this core *cannot* be limited in favor of ethical or practical considerations" (CJ, 85). In this way, Forst speaks of a "threshold of reciprocity and generality" that legal norms must meet in order to be valid (CJ, 85). He makes a similar point with respect to the political context, which he discusses in terms of an account of deliberative democracy understood as "the rule of generally justified reasons" (CJ, 123). Here, too, morality serves as a threshold context:

> Particularly with problems in which moral questions play a role. . . . the moral points of view must take precedence; they must not be sacrificed to ethical or, even worse, pragmatic considerations. The emphasis on this strict criterion thus derives not from the neglect of the ethical constitution of persons and the contextless ideal of "pure" discourses but from the special significance of the moral protection of persons in their concrete identity. Political discourses are not moral discourses but are concerned with diverse material; they must not however give wrong answers to moral problems.
>
> (CJ, 126, translation modified)

Forst's account of the political is thus sensitive to context inasmuch as he maintains that certain claims of social justice—for example, claims about how social inequalities can be justified, if they can be—are relative to the particular social context within which they are lodged—for example, because claims that aim to justify inequalities must be justified to the worst-off members of that society. However, this is not the same as saying they are relativistic because central to Forst's view is the idea that there are some basic rights that all persons have qua moral persons and that these are justified in every society (CJ, 145).

In other words, in different ways, the ethical, legal, and political contexts all refer back to an overarching "context," that of morality. Although Forst claims to be charting a course between (liberal) universalism and (communitarian) contextualism, and he even goes so far as to describe his view as a "contextualist universalism," an examination of how he understands the moral "context" serves to clarify in what—extremely limited—sense his view can be considered a contextualist one. Against communitarian critics, Forst argues that his theory of justice as the right to justification does not bottom out in a particular conception of the good, where the good is defined in terms of self-determination or individual freedom. Rather, Forst maintains that his contextualist universalism "connects formal universalism and substantive contextualism by means of the idea that universal principles establish a formal framework that is constantly reiterated in a different manner in contexts of political communities, in their self-understandings, practices, and institutions" (CJ, 167). Contextualist universalism imposes two kinds of moral constraints on social contexts: first, it imposes the internal restriction that communities can claim legitimacy for themselves only if their core components are generally recognized by their community members as justified (CJ, 171); and, second, it imposes the external restriction that ethical or political communities must not contravene a certain set of minimal moral norms that recognize all human beings as moral persons (CJ, 171–172). These minimal moral norms are grounded in a principle of practical reason that does not, on Forst's view, express a particular conception of the good or a contingent set of shared understandings.

To be sure, this conception of practical reason is open to contestation and revision. Hence, Forst maintains, the principle of practical reason should be interpreted "*recursively* and *discursively*: in the absence of metaphysically validated normative principles, moral-universal justification can be located only in a process of reciprocal rational argumentation that is in principle unfinished. If the alternatives of moral realism and relativism are to be equally avoided, then norms of justice must, as it were, 'earn' their universal claim to validity" (CJ, 176). Nevertheless, Forst's contextualist universalism consists in a nested hierarchy of normative contexts. Validity claims are situated within specific contexts of justification—ethical validity claims must be justified to members of ethical communities with shared conceptions of the good, legal validity claims to members of political communities, and moral validity claims to all moral persons—but one context overrides the rest and provides the moral threshold of reciprocal and general justification that the other contexts cannot breach. This is the "context" of "the unlimited community of all moral persons" (CJ, 196).[10] Even if one were to accept that the moral context qualifies as a context in the relevant sense—which is far from clear to me, given that it is defined as the all-encompassing context of all contexts—this context is, in turn, rooted in a conception of practical reason that is clearly not understood in contextualist terms.

> In the absence of "ultimate" reasons, the very point of morality "without a bannister [sic]" is found in this self-critical recursive "unconditionality" of reason. By reason of its procedural character, the principle

> of general justification does justice to the substantive conceptions of the good of persons in communities, without resting on a theory of the good: regarding questions of ethical self-determination, equal rights, political autonomy, and moral integrity, it refers to contexts that are filled in concretely by ethical persons on the basis of their identities, by legal persons in mutual respect for personal autonomy, by citizens in political self-determination, and by moral persons in reciprocal recognition. . . . In this complex view of different contexts of practical questions and reciprocal recognition there lies the possibility of a connection between universalism and contextualism.
>
> (CJ, 229)

Thus, in Forst's work, the connection between universalism and contextualism amounts to this: a universalist conception of practical reason serves as the basis for a universalist conception of the "context" of morality that can then be concretely filled in, in various ethical, legal, and political contexts, so long as they don't contravene the requirements of morality or of practical reason. Moreover, the account of practical reason on which the whole edifice rests is, as Forst admits, "context-sensitive but not contextualist" (CJ, 237).

PRACTICAL REASON, AUTHORITARIANISM, AND SUBJECTION

But the limits of Forst's contextualism also reveal a potential problem for his constructivist strategy for grounding normativity. After all, if moral constructivism ultimately rests on some view about practical reason, then isn't the problem to which constructivism is supposed to offer such an elegant solution—namely, how to ground the validity of our moral judgments in a way that avoids relativism but without recourse to moral realism or foundationalism—just shifted back a level, to the level of the account of practical reason? Since that account of practical reason is a normatively laden one, can't we just ask what grounds the appeal to the normative content of the account of practical reason itself? If, in an effort to avoid moral realism, one answers this question, as Forst does, by saying, in effect, "this is just what it means to be a practical reasoner, as revealed by my reconstructive argument," then the norms that are taken to be constitutive of practical reason threaten to become arbitrary,[11] or, even worse, authoritarian. As Adorno points out in his critique of Kantian moral philosophy, to insist that "the given nature of the moral law should not be open to further questioning" is an "authoritarian gesture" which asserts that "the fact *that* it [that is, the moral law] exists is actually the most powerful proof of its validity" (PMP, 95). Raising this point need not reveal, on the part of the critic, a "foundationalist desire for a metaphysical security we cannot have," as Forst suggests (JJ, 182). After all, it is Forst who is committed to the project of providing a strong philosophical justification or grounding for our normative principles or ideals;[12] thus, it would seem to be a problem for his view, *by his own lights*, if that justification should turn out to rest on an arbitrary foundation. If, by contrast, we let go of the project of offering a strong philosophical grounding of normativity and understand practical reason in a more open-ended, practical, and political way, then the worry about arbitrariness may well come to seem misplaced as well.[13]

In response to the worry about arbitrariness, Forst insists that "all we have is the best account of the principles of the practice we call the use of reason, and there is no God or eternal truth that dictates that to us" (JJ, 182). But here the worry about authoritarianism reemerges in a slightly different form. Who, after all, are "we," and how does that "we" go about determining which account of practical reason is the best? Can we be confident that "our" conceptions of practical reason are free of ideological distortions? Nor should this be seen as an empty worry, since there has been a great deal of criticism over the last thirty years or more, from feminist, queer, postcolonial, and critical race theorists, of the very conception of practical reason on which Forst's moral constructivism rests.[14] Such critiques claim that the Kantian Enlightenment conception of practical reason explicitly or implicitly excludes, represses, or dominates all that is associated with the so-called Other of reason, whether that be understood in terms of madness, irrationality, the emotions, the affects, embodiment, or the imagination, all of which are symbolically associated with black, queer, female, colonized, and subaltern subjects. These symbolic associations serve both to rationalize and to justify existing relations of racial, heterosexist, and ethnic oppression and domination—by defining women, blacks, queers, colonized, and subaltern peoples as not rational and therefore as not fully human—at the same time that they reinforce certain stereotypical understandings of black, queer, feminine, and subaltern identity as closer to nature, more tied to the body, more emotional, more prone to madness, irrationality, and violence, and so on. This shows the extent to which the Kantian notion of practical reason has been closely bound up with pernicious notions of progress, inasmuch as it has provided the benchmark with respect to which black, female, queer, colonized, and subaltern subjects have been judged to be sufficiently civilized, mature, developed, or capable of autonomous self-rule.[15] Moreover, as James Tully has argued, Kantian and neo-Kantian metanarratives, precisely because of their formal, abstract, universal, necessary, and obligatory character, "cannot recognize and respect any other of the plurality of narratives, traditions or civilizations as equal yet different, and enter into a dialogue with them on equal footing."[16] They are, Tully suggests, imperialist in their very form, precisely as *meta*narratives.

The argument I am making here might best be thought of as a kind of pessimistic induction. The thought is that, given that conceptions of practical reason have had these exclusionary effects and have been entangled in and served to justify relationships of domination in the past, we should reasonably worry that whatever conception of practical reason we now endorse will turn out to have similar biases built into it that we are not now in a position to see, and thus will not be as formal, abstract, or universal as we think. The point of this pessimistic induction is not to suggest that practical reason is always or necessarily a tool of domination, nor is it to claim that those who endorse the ideal of practical reason while admitting to its ideological misuses in the past are mired in paradox (see JJ, 181). Rather, it is to make the more modest claim that coming to appreciate the extent to which all of our previous conceptions of the reasonable "have been exclusionary, one-sided, racist, paternalistic, etc." (JJ, 181), as Forst himself admits, should serve to undermine our confidence that we have now hit upon a conception of the reasonable that is not so entangled with domination.[17] And this, in turn, should make us doubtful about our ability to articulate a conception of practical reason "as such,"[18] one that aims to establish, as Forst's account does, that by virtue of the very act of engaging in practical reasoning, regardless of the particular historical or cultural context in which I find myself, I thereby commit myself to providing justifications for my actions and my normative commitments, justifications that are guided by the normative constraints of reciprocity and generality.[19] Although Forst denies that we have access to an ahistorical, transcendent, pure notion of reason or even to a point of view from which we could settle the question of whether "our" conception of practical reason is either historically necessary or historically contingent,[20] his account of practical reason as such has the formal, abstract, necessary, universal, and obligatory character that Tully identifies as imperialist in form.

For another way to see the problem with Forst's overly abstract conception of practical reason as such, consider his account of the space of justification, understood as a space populated with "reasonable, autonomous, and moral beings who must be able to account for their actions to one another" (RJ, 22). How, after all, by what mechanisms and for what motivations, do individuals enter such a space? In contrast to neo-Humeans such as Bernard Williams, Forst insists that the reasons for taking up the moral point of view cannot be external, in the sense of fear of external sanctions or guilt or considerations of self-interest. And this is so because "a categorical and unconditionally valid morality cannot stand on an instrumentally or ethically hypothetical foundation. It requires an *unconditioned ground*" (RJ, 34). So, the motivation for taking up the moral point of view has to be "respect for the fundamental right to justification of every autonomous moral person" (RJ, 37), which Forst characterizes as a "second-order practical insight" that is "fundamental for morality" (RJ, 37). Through this insight, "humans recognize themselves and each other reciprocally as members of the moral community of justification that includes all human beings, as autonomous and responsible beings, endowed with reason, who are members of a shared (and commonly constructed) space of justifying reasons" (RJ, 37–38).

On Forst's view, one cannot arrive at this insight into what it means to be moral by being convinced that doing so is in your interest, for the phenomenon of being moral "consists in the fact that anyone who realizes that he is morally obligated toward others also knows that he cannot have reasons for this obligation rooted in primarily self-regarding empirical interests, such as the avoidance of sanctions" (RJ, 58). In support of this point, Forst paraphrases Heidegger's attempt to dissolve (rather than solve) the problem of epistemological skepticism about the external world. As Heidegger famously argued, the problem of skepticism arises only if one accepts an artificial and problematic view of the relationship between subject and object, whereby the subject is understood as a unique kind of being, set over against a world of objects.[21] Once one sets things up in that way, the subject is separated from objects by a chasm that it can never quite manage to get back across; it is forever after plagued by skeptical worries about whether its experience of the world in fact matches up with the way the world really is. Heidegger's (dis)solution of this problem rests on showing it to be a false problem, based on an abstraction from our primordial way of existing, which is to be immersed in the world, to experience our being-in-the-world as a unified phenomenon. Forst attempts to run an intriguing parallel argument with respect to moral skepticism. As Forst puts it, "From the perspective of someone who understands himself as a moral being, from the perspective of moral 'being-in-the-world,' so to speak, this question [that is, why be moral?] does not even arise; and someone who does not understand himself morally can never be brought to see the point of morality in this way [that is, by means of external sanctions]" (RJ, 104).

But notice that there is a crucial disanalogy between epistemological and moral skepticism that Forst does not acknowledge, and it is a difference that casts doubt on Forst's strategy here. The difference is this: no one starts out in life a skeptic about the reality of the world. Quite the contrary, we all start out in life as naïve realists, who experience ourselves as immersed in the world in just the way that Heidegger's phenomenology attempts to recover. As anyone who has taught introduction to philosophy knows quite well, a good deal of sophisticated philosophical argumentation is typically necessary in order to motivate skeptical doubts about our knowledge, and those doubts tend to dissipate all too easily as soon as we leave the philosophy classroom, which, as Hume noted, we quite naturally do by opening the door rather than the window. But in the case of moral skepticism, the situation is much less clear. Although some recent work in empirical psychology has attempted to suggest otherwise, there is at least some reason for thinking that we *do* all start out life as moral skeptics, or at least as creatures who do not yet inhabit the moral point of view. Anyone who has spent a significant amount of time with toddlers has some experience with this phenomenon. Children have to be *socialized into* morality and the central mechanism for this socialization is precisely the threat of sanctions (whether positive or negative), which (if all goes well) leads through the mechanism of guilt to the internalization of structures of parental authority. This basic insight is found not only in the work of Nietzsche and Freud; it is also central to the first generation of the Frankfurt School. As Horkheimer and Adorno put it, "Humanity had to inflict terrible injuries on itself before the self . . . was created, and something of this process is repeated in every childhood" (DE, 26). However, lest one think that this is an overly authoritarian view of parenting that is best left behind (JJ, 185), let me emphasize that such sanctions need not be negative—rewarding children for doing the right thing is every bit as much a sanction as punishing them for doing wrong—and that this basic idea is also central to the work of considerably less pessimistic or ambivalent theorists of moral development such as Lawrence Kohlberg and even Habermas.[22]

Forst acknowledges that there's a degree of socialization required here but insists that this socialization is benign: "To become part of such contexts means to learn to recognize what justifications are, when one owes them, and to whom. Such processes of formation do not 'ram' an 'absolute must' into us in an inexplicable manner. . . . Rather, they constitute the way in which we are as fellow human beings and through which we become individual persons" (RJ, 61). But he offers no discussion of how one is socialized into the space of moral reasons, nor does he acknowledge the role that accepting and internalizing the superior power of the parent, who stands in for the normative authority of the social order, necessarily and inevitably plays in this process as a result of the child's radical dependence on her parents. Nor does he appreciate the fact that *from the point of view of the child*, these formation processes *necessarily* have an element of inexplicability and arbitrariness to them; the child can only appreciate the reasons that justify such socialization processes and legitimize the authority on which they rest *after the fact*, after she has taken up a position within the space of reasons and adopted the moral point of view.[23] The threat of parental or social sanctions—whether positive or negative—and the mechanisms of guilt and shame play a crucial role in this process. Until that point is reached, parental reasons, from the point of view of the child, all seem to rest on one ultimate ground: because I said so.

Here I am once again echoing a point that Adorno, building on the insights of psychoanalysis, makes in his critique of Kantian moral philosophy. Adorno argues that Kant appeals to our experience of duty or of obligation as "the most powerful reason for us to recognize the moral law and to acknowledge that some such thing as conscience really does exist"; however, in so doing, Kant "falls into a trap of his own making," inasmuch as "the actual existence of compulsive behavior of the kind that is commonly covered by the concept of conscience tells us nothing about the legitimacy of this authority" (PMP, 81). That authority, which is the ultimate ground of normativity in this Kantian picture, is not an unconditioned but rather a contingent ground; "it cannot, therefore, be regarded as the rightful source of the moral" (PMP, 83). In short, there is an "element of heteronomy at the heart of Kant's so-called doctrine of autonomy" (PMP, 83). Indeed, one might go so far as to say that heteronomy is the condition of possibility for (Kantian) autonomy. If this is the case, then the space of (autonomous) reasons is *also* a space of (heteronomous) power in the sense that it is constituted through a certain kind of power relation that can only be justified to the participants after they have entered it and accepted its demands and constitutive norms.[24]

The conclusion we should draw from this is *not* that all authority is illegitimate, that we shouldn't discipline children, or that freedom means a wild, schizophrenic, anarchic transgression of the boundaries of moral personhood. Rather, the conclusion is a more complicated one: that power relations are constitutive of subjectivity and moral personhood, that power relations provide the condition of possibility for entering the space of reasons in the first place, which means that the space of reasons is, in a slightly different sense from the one delineated above, always already a space of power. Moreover, and here we can connect this worry about how one enters the space of reasons to the previous discussion about the potentially authoritarian and exclusionary nature of our conceptions of practical reason, the power relation at issue here isn't merely a structural feature of the dependency relation that obtains between young children and their parents. Inasmuch as parents stand in for and are themselves profoundly shaped by the normative demands of the existing social order—by socializing their children to take up particular gender, race, sexual, and cultural identities, for example, in ways that they may not even themselves endorse or even fully comprehend—parental authority is not easily disentangled from existing relations of social authority, dominance, and hegemony. Hence, although it would be too strong to view the process of subjection as per se subordinating, in societies that are highly stratified by identity-based forms of dominance and subordination such as those of race, gender, and sexuality, this process often entails being socialized into taking up positions of subordination. Moreover, the structural dependence of the child on the superior power of the parent for its own survival and development as an intact subject renders the child systematically vulnerable to subordination, since the child so desires the social recognition that comes with having a stable social identity that she will attach to a subordinating form of identity rather than not attach at all.[25] As Fanon's work brilliantly shows, these intertwined dynamics of recognition, subjection, and subordination are at work in colonial contexts, where they help to produce what Fanon calls "the inferiority complex" of the black man, a complex that is instilled through a process of "internalization or rather epidermalization."[26] As a result of this colonial form of subjection, Fanon contends, "what is called the black soul is a construction by white folk," and the goal of Fanon's critique must be a liberation of "the black man from himself."[27]

As I mentioned above, the critique of the overly abstract Kantian conception of practical reason and normativity can be launched from a variety of theoretical perspectives, including, as Fanon's work shows, from the direction of post- or decolonial theory. In some ways, the line of thought that I have been sketching here dovetails with a communitarian critique of Forst's Kantian account. Although I would not characterize my own position as communitarian,[28] it is worth considering this critique if only because Forst's response to it is, in my view, revealing. The communitarian critique could be thought of as starting from the question of what, after all, we are being socialized into when we are being socialized into the space of reasons. Are we being socialized into a reasoning practice that allows us to arrive at or at least approximate a truly universal, context-transcending perspective, one that affords us a genuinely critical perspective on any form of life whatsoever, including our own? Or are we being socialized into a particular form of life, one that is rooted in and carries with it both the ethical values and, perhaps, the ideological biases of that form of life? Is the community of beings who argue a truly universal community, or is it reflective of a particular, and particularly modern, Western, post-Enlightenment form of life? And if the latter, then might the freestanding conception of practical reason that serves as the foundation for Forst's theory of justice turn out to be not so freestanding at all? Might it not implicitly presuppose the superiority of the particular Western, post-Enlightenment form of life in which it is rooted and thus rely on the very kind of historical truth claim that Forst claims to eschew?

Forst considers such worries in his discussion of Charles Taylor's work, since Taylor argues that belief in the power of reason and the autonomous subject are not, in fact, universal moral values, but rather part of the uniquely modern spirit or identity (RJ, 73–74).[29] Hence, on Taylor's view, the normative concepts such as practical reason and autonomy that undergird universalistic Kantian moral theories are themselves rooted in thick ethical values or constitutive goods of a particular form of life, namely, the modern (European) form of life. In response to Taylor, Forst insists that the validity of morality cannot be grounded in this way, since "morality is about a sphere of categorically binding norms whose observance is not required for the sake of *one's own* good, but is *unconditionally* required for the sake of the good of *others* according to the criteria of reciprocity and generality" (RJ, 74). Morality and its central principle, the principle of justification, must be grounded instead in "practical reason itself" (RJ, 74). However, to the non-Kantian, this response sounds a bit like emphatically stamping one's foot, inasmuch as it presupposes precisely what is supposed to be at issue here, which is whether or not the validity of the moral can have an unconditioned ground, whether or not it can be defended independently of any and all thick, culturally specific conceptions of the good. The most that Forst seems entitled to say at this point is that in order to count as a genuine morality in his neo-Kantian sense of that term, a system of normative principles would have to have an unconditioned ground; but claiming that this is a necessary feature of morality as such is not, by itself, sufficient to show that this unconditioned ground actually exists. It is worth noting that part of Taylor's historical story is about the "belief in the power of reason of the autonomous subject" as one of the goods particular to modernity (RJ, 74). If Taylor's historical genealogy is plausible, then even Forst's account of practical reason comes from somewhere, is rooted in a particular point of view, something like the point of view of European Enlightenment modernity.[30] And in that case, the communitarian challenge is a serious one—and it isn't just about how to draw the distinction between ethics and morality, as important as that issue may be.[31] Rather, it is about whether all attempts, such as Forst's, to articulate morality in the strong universalist and categorical sense are not, in fact, thick, particular, ethical values and substantive conceptions of the good in disguise.

To be sure, Forst criticizes Taylor by saying that "excluding a Hegelian recourse to the absolute, [Taylor's] narrative reconstruction of the goods underlying modern identity is confronted with the problem of justifying the validity of this kind of ethics" (RJ, 74). This is the same basic argument that he offered against the communitarian critique of universalist, Kantian conceptions of morality in his earlier work (CJ, 215–229). But notice that this is only true to the extent that one understands validity in the fairly demanding sense that Forst himself does. If, by contrast, one is comfortable with a less demanding, more contextualist conception of normative validity, one that is indexed more to particular and local conceptions of practical reason rather than the idea of practical reason as such, then perhaps one wouldn't have to have recourse either to a Hegelian theory of the absolute or to the Kantian notion of an unconditioned ground. I will come back to this issue in the concluding chapter of this book.

PUTTING FIRST THINGS FIRST: POWER AND THE METHODOLOGY OF CRITICAL THEORY

In the previous section, I argued that Forst's conception of practical reason obscures rather than illuminates reason's various entanglements with certain kinds of power relations, particularly with forms of authoritarianism and subjection that are found in various relations of subordination and that assume particularly pernicious forms in the context of colonialism. And yet, Forst himself insists that what distinguishes his framework for critical theory from alternatives is its ability to foreground questions of power (JC, 109–125). As he puts it, the first question of justice is the question of "the justifiability of social relations and the distribution of the 'power of justification' within a political context" (RJ, 11). This insight is central to a critical theory of justice, which insofar as it is critical must also be radical, that is, it must uncover the roots of social injustice. The first good of a critical theory of justice is therefore "the socially effective power to demand, question, and provide justifications, and to turn them into the foundations of political action and institutional arrangements" (RJ, 11). Hence a critical theory of justice that puts the issue of justification at its center is one that, as Forst puts it, puts "first things first," where this means that it puts the issue of "justificatory power" first (JC, 120). Justice, Forst rightly insists, is a matter not of the distribution of goods but of the subjection of some individuals to the domination or arbitrary rule of others.[32] Thus the first question of justice is the question of power.

And yet, it is far from clear that Forst succeeds in putting first things first. The reasons for this have mainly to do with Forst's conceptualization of power. In *The Right to Justification*, Forst tends to present justificatory power as something normatively positive and empowering, and to link it to the ability on the part of subjects of domination or arbitrary rule to demand justification for their situation. In this vein, he claims that justificatory power is "the highest good of justice (though one that cannot be distributed like a material good)" and he defines it as "the 'discursive' power to provide and to demand justifications, and to challenge false legitimations" (RJ, 196). As a result, his formulation of justificatory power in that text is open to the criticism that it overemphasizes reason's emancipatory potential and underemphasizes the subordinating power of justification, that is, the ways in which conceptions of practical reason and practices or orders of justification can and do serve to entrench, rationalize, and legitimate relations of domination by defining female, queer, and subaltern subjects as irrational or unreasonable.[33] However, Forst claims in response to this line of criticism that his more recent work articulates a more complex and ambivalent conception of power that is attentive to both the empowering and the subordinating effects of justificatory power (JJ, 178).

In this recent work, Forst continues to equate power with justificatory power, though he now describes such justificatory power in normatively neutral terms. For him, the concept of power describes "what is going on when someone acts for certain reasons for which others are responsible—that is, reasons that he or she would not otherwise have had and that still characterize him or her as an agent for whom alternatives of action remain open, though possibly less than before" (NP, 2). To be subjected to power means to be moved by reasons that others have given me and that motivate me to think or act in some way that I would not otherwise have done.[34] Hence, power, for Forst, is noumenal, which means that it exists in the realm of justifications. But, unlike in his earlier discussions of justificatory power, Forst now conceives of noumenal power as a "normatively neutral notion of power that enables us to distinguish more particular forms of power, such as rule, coercion, or domination" (NP, 1). Power, on this view, "rests on recognized, accepted justifications—some good, some bad, some in between" (NP, 6). In other words, the justifications on which power rests may be "well-founded and collectively shared with good reasons, or they can be merely 'overlapping,' or they can be distorted and ideological" (NP, 7).

Forst thus defends a cognitivist account of power, according to which "power is what goes on in the head, and what goes on is recognition of a reason to act in a certain way."[35] Physical force thus serves as the limit for power; when power turns into physical force, the noumenal character of power vanishes. Unlike physical force or violence, power, for Forst, rests on recognition, specifically, the recognition by the target of power that the actions of another agent or other agents give her a reason to think or act in a particular way. To use one of Forst's examples, for a blackmailer to exercise power over his target, the target must recognize the threat of blackmail as real or serious and thereby take it as a reason to change his actions; otherwise, the threat disappears and the power of the blackmailer vanishes. Power not only rests on perceived or recognized justifications; it "exists only when there is such acceptance" (NP, 6).

Although the fact that Forst's more recent conceptualization of power is normatively neutral does allow him to address the ideological and dominating potential of justificatory power, its overly cognitivist understanding of power has some problematic implications when it comes to theorizing social subordination and oppression. For one thing, to say that power rests on the recognition of reasons or justification on the part of the person over whom power is exercised seems to imply an account of power where no one can oppress you without your permission that puts too much responsibility for upholding relations of dominance on those who are subordinated to the power of others. In a way that is strangely reminiscent of Sartrean notions of absolute freedom and responsibility, Forst seems committed to saying that I can be free (that is, not subject to power) even if I am oppressed or colonized or facing a line of tanks, since it is up to me to decide whether I regard my oppression or colonization as being justified or whether I respect the authority of those who are giving orders to the people driving the tanks—roughly, as Sartre would have put it, what my situation means to me. There is a sense in which this is a true, even a compelling thought, but the fact that it can be invoked *in any situation whatsoever* suggests that the definition of power on which this claim rests does not give us the kind of analytical precision or clarity that we might hope for in a critical theory of power.

When used to analyze relations of oppression and domination, this way of conceptualizing power seems to imply that, for example, I am subject to masculine domination only insofar as I recognize it as being justified (whether that justification rests on good or bad reasons). But it seems to me that I can be subject to gender-based subordination whether or not I personally recognize it as justified, whether or not I take it as giving me a reason to act in a certain way or not, so long as enough people around me do accept it as legitimate and take it as a reason for their actions. I can still be taken less seriously as a philosopher, paid less than my male colleagues, subjected to sexual harassment, and so on, even if I do not myself recognize or accept the justifications for male dominance. In that way, gender subordination is strikingly disanalogous to Forst's blackmail example. As formulated, Forst's view implies that individuals can decide for themselves whether or not others have power over them, but this seems implausible, so perhaps it isn't what he has in mind.[36] However, even the somewhat more plausible claim that it is not individuals but collectives—say, some particular group of women or even women as a whole—who can collectively decide to stop recognizing the authority of those who are attempting to subject them to masculine domination and thereby make the power disappear is far from intuitively obvious. Certainly groups can try to refuse or to challenge certain kinds of justifications or reasons for subordination, but whether these collective refusals could possibly succeed is an open question. Feminists have been openly questioning and critiquing justifications for masculine power and privilege for decades, and yet such power remains stubbornly entrenched.

However, the main issue that I want to focus on here is rather different. Inasmuch as Forst defines power as "a way of binding others through reasons" (NP, 16), it isn't clear that his account of power can make sense of the role that power plays in constituting the space of reasons in the first place. That is, it isn't clear that his account of power can make sense of the dynamics of subjection that I discussed in the previous section. To be sure, Forst acknowledges that "even the most powerful individuals or groups cannot determine or close off the space of reasons entirely—that would be a task for the gods or a Leviathan as Hobbes imagined it. To have power means to rule in the space of reasons; but, given the plurality of human life, this is not absolute rule" (NP, 17). On this model, domination can be understood as the attempt to close off the space of reasons for some persons, but by definition this is an attempt that can never fully succeed. And yet, insofar as he defines power as rule *in* the space of reasons, Forst clearly does not understand it as rule *through* the constitution of the space of reasons. Thus, he seems either to rule out or to thoroughly domesticate the idea of subjection as a form of power, since subjection, understood as the becoming of subjects in and through a process of subjection to power relations, is the means by which individuals are given entry to the space of reasons. As Martin Saar has put this point, summing up the implications of a more constitutive, Foucaultian conception of power for thinking about the discursive space of reasons:

> Doesn't the discursive performance of the speaking, reason-exchanging subject necessarily rely on a multiplicity of practices not of its own making and not at its disposal? But are we then not required to admit that an intimate bond connects discourse, the space of reasons, and its social conditions, the realm of power? But this would mean that discourse is a realm of power and nothing sealed off from it. Being made, and being made possible by social practices (all of which will include exclusions, regulations, normalizations); discourse and reason are products of constitutions and therefore of power, and not even being right will help us from not being totally free.[37]

I suspect that this line of thought would be anathema to Forst, whose division of labor between the constructive and the critical tasks of a theory of justice seems designed to avoid precisely the sort of considerations about the intertwining of the space of reasons and the space of power that I've been suggesting. This brings me to my second challenge, concerning the methodology of critical theory. According to Forst, the constructive part of the theory of justice "lies in identifying the premises, principles, and procedures of the project of establishing a (more) just society" (RJ, 117); the critical part "lies in uncovering false or absent justifications for existing social relations and the corresponding relocation of the *power of justification* to the subjects themselves" (RJ, 117). The centerpiece of the constructive part of the theory is the justification of a just basic structure, which rests on the constructivist account of the principle of justification and the reconstructivist account of practical reason. The centerpiece of the critical part of the theory of justice is the "analysis and critique of legal, political, and social relations that are not reciprocally and generally justifiable. It requires a *critique of relations of justification* in a double sense, namely, both with respect to the real, particularly institutional possibility of discursive justification and (in terms of discourse theory) with regard to allegedly 'generally' accepted and acceptable results, that in truth are missing a sufficient grounding" (RJ, 121).

The advantage of distinguishing between the constructive and the critical tasks of a theory of justice in this way is relatively clear: it allows Forst to confine questions of the relations of domination in existing social relations to the critical part of the theory, allowing him to focus in the constructive part on the normative defense and elaboration of the principle of justification and the corresponding conception of practical reason. This enables Forst to develop a strong normative foundation on the basis of which power relations can be critically assessed. But the shortcomings of such an approach, at least from the point of view of critical theory, are, in my view, equally clear. This sort of approach seems to be a clear instance of political philosophy as applied ethics.[38] The strategy is to develop and defend a normative philosophical framework that rests on independent—freestanding—grounds and then, in a second step, to apply this theory to the task of criticizing existing social relations. In Forst's work, the freestanding normative philosophical framework is the right to justification, a right that is grounded, in turn, in his account of practical reason. This account provides the normative resources needed to transform the analysis of power as noumenal into a critique of actually existing power relations in society by means of developing a "*critical theory of relations of justification*" (NP, 17).

The merits of such an approach as a general method for doing political philosophy are debatable.[39] The more specific question that I would prefer to focus on here has to do with the merits of adopting this sort of approach when what one endeavors to do is to offer a critical theory of justice that puts first things first by putting the question of power at its center. Can an approach such as this do justice to the depth and complexity of power relations, especially as these pertain to the conditions and practices of justification and practical reasoning and the ongoing entanglements of such notions in the subordination of women, queers, racial minorities, and subaltern subjects? Can it illuminate the power investments and normative exclusions on which the conceptions of justification and of practical reason so often seem to rest? Can it make sense of the notion of subjection, understood as a phenomenon of power that shapes and constitutes the space of reasons as such and, in so doing, renders some individuals systematically vulnerable to subordinating forms of identity?

In order to further motivate such questions, let's consider two specific contexts in which Forst's analyses of the right to justification, practical reason, and noumenal power seem to obscure rather than illuminate relations of power. First, as Kevin Olson has recently argued, drawing on the work of Pierre Bourdieu, the ideas of discourse and justification at the center of Forst's theory of justice can be seen to have an implicit class bias. Within such contexts, paradigms of discursive justification are, Olson argues, the ruling ideas of a ruling class of knowledge experts: politicians, policy experts, journalists, writers, and academics. Members of such professions have high cultural capital and are extremely skilled in the public use of reasons. They place a high value on giving and asking for reasons because discursive reason-giving is so central to their own practices. "From this perspective," Olson writes, "justification is not a basic human right, but a mode of practice that is the expert domain of others. It does not recognize one's basic humanity, but implicitly universalizes a vision of humanity whose signature characteristics are most comfortably practiced by the members of elite groups."[40] Olson suggests that Forst is guilty of what Bourdieu calls the "unconscious universalization of the particular case."[41] The result is a picture of justice only a philosopher (or another member of the class of knowledge experts) could love. This unconscious universalization of the particular practice of discursive reason giving amounts to what Olson calls "a cultural imperialism *within* developed societies: not the imposition of Western ideals on the rest of the world, but the imposition of the ideals of the thinking and talking classes on the rest of society."[42] This means that, precisely by framing justice in terms of the right to discursive justification, Forst's theory may unwittingly reproduce certain class-specific power relations, power relations that are obscured rather than revealed by his noumenal conception of power.

With reference to Olson's point about cultural imperialism, consider Gayatri Spivak's analysis of the complexities of political discourse between hegemon and subaltern. Recall that Spivak's famous question—can the subaltern speak?—arises in the context of her attempt to theorize the subject position of the female subaltern subject in debates about the practice of sati, or the self-immolation of widows during the British colonial rule over India.[43] Such female subaltern subjects are, Spivak argues, caught in an impossible double bind in which their agency is systematically effaced: either they submit to the patriarchal norm that defines virtuous femininity in terms of self-denial or they allow themselves to be "saved" by the British imperialists; either they define themselves as subjects on patriarchal terms or they allow themselves to be constituted as objects of imperialism: "The abolition of this rite [sati] by the British has been generally understood as a case of 'White men saving brown women from brown men.' White women. . . . have not produced an alternative understanding. Against this is the Indian nativist statement, a parody of the nostalgia for lost origins: 'The women wanted to die.' . . . The two sentences go a long way to legitimize each other" (CPR, 287). Spivak's main point is that in neither of these two sentences does one encounter the voice of the women who want to perform such acts. Under such conditions, Spivak suggests, we must call into question the assumption that is implicit in Forst's account of justificatory power and its attendant deliberative conception of politics, namely, that "the oppressed, if given the chance, . . . *can speak and know their conditions*" (CRP, 269). Although Spivak does venture to say, in response to this question, that the subaltern cannot speak (CPR, 273), she also acknowledges that this is "an inadvisable remark" (CPR, 308). But even if we don't go quite so far as to say that the subaltern cannot *speak*, it seems clear that the kinds of subaltern subjects that Spivak has in mind—not only the women who wanted to immolate themselves, but also the "men and women among the illiterate peasantry, Aboriginals, and the lowest strata of the urban subproletariat"—cannot *be heard* by those who occupy positions of power and privilege (CPR, 269).

Spivak's critique calls our attention not only to the vast differences of power and privilege across the (post)colonial divide, but also to the vast differences of power and privilege *within* the category of postcolonial subjects. It is not only privileged Westerners who cannot hear subaltern subjects, but also postcolonial elites. This points to what James Tully calls the "multiplex" character of the distinction between "hegemon" and "subaltern," to the ways in which such categories are "dispersed across complex, criss-crossing and overlapping fields of unequal and mutually constitutive relationships of interplay. They are not conveniently located in the West and the non-West or the North and South, but within and across these binary categories of colonial geography, dividing subaltern (and hegemonic) societies into complex hegemonic-subaltern classes and ethnicities."[44] Just as developed societies are fractured along lines of class (though not only along such lines), as in Olson's analysis, Spivak insists that "the colonial or postcolonial subaltern is defined as being on the other side of difference, or an epistemic fracture, even from other groupings among the colonized" (CPR, 309), for example, from the "self-marginalizing or self-consolidating migrant" who writes postcolonial theory (CPR, 6).

Spivak's analysis of the subaltern raises questions not only about discursive justification but also about the narratives of progress and development that have typically served to make some voices audible while silencing or drowning out others. After all, the virtuous British repeatedly described and justified their mission of saving female subalterns by appealing to narratives of progress and civilizational superiority, and such assumptions continue to inflect many contemporary versions of the project of imperial feminism that positions white Western feminists as the saviors of brown women.[45] Such narratives of progress and civilizational superiority are, once again, quite prominent in Kant; as McCarthy has argued, it is Kant's developmentalism that enables him to reconcile his normative universalism with his liberal imperialism, by positing Africans, Native Americans, and Asians as not yet capable of autonomous self-rule and therefore as people in need of being spoken for. Thus, Spivak allows us to see how the issues of practical reason, discursive justification, and narratives of progress are deeply intertwined. As such, her work raises the possibility that Forst's own view, while claiming to be grounded in a constructivist conception of normativity precisely so as to avoid the difficulties that arise for Honneth's more historicist approach and precisely in an effort to address the kinds of postcolonial critiques of progress discussed above, nevertheless ends up in much the same place: implicitly relying on a thick, historically specific conception of the good that undergirds its conception of practical reason and that is deeply bound up with teleological progress narratives while disavowing those very connections.

This multiplex situation of the postcolonial subaltern in relation to postcolonial elites and privileged members of hegemonic societies poses formidable difficulties for the theorist who is trying to analyze and critique relations of dominance and subordination in and across post- and neocolonial contexts. I take it that Spivak's main point is to call our attention to these difficulties and to the epistemic violence that we so easily do even when we attempt to construct a theory of justice that takes into account the perspectives of subaltern subjects. This is why she continually speaks of the "(im)possible perspective of the native informant" (CPR, 62), a perspective that is, in her view, continually foreclosed not only by Kantian universalism,[46] but also by radical postcolonial critique, insofar as the latter has the tendency simply to reverse and therefore implicitly to legitimate the colonial attitude (CPR, 39). As Spivak puts it: "No contemporary metropolitan investigator is not influenced by [the masculine-imperialist ideological formation].

Part of our 'unlearning' project is to articulate our participation in that formation—by *measuring* silences, if necessary—into the *object* of investigation" (CPR, 284). This is a matter precisely of acknowledging "our complicity in the muting, in order precisely to be more effective in the long run" (CPR, 309). However, it isn't clear that a theory that understands power in wholly cognitivist and noumenal terms, defines justice as the right to justification, and links justice to a strong conception of normative progress can be of much help in this unlearning project. Such a theory may be quite useful in providing ways of assessing the reasons or justifications that are given *within* political discourses, but it doesn't seem to be much help in the project of measuring the silences and normative exclusions that constitute the space of reasons within which demands for justification are raised. Although Forst readily acknowledges that particular justifications may be problematic or ideological or may serve the interests of those in power, there is seemingly no room in his theory for the thought that our ideal of justification itself rests on a set of social practices that are shot through with normative exclusions.[47] As such, this theory not only fails to fully illuminate certain kinds of power relations in which we as theorists of justice are ourselves implicated, including the kinds of class divisions that Olson cites and the multiplex postcolonial power relations that Spivak and Tully analyze; it also, by virtue of that failure to illuminate, runs the risk of reproducing them.[48]

In response to this line of criticism, Forst turns the tables and insists that it is his critics who disrespect and even infantilize working-class or subaltern subjects by suggesting that they are not discursively competent or are incapable of demanding or offering justifications. In so doing, Forst asserts, these critics reproduce their own form of cultural imperialism (JJ, 192). In a similar vein, Forst challenges those critics who claim that a justificatory conception of practical reason is rooted in a particular form of life, namely, à la Taylor, the form of life characteristic of European Enlightenment modernity. Forst accuses such critics of mixing up genealogy and validity, and thus of implicitly claiming "that people in non-European societies in the past or the present have no justifiable claim to be respected as moral equals, or at least that they speak a foreign, 'Western' moral language when they make such claims. The result would be to exclude those who struggle for emancipation in such societies from the realm of justifications; it would disenfranchise them morally, for they would be seen to have the wrong, non-European passport to properly speak the language of 'European' morality" (JJ, 183; see also JC, chaps. 2 and 3). On Forst's view, the structure of demanding justifications belongs to the "deep grammar" of social conflict, and as such is an essential part of all emancipatory struggles; thus, it cannot be said to belong to any particular form of life: "The language of emancipation and of no longer wanting to be denied one's right to be a participatory equal is a universal language spoken in many tongues" (JJ, 184).

But it seems to me that Forst has constructed a straw man here. He is absolutely right that no one owns the concept of justification, or even the language of European morality. To the extent that such concepts, practices, and ideas have proved and continue to prove useful in struggles against domination, critical theorists should regard them as important critical emancipatory tools. But acknowledging this point in no way requires that we accept his abstract Kantian picture of practical reason as such or of the context-transcendent metacontext of moral justification or the foundationalist account of normativity that these notions support. Rather, one can acknowledge that practices and languages of justification are used in a variety of different historical, cultural, and social contexts, and that although these practices are embedded in particular social and cultural forms of life and in the webs of value that suffuse such forms of life with substantive normative content, these forms of life are also open and porous and entangled with one another. Nevertheless, the webs of value that suffuse these forms of life help to determine what can count as a reason in a particular justificatory context or order of justification. Indeed, one could argue that such a picture is required if we really want to understand justification as a *social practice*, as Forst himself suggests we should. In fact, this is precisely the picture found in the sociological work of Boltanski and Thévenot, who identify a plurality of what they call "principles of equivalence" operating within specific orders of justification, each recognized as universal within its own order and formally incompatible with one another. Critique, for them, is either internal, in which case it relies on standards internal to a specific order of justification, or external, in which case the standards of one order are used to critique a situation in another order, but it neither requires nor entails reference to an overarching context of justification that transcends and unifies all of the diverse orders of justification.[49] The picture here is one of specific languages of justification supported by particular sets of practices of reasoning, with no one overarching context or metacontext that purports to transcend them all and by appeal to which one can easily translate from one context or order to another, but where the justificatory norms from one context can be and often are used to critique situations that arise in others.[50]

Such a picture is better suited, I think, to acknowledging Spivak's central point, which is the ongoing need to critically interrogate the power investments and normative exclusions of our own practices and languages of justification. To appeal to a metacontext of justification that ex hypothesi transcends all of the messy, power-laden social practices of justification in which we engage is to fail to acknowledge one of the central insights motivating Spivak's critique, which I would characterize in the idiom of standpoint theory: domination, when viewed from above, looks an awful lot like equality.[51] This is why any and all claims to have accessed a categorical normative point of view unsullied by and unentangled with power relations and reflective of a genuinely universal conception of practical reason can so easily seem like a power play.[52] Those of us in positions of privilege—academic elites within our own culture, hegemons in relation to subaltern subjects—should be especially mindful of the dangers attendant upon such claims, and we should work hard to problematize our own point of view, to consider the ways in which such claims might implicate us in relations of domination and structures of normative exclusion even—and perhaps especially—as we attempt to theorize justice on behalf of subaltern subjects.[53] This goes double for those of us committed to the emancipatory project of critical theory. But note that this does not amount to a self-contradictory rejection of the norms of practical reason. Rather, it might just as easily take the form of what Spivak calls a vigilant and persistent "critique of what we cannot not want" (CPR, 110), by which I mean a persistent critical interrogation of the power investments and effects of our own normative commitments and ideals. Such a critique need not compel us to give up those ideals but it might lead us to inhabit them differently, to take up a different stance with respect to them. I will explore a possible way of inhabiting the ideal of practical reason differently, one that is more compatible with the kind of critical stance called for by Spivak, in chapter 6.

In response to the kinds of concerns about the entanglement of practical reason with power relations that I have raised throughout this chapter, Forst would no doubt say that even granting such concerns, we still have no other resource on which to rely in analyzing and critiquing such entanglements but reason itself. As he puts it, "A morality of justification is a morality that can be criticized and revised in its details: a human morality 'without a banister' that cannot in principle exclude the possibility of failures and errors. There is, however, *only one* 'authority' for revising any reasons that no longer seem defensible: reason itself" (RJ, 39). Indeed, in his reply to an earlier version of this chapter, Forst wrote: "However 'scandalous' or 'impure' social and historical forms of reason have been and as much as we need to critically reflect on the blind spots of our own notions of the 'reasonable,' *there is no other faculty* of seeing through that but the always imperfect and yet infinitely improvable finite faculty of reason" (JJ, 181–182). Moreover, in his more recent work, Forst characterizes this distinction between the impure forms of reason embedded in social reality and the infinitely improvable faculty of reason as a distinction between "two worlds": "the social reality, on the one hand, and an ideal normative dimension in terms of which it is criticized in part or radically, on the other" (JC, 95). The practice of critique, Forst suggests, both relies on such a distinction and "forms the link between these two worlds" (JC, 96–97; see also JJ, 189–191). The two-worlds image is Forst's way of capturing the dialectic between immanence and transcendence, and of making sense of context-transcending ideals that are nevertheless formulated and invoked in historically specific contexts.

My full response to these claims will emerge through the remainder of this book, but for now, let me give some indications of the direction of the argument: First, I'm very skeptical of the two-worlds talk, for the basic reason that, Forst's protestations to the contrary notwithstanding, such talk carries with it assumptions of metaphysical and normative purity. I also think it is indicative of the kind of splitting between the constructive and the critical tasks of theory that leads to the problematic model of political theory as applied ethics that I discussed above. Through my reading of Foucault and Adorno in the next chapter, I offer a way of thinking about critique that does not rely on this two-worlds imagery but rather understands critique as a wholly immanent, this-worldly practice of opening up lines of fragility and fracture *within* the existing social world. Second, I'm not convinced that reason is our *only* means of critiquing ideological justifications. As both Adorno and Foucault knew quite well, works of art or other kinds of imaginative world disclosures that allow us to see our social world in a new way or expand our moral imagination can also serve to critique ideological conceptions of reason or forms of subjection to power relations.[54] To be sure, Forst could always say that these are reasons, too, at least in his sense of that term—just as he claims that seductions and threats are reasons—but this, I fear, threatens to make reason into the night in which all cows are grey, and thus to make us lose our grip on the kind of work that practices of reason-giving can (and cannot) do. Third, even if we grant Forst his claim that reason is all "we" have, that reason is self-correcting, and that we can't do critique without it, this does not mean, as I've just argued, that we have to agree with his specific conception of practical reason or with his foundationalist understanding of the role that practical reason plays in relation to our normative principles. The pessimistic induction offered above should compel us to acknowledge the ongoing possibility that "our" ideals and practices of reasoning are entangled with power relations and forms of epistemic violence; this, in turn, should lead us not to abandon the ideal of practical reason but to conceptualize it differently, in a more humble, contingent, and modest or self-effacing way.[55]

This alternative account of the relationship between power, justification, and the space of reasons is in line with an alternative conception of the methodology of critical theory: not an approach that envisions critical theory as a kind of applied ethics, but rather an approach that takes the distinctiveness of critical theory to lie in its understanding of practical reason as impure, by which I mean embodied and embedded in history, culture, society, language, and so on, which is to say, entangled with power relations. On this view, the methodological distinctiveness of critical theory lies precisely in its attempt to grapple with the essential tension between reason and power relations, an essential tension that needs to be confronted not just at the empirical level but also at the conceptual level.[56] In other words, the methodological distinctiveness of critical theory rests in its acknowledgment that, as Foucault once put it, we are "fortunately committed to practicing a rationality that is unfortunately crisscrossed by intrinsic dangers" (SKP, 358). For Foucault, the task of critical thought is precisely to think through this spiral. In a similar vein, Adorno might have said that this is a contradiction that has its roots in the social world that we inhabit, and the aim of critical thought is not to cover over but rather to reflect on such contradictions. As I will explore in the next chapter via my discussion of Adorno and Foucault, such an approach to critical theory could actually be seen as more fully reflexive than the approach to political philosophy as applied ethics, insofar as it has built into itself a genealogical reflection on the contingent and possibly ideological grounds of its own theoretical formation.[57]

Finally, the next chapter will return to and complicate further Forst's understanding of the dialectic of progress. Recall that, on Forst's view, the dialectic of progress arises because every critique of progress necessarily relies on the concept of progress to formulate its critique. Hence one cannot be against progress without also being for it. Similarly, every appeal to progress should generate a critique of its ideological blind spots. Hence those who are for progress should also be critical of the very discourses of progress to which they (necessarily) appeal. I already noted the asymmetry between these two poles of the dialectic of progress: even if it is true that one cannot be against progress without being for it, one can be for progress without being against it, and this is one of the things that has given the discourse of progress such a bad name. But we should take care in assessing Forst's transcendental argument that one can only be against progress by being for it. This argument trades on a conflation between the two distinct conceptions of progress delineated in chapter 1. Post- and decolonial critics of progress are "against" the backward-looking idea of progress as a historical "fact" about the developmental process that has led up to European modernity, for it is this account of progress that frames traditional or nonmodern subjects as what Chakrabarty calls "human embodiments of the principle of anachronism."[58] By making such a critique, they may well be implicitly claiming that it would be better if we gave up this problematic bit of imperialist ideology, and in that sense it may be true that they are implicitly appealing to some sort of notion of progress. But notice that the notion that they are appealing to here is not a backward-looking one but rather a forward-looking conception of progress as a moral-political imperative or a future goal toward which we strive. Not only that, but it is far from clear that such critics of progress as a historical "fact" must, as Forst implies, defend their implicit forward-looking claims about progress by appealing to such strong notions as categorical normativity and universal conceptions of practical reason. I will return to these issues in the concluding chapter. These considerations suggest a possibility opened up by Adorno's rather different account of the dialectic of progress, namely, that forward-looking progress may be possible only once we have abandoned the backward-looking conception of progress, or, as Adorno more pithily puts it, that "progress occurs where it ends" (P, 150).

5

From the *Dialectic of Enlightenment* to the *History of Madness*

FOUCAULT AS ADORNO'S OTHER "OTHER SON"

As I discussed in chapter 1, unlike Habermas, Honneth, and Forst, the thinkers of the first generation of the Frankfurt School were extremely skeptical about the idea of historical progress. Recall that for Adorno, the catastrophe of Auschwitz makes "all talk of progress towards freedom seem ludicrous" and even makes the "affirmative mentality" that engages in such talk look like "the mere assertion of a mind that is incapable of looking horror in the face and thereby perpetuates it" (HF, 7). Importantly, Adorno doubted not that progress as a forward-looking moral-political imperative was *possible*, but rather that any sense could be made of backward-looking claims that progress as a historical "fact" is *actual*, and he was extremely critical of the ways in which belief in the latter easily becomes a kind of ideological mystification that stands in the way of attempts to achieve the former. This is what motivates his paradoxical-sounding claim that "progress occurs where it ends" (P, 150). Adorno's skepticism about any and all backward-looking claims about historical progress is shared by one of the other great historico-philosophical thinkers of the late twentieth century, Michel Foucault. Already in his first major philosophical work, the *History of Madness*, Foucault announced his intention to write a history that would "remove all chronology and historical succession from the perspective of a 'progress,' to reveal in the history of an experience, a movement in its own right, uncluttered by a teleology of knowledge or the orthogenesis of learning" (HM, 122). Foucault's skepticism about claims to progress was motivated less by a moral reaction to the horrors of the twentieth century—though clearly there *is* a moral sensibility at work in his analyses of the ways in which progress in the human sciences is predicated upon the exclusion of madmen, social deviants, homosexuals, and other "abnormals"—than by the philosophical point, also made by Adorno, that traditional conceptions of historical progress presuppose a suprahistorical, atemporal point of view that we now know to be a metaphysical illusion.

In this sense, both Foucault and Adorno can be understood as attempting to break out of—at least a certain interpretation of—Hegelian philosophy of history and its closely related conception of dialectics. And yet Foucault, like Adorno, remained firmly committed throughout his career to the basically Hegelian thought that philosophy—understood as a project of critique—is a historically situated endeavor, that philosophy consists in a critical reflection on our historical present that makes use of conceptual tools that are themselves the products of history. In this sense, both thinkers can be understood as attempting to think through the possibilities for a thoroughly historicized understanding of critical philosophy once we no longer have recourse to the notion of the Absolute, that is to say, to think through Hegel but also beyond him. For these reasons, and others that will be explored in this chapter, Foucault can and should be thought of as Adorno's other "other son."[1]

Precisely because of their skepticism about progress, Adorno and Foucault are often read as offering a negative philosophy of history, a *Verfallsgeschichte*, a conservative story of history as a process of decline and fall that is, as Habermas put it, "insensitive to the highly ambivalent content of cultural and social modernity" (PDM, 338). Habermas maintains that Adorno and Foucault follow Nietzsche in collapsing the distinction between validity and power, and that this leads them to a totalizing critique or abstract negation of the normative content of Enlightenment modernity.[2] In what follows, I argue, contra Habermas, that the critiques of progress found in Adorno and Foucault are in service of a broader project of immanent critique that aims not at an abstract negation of the normative inheritance of modernity but rather at a fuller realization of that inheritance. Inheritance is understood here in the Derridean sense as something that is reaffirmed in and through its radical transformation: "inheritance," Derrida reminds us, "is never a *given*, it is always a task."[3] In other words, the critique of progress in Adorno and Foucault is in service of an immanent critique of modernity that aims to compel those who have inherited the project of the Enlightenment to live up more fully to its own normative ideals of freedom, inclusion, and respect for the other. The aim of this chapter is to recover this theme in the work of Adorno and Foucault and to give some indication of its value for a critical theory that aims to decolonize itself.

I should emphasize at the outset, however, that my aim here is neither to compare Adorno and Foucault (though I will of course point out some commonalities and some differences along the way) nor to synthesize them (though I will be weaving together some of their insights). Rather, the aim of this chapter is to recover some of the insights of Adorno's philosophy of history and his moral philosophy read in conjunction with Foucault's early work on history to construct an alternative framework for thinking through the relationship between history and normativity. I also hope to press these insights into the service of addressing some of the problems, diagnosed in previous chapters, that contemporary critical theory has encountered in its attempt to ground normativity in either a deflationary, pragmatic, and contingent but still broadly speaking Hegelian account of historical progress or a neo-Kantian conception of practical reason. This may seem like a strange or quixotic project not only because it is it often assumed that Adorno and Foucault had totalizing negative philosophies of history that were tied to romantic and ultimately conservative attempts to reclaim some mythic past, but also because it is often assumed that neither thinker makes a serious contribution to normative theorizing. Adorno's overwhelming negativism and his cultural pessimism are thought to place him outside ethics, and Foucault's paranoia about power and his cryptonormativism are said to render him normatively confused.[4] I hope that this chapter will give the reader some reasons to rethink this received wisdom regarding these two thinkers, but I won't be attempting a full-scale reconstruction of either, much less both, of their positions on morality or ethics here, since such a project would require a separate book. In the case of Foucault, I have attempted to reconstruct his normative position in some of my previous work;[5] in the case of Adorno, I will lean on some excellent recent reconstructions of his normative project.[6] As I said, my main focus here will be on mobilizing some of Adorno's and Foucault's insights to construct an alternative to the Hegelian and Kantian accounts of the relationship between normativity and history that have been put forward by Habermas, Honneth, and Forst, and to suggest how this alternative can be useful for the project of decolonizing critical theory.

I begin by briefly reconstructing the alternative histories of Enlightenment modernity presented in Horkheimer and Adorno's *Dialectic of Enlightenment* and Foucault's *History of Madness*. My goal is to read these two texts contrapuntally: keeping in view their distinct and divergent aims, while nonetheless bringing out their rich harmonies. Next, I sketch out the distinctive alternative methodology for the philosophy of history that can be reconstructed from the work of Adorno and Foucault. This methodology weaves together vindicatory and subversive genealogies—and, as such, it reconstructs history as a story of *both* progress *and* regress *at the same time*—in service of a distinctive genealogical aim: a critical problematization of our present historical moment. This problematization of our historical present has a normative point, namely, the fuller realization of the normative inheritance of the Enlightenment, in particular, the norms of freedom and respect for the other. Finally, I consider how conceptualizing the relationship between history and normativity in this way can open critical theory up to a more fruitful dialogue with post- and decolonial theory.

THE DIALECTIC OF PROGRESS: ADORNO AND THE PHILOSOPHY OF HISTORY

The *Dialectic of Enlightenment* opens with a thunderbolt: "Enlightenment, understood in the widest sense as the advance of thought, has always aimed at liberating human beings from fear and installing them as masters. Yet the wholly enlightened earth is radiant with triumphant calamity" (DE, 1).[7] The source of the fascist and totalitarian regression to barbarism that Horkheimer and Adorno witnessed as they wrote this text in the early 1940s, against the backdrop of the war and the horrors of Nazism, is not merely the concrete historical or institutional forms of enlightenment thinking; it appears to be enlightenment rationality itself, which they describe as "corrosive" and "totalitarian" (DE, 4). The key to this shocking claim lies in the meaning of the term "enlightenment." It refers not—at least not exclusively and not even primarily—to the historical epoch of European Enlightenment that began in France and flowered in Germany in the eighteenth century, but rather to a more general process of progressive rationalization that enables human beings to exercise greater and greater power over nature, over other human beings, and over themselves. It is the latter meaning of "enlightenment" that allows Horkheimer and Adorno to link enlightenment rationality with a will to mastery, control, and the domination of inner and outer nature; this will to mastery comes to fruition in the historical period known as the Enlightenment, but it does not originate there.

To be sure, Horkheimer and Adorno also hold out some hope for a positive conception of enlightenment. For instance, in their preface, they claim that their goal is to enlighten enlightenment about itself by unmasking its self-destructive tendencies. In this context, they readily acknowledge that "freedom in society is inseparable from enlightenment thinking" (DE, xvi). And yet, they continue, "the very concept of that thinking . . . already contains the germ of the regression which is taking place everywhere today" (DE, xvi). Enlightenment must *reflect* on this "regressive moment" lest it "seal its own fate" and descend completely into barbarism (DE, xvi). Through an analysis of the intertwining of enlightenment rationality and a social reality permeated with relations of oppression and domination, Horkheimer and Adorno aim to "prepare a positive concept of enlightenment which liberates it from its entanglement in blind domination" (DE, xviii).

However, as many commentators have noted, the text offers only a few glimpses of this positive conception of enlightenment, and even those emerge more or less indirectly. One such indirect glimpse comes in the excursus "Juliette or Enlightenment and Morality," where Horkheimer and Adorno argue that the "dark writers of the bourgeoisie" such as Nietzsche and the Marquis de Sade expose the inherent amorality of enlightenment. Unlike the apologists for the bourgeoisie, Nietzsche and Sade did not shy away from the consummation of enlightenment's means-end, coldly calculative mode of thinking in immoralism: "While the light-bringing writers protected the indissoluble alliance of reason and atrocity, bourgeois society and power, by denying that alliance," Horkheimer and Adorno write, "the bearers of darker messages pitilessly expressed the shocking truth" (DE, 92). In their proclamation of "the identity of power and reason, their pitiless doctrines are more compassionate than those of the moral lackeys of the bourgeoisie" (DE, 93). This last passage is ambiguous (perhaps intentionally so), but it suggests that by proclaiming the identity of power and reason, Nietzsche and Sade hold up a mirror to enlightenment that enables enlightenment to reflect on its own regressive tendencies and thus "opens to view what lies beyond it" (DE, 92). This further suggests that Horkheimer and Adorno's own position is not that power and reason are identical. It is true that this is what Sade and Nietzsche proclaim, but in doing so they are acting not as enemies of enlightenment, but rather in service of its rescue. Moreover, the "light-bringing writers," the "apologists" for enlightenment and the bourgeoisie, who deny the alliance between reason and power by espousing "harmonistic doctrines," in so doing unwittingly *reinforce* that alliance (DE, 92). Thus, the idea of holding up a mirror to enlightenment so that it can become aware of its regressive tendencies goes together with the relatively hopeful note on which the book ends: "Enlightenment itself, having mastered itself and assumed its own power, could break through the limits of enlightenment" (DE, 172). The possibility of breaking through the limits of enlightenment with the very tools of enlightenment itself is connected to a nonviolent, open-ended form of reflection or reconciliation that is exemplified by (though perhaps not limited to) aesthetic mimesis.

This dialectical relationship between the negative, totalitarian, regressive, barbaric, and amoral aspects of enlightenment and its positive, reflective, and emancipatory aspects, between enlightenment as domination and enlightenment as the capacity for rational self-reflection, is the philosophical core of the book. Consistent with Adorno's later notion of negative dialectics, however, this dialectic does not aim at a dialectical reconciliation or resolution. Although there is a notion of reconciliation present in Adorno's work, and although this notion is tied to the idea of enlightening enlightenment about itself—or, as Adorno puts it in *Negative Dialectics*, transcending the concept "by way of the concept" (ND, 15)—reconciliation, for Adorno, stands in an aporetic relationship to the unreconciled world that we live in and thus can be neither conceptualized nor represented but can only be glimpsed indirectly through the illumination provided by some works of modern art.[8] Thus the aim of the *Dialectic of Enlightenment* is not to *resolve* what we might call, following Max Weber, the paradox of rationalization—that is, the fact that enlightenment rationality is predicated on the domination of inner and outer nature and that domination in modernity is predicated on rationalizing itself—but rather to *call our attention to that very paradox*. As Adorno noted in his lectures on moral philosophy, dialectical thinking is precisely "the refusal to accept the denial or elimination of contradictions. . . . Instead it makes contradiction into an object or theme of philosophical reflection itself" (PMP, 79).[9] At a conceptual level, the structure of the dialectic of enlightenment is that of a contradiction or an aporia. As Horkheimer and Adorno state in their preface:

> The aporia which faced us in our work thus proved to be the first matter we had to investigate: the self-destruction of enlightenment. We have no doubt—and herein lies our *petitio principii*—that freedom in society is inseparable from enlightenment thinking. We believe we have perceived with equal clarity, however, that the very concept of that thinking, no less than the concrete historical forms . . . with which it is intertwined, already contains the germ of the regression which is taking place everywhere today. (DE, xvi)

The *Dialectic of Enlightenment* thus strives to articulate and reflect upon a contradiction that its authors take to be central to modern,

Western societies: enlightenment rationality is both freedom and unfreedom or domination at the same time. This contradictory truth can only be expressed through an aporetically structured argument.[10]

But this brings us to the difficult question of the *status* of this aporetic relationship between enlightenment rationality and domination: is it a conceptual aporia, one that results from the structure of reason or rational thinking as such, or is it a historically emergent, contingent aporia, a function of the particular ways in which the notion of enlightenment rationality as it emerged in European culture in the eighteenth and nineteenth centuries was bound up with specific historical and social conditions that led it to be intertwined with bourgeois coldness and with the domination of inner and outer nature? Note that this question is hovering in the background of Habermas's charge that "anyone who abides in a paradox on the very spot once occupied by philosophy with its ultimate groundings is not just taking up an uncomfortable position; one can only hold that place if one makes it at least minimally plausible that there is *no way out*" (PDM, 128). If the relationship between reason and domination is a conceptual aporia, and if this means that reason is reduced to domination, then either there is no rational way out, in which case the way out can only be found through a nostalgic return to a romanticized understanding of magic or mimesis, or the way out can only be found by articulating an alternative conception of reason, as Habermas attempts in his own conception of communicative rationality.[11] If, however, the relationship between reason and domination is historically contingent, and if it doesn't involve a reduction of reason per se to domination, then the paradox emerges from a certain process of rationalization and is not internal to reason as such.

What is interesting about Horkheimer and Adorno's understanding of enlightenment is their attempt to theorize its dialectic, in Hegelian fashion, as *both* conceptual *and* historically contingent. After all, as Adorno never tired of pointing out, the great lesson he learned from Hegel is that concepts cannot be grasped independently of their concrete historical content (H, 53–88; see also EF, 10–11).[12] The mediation between the conceptual and the historically contingent helps to illuminate Horkheimer and Adorno's persistent (if underdeveloped) faith in the positive concept of enlightenment, and its relationship to freedom. The dialectic of enlightenment is presented in conceptual terms, for example, in a passage that I have already quoted: "the very concept of [enlightenment] thinking, no less than the concrete historical forms, the institutions of society with which it is intertwined, already contains the germ of the regression which is taking place everywhere today" (DE, xvi). In this sense, Horkheimer and Adorno do posit an essential tension between enlightenment rationality in the broad sense and power relations understood as the control or domination of inner and outer nature. As I suggested above, this is the fundamental conceptual aporia that Horkheimer and Adorno are trying to illuminate. And yet the particular historical unfolding of this entanglement that has led to the barbarism and totalitarianism of the twentieth century must be understood as historically contingent. Indeed, Horkheimer and Adorno sharply criticize any philosophy of history that claims to know the telos of historical development. "With determinate negation," they write, "Hegel gave prominence to an element which distinguishes enlightenment from the positivist decay to which he consigned it. However, by finally postulating the known result of the whole process of negation, totality in the system and in history, as the absolute, he violated the prohibition and himself succumbed to mythology" (DE, 18). Notice that the prohibition that Hegel is said to have violated is not just a prohibition on positing absolute knowing as the end point of the historical development of reason; rather, it is a prohibition on positing *any* end point, *any* final reconciliation, whether positive or negative, to the dialectical process. Hence, although Adorno was sharply critical of the tendency of Hegel's philosophy of history to justify the status quo (H, 85), his conceptual argument against Hegel goes further than this: "The philosophical anticipation of reconciliation is a trespass against real reconciliation. . . . A seamless system and an achieved reconciliation are not one and the same; rather, they are contradictory: the unity of the system derives from unreconcilable violence" (H, 27). This conceptual point applies not only to positive philosophies of history such as Hegel's own, but also to negative philosophies of history that hold on to mirror-image epistemological and metaphysical assumptions about the directedness of history.

Thus it would be a mistake to read *Dialectic of Enlightenment* as a negative philosophy of history. Rather, the particular path that has been taken by the dialectic of enlightenment in European modernity should be understood as a *contingent* historical process: the emergence of modern, technologically oriented science, of capitalism and the bourgeois morality and forms of social organization that rationalize it, of the culture industry as a mechanism for placating an oppressed majority, and of virulent forms of anti-Semitism. The concept of enlightenment in a broad sense is entangled with power relations, and in that sense, it carries within itself the seed or the germ of its own regression, or represents the system *in nuce*. But the particular way that this relationship has been worked out in the history of the West—in such a way that the potentials for reification, regression, and domination that are present in the concept of enlightenment have grown and blossomed into full-fledged barbarism—is contingent. As Adorno would later summarize the main claim of the text: "The dialectic of reason or the dialectic of Enlightenment is a matter of such profound importance in history, so much so that we must conclude—and perhaps I exaggerate in order to make the point—that, *in the historical form in which we encounter it to this day*, reason is both reason *and* unreason in one" (HF, 45, emphasis added). Within that contingent historical form, "adaptation to the power of progress furthers the progress of power, constantly renewing the degenerations which prove successful progress, not failed progress, to be its own antithesis. The curse of irresistible progress is irresistible regression" (DE, 28).[13]

The cause of enlightenment's reversion to myth is "the fear of truth which petrifies enlightenment itself" (DE, xvi). What is the truth that enlightenment fears? Perhaps it is precisely its entanglement with domination. By holding up a mirror to this aspect of enlightenment, Horkheimer and Adorno hope not to disentangle reason and power once and for all, but rather to render reason self-aware of its inevitable entanglements with power. Hence, their positive concept of enlightenment aims to liberate us not from the entanglement with power per se, but rather from the "entanglement in *blind* domination" (DE, xviii; see also 33). What good would overcoming this blindness do? It would enable us to see that "although humanity may be unable to interrupt its flight away from necessity and into progress and civilization without forfeiting knowledge itself, at least it no longer mistakes the ramparts it has constructed against necessity, the institutions and practices of domination which have always rebounded against society from the subjugation of nature, for guarantors of the coming freedom" (DE, 32).

On this way of understanding the historical and conceptual dimensions of the dialectic of enlightenment, there may well be certain dangers that cannot be wholly purged from enlightenment rationality understood in the broadest sense, but this does not mean that enlightenment's descent into fascist barbarism was inevitable. On this reading, then, Horkheimer and Adorno are not wedded to a negative philosophy of history, nor does their invocation of the positive concept of enlightenment amount to a simple mistake or confusion. On their understanding, the concept of enlightenment is not in itself barbaric or totalitarian; rather, it is deeply *ambivalent*, in the sense that it contains the *potential* to descend into barbarism and totalitarianism. But it contains other potentials as well, including the potential to reflect on its own regressive tendencies, to hold up a mirror to itself, and thus to break through its own limits. As Adorno put it, "Only through reflection can reflective thought get beyond itself" (H, 73). The contingent, historical story of the descent of enlightenment into barbarism is told in a thoroughly pitiless fashion because "only thought which does violence to itself is hard enough to shatter myths" (DE, 2). But through their lack of pity, Horkheimer and Adorno compassionately hold up a mirror to the particular historical configuration that enlightenment rationality has taken for us, thus giving us an anticipatory glimpse of the possibility of a genuine reconciliation—a nonviolent, nontotalizing, mimetic togetherness of identity and the nonidentical—that lies beyond it.

Implicit in the *Dialectic of Enlightenment*, then, is a dialectical conception of progress where a narrative of past regression—what we might call regress as a historical "fact"—is employed in service of progress as a forward-looking moral-political imperative, where "what is at stake," as Horkheimer and Adorno put it, "is not conservation of the past but the fulfillment of past hopes" (DE, xvii). In his later work, Adorno develops this dialectical account in more detail and spells out its relation to freedom. As Benjamin pointed out in "On the Concept of History," the idea of historical progress refers not to progress in some specific domain but rather to the progress of humanity itself; in this way, the idea of historical progress depends on the idea of humanity. However, following Benjamin,[14] and in light of the general slaughter bench of history and the catastrophic events of the twentieth century, Adorno maintains that precisely this idea of humanity cannot now be presumed to exist: "No progress is to be assumed that would imply that humanity in general already existed and therefore could progress. Rather progress would be the very establishment of humanity in the first place, whose prospect opens up in the face of its extinction" (P, 145). Central to Adorno's dialectical conception of progress is the idea that the belief in progress as a historical "fact"—the idea that humanity has progressed in the past and that our present form of life is the result of such progress—stands in the way of progress as a forward-looking moral-political imperative, because such a belief leads to an "idolization of history" that blinds us to its own ideological bases (P, 147). As a result, our challenge is to face up to what Adorno calls "the absurdity that it is progress itself that inhibits progress" (P, 147). And, if this is the case, we should accept the "heterodox and even heretical view" that "progress occurs where it comes to an end" (HF, 153).

Hence, for Adorno, progress has an antinomian structure; the concept of progress is riven by a tension between the concrete actuality of history, which gives the lie to all claims of progress as a historical "fact," and the forward-looking, utopian promise of redemption or reconciliation as a moral-political imperative. The antinomy leaves us with a practical difficulty: "Too little of what is good has power in the world for progress to be expressed in a predicative judgment about the world, but there can be no good, not a trace of it, without progress" (P, 147). Sober contemplation of history offers us no rational basis for our belief in the possibility of progress—as Adorno puts it rather bleakly, "We can find nothing in reality that might help to redeem the promise inherent in the word 'progress'" (HF, 143)—but we can't do without that belief either, and, to that extent, we can't entirely do away with the thought of redemption or reconciliation. In connection with this point, Adorno is harsh in his assessment of those, like Heidegger, who would conclude from their reading of history that progress in the future is impossible or, worse, undesirable. Such a view "is sustained by the false inference that because there has been no progress up until now, there never will be any" (P, 153). This amounts to a "translation of historical desperation into a norm that must be adhered to," and it echoes the "abominable construal of the theological doctrine of original sin, the idea that the corruption of human nature legitimates domination, that radical evil legitimates evil" (P, 153). This is a "self-righteous profundity" that "takes the side of the terrible" (P, 153). Although such pessimistic denials of the possibility of progress draw the wrong lesson from the sober reading of history that Adorno also endorses, they nevertheless provide "an antidote to the mythology" from which theories of progress suffer (P, 153). What is called for is neither the mythological faith in the actuality of progress as a "fact" nor the pessimistic denial of its possibility in the future, but rather a "doctrine of progress that has been brought to self-consciousness" (P, 153).

Adorno negotiates this antinomy by means of what Brian O'Connor calls a "negativistic theory of progress" where progress equals the avoidance of catastrophe.[15] This is connected to what Adorno calls the new categorical imperative: that there should never again be an Auschwitz (ND, 365). As Adorno put it:

> I believe that you should start by taking progress to mean this very simple thing: that it would be better if people had no cause to fear, if there were no impending catastrophe on the horizon—if you do this, it will not provide a timeless, absolute definition of progress, but it will give the idea a concrete form. For progress today really does mean simply the prevention and avoidance of total catastrophe.
>
> (HF, 143)

If progress, like the new categorical imperative, is understood negativistically, as the avoidance of catastrophe, then the possibility of progress is connected to what James Gordon Finlayson has called

Adorno's "ethics of resistance."[16] As Finlayson explains it, Adorno's ethics of resistance consists in "various strategies of self-conscious non-cooperation with institutionalized forms of social unfreedom and with prevailing norms and values," where these strategies aim "first and foremost to prevent the worst, where the worst is the 'repetition of Auschwitz' or something similar."[17] As Adorno puts it, the concept of progress "calls for a critical confrontation with society as it actually exists" (HF, 149–150); progress demands "resistance to the perpetual danger of relapse. . . . at all stages" (P, 160; see also HF, 172). Adorno's forward-looking conception of progress as an imperative is thus framed negativistically and presents us with a set of minimal conditions that are necessary for averting catastrophe.

Crucially, however, this negativistically framed, forward-looking conception of progress rests not on an abstract negation of reason—even once we have uncovered reason's entanglement with domination—but rather on a further reflexive realization of reason. As Adorno puts it: "The explosive tendency of progress is not merely the Other to the movement of a progressing domination of nature, nor just its abstract negation; rather it requires the unfolding of reason through the very domination of nature. Only reason, the principle of societal domination inverted into the subject, would be capable of abolishing this domination" (P, 152). This is connected to the idea that despite the absurdity of all backward-looking claims to progress as a historical "fact," it is only now, under conditions of late, capitalist modernity, now that we have followed the trajectory from the slingshot to the atomic bomb, that we have developed the material and technological capacities to make progress in meeting the basic human needs of the whole population (see P, 153). But it also evinces Adorno's belief that progress as a moral-political imperative can only be achieved through a *rational* reflection on reason's own limits and blind spots. In other words, the goal of philosophy, for Adorno, is to "achieve through reflection on its own activity the consciousness that could lead it out of this web of delusion in a non-arbitrary manner. . . . By using its own methods, philosophy would be enabled to understand the ways in which it is embroiled with forces that are in conflict with what it truly desires" (HF, 169). Philosophy, in other words, "is faced with the challenge of transcending itself" (HF, 170).

DE-DIALECTIZING HEGEL: FOUCAULT AND THE HISTORICAL *HISTORICAL A PRIORI*

A similar attempt to reflect rationally on the limits and blind spots of reason in service of a *critique* of reason that foregrounds the ongoing spiral of rationality and power is also at the center of Foucault's early masterpiece, the *History of Madness*. But showing this to be the case requires countering both Foucault's harshest critics and some of his most ardent supporters, who tend to interpret Foucault as advocating a rejection of reason in favor of a romantic embrace of unreason or madness.[18] Foucault has, I suggest, a fundamentally ambivalent stance toward reason, one that is well expressed in a passage from his late work to which I have already referred: we are "fortunately committed to practicing a rationality that is unfortunately crisscrossed with intrinsic dangers" and the task of critical thought is "precisely to accept this sort of spiral, this sort of revolving door of rationality that refers us to its necessity, its indispensability, and, at the same time, to its intrinsic dangers" (SKP, 358). Moreover, the aim of this critique of the spiral of rationality and power is to open up a space of freedom between ourselves and our historical a priori. My goal in this section is to show that this ambivalent conception of reason and the related understanding of critique as part of the undefined work of freedom, expressed explicitly in Foucault's later work, are already implicit in the *History of Madness*.[19] What interests me most about this text, in the context of the present discussion, is that, like Adorno's philosophy of history, it can be understood as a distinctly Hegelian attempt to take up and radically transform Hegelian philosophy of history from within.

Foucault's critique of History—where History with a capital *H* refers to the Hegelian account of history as the progressive realization of reason—is central to understanding both his critique of reason and his account of freedom. Indeed, Foucault's historical method cannot be understood except in relation to the Hegelian notion of history that he rejects: the notion of History as the story of reason's dialectical self-realization as it progresses toward Absolute knowing. The problem with this conception, as Foucault sees it, is that it presupposes a "suprahistorical perspective" from the point of view of which "the finally reduced diversity of time" is translated into "a totality fully closed upon itself," and all of the myriad "displacements of the past" are recognized and reconciled (NGH, 379). However, Foucault's alternative understanding of history implies neither a rejection of reason nor a romantic idealization of unreason as the outside of this rational, progressive, teleological conception of History. Although there is an important connection between unreason and freedom in the *History of Madness*, Foucault is not committed to the simplistic claim that freedom is the embrace of unreason (let alone madness). Rather, as I shall argue, the figure of unreason serves to illuminate lines of fragility and fracture in our historical a priori; the indirect illumination provided by the figure of unreason serves to opens up spaces of freedom within our historical a priori and allows us to see not only that our present is contingent but also how it has been contingently made up through complex historical events.[20]

Lynne Huffer astutely points out that the *History of Madness* is best understood as an attempt at "de-dialectizing Hegel," by "undo[ing] Hegel from within."[21] How does Foucault attempt this de-dialectizing of Hegel in the *History of Madness*? And what are its implications? There are several important elements. The emphasis on discontinuity over continuity in thinking about historical change is certainly one such element;[22] this aspect of Foucault's historical method became quite prominent in his later, explicitly "archaeological" period, though it was subsequently abandoned in favor of a genealogical analysis of historical transformation.[23] Like Adorno, Foucault also steadfastly refuses to assume that history should be understood under the idea of progress toward some end point or goal. But perhaps even more important than either of these two elements, and less often noticed, is Foucault's attempt to *historicize* Hegel's philosophy of history, to offer a genealogy of the Hegelian notion of History.[24] This is, to be sure, a paradoxical project, one that requires the genealogist to "change roles on the same stage" (NGH, 384). Writing a genealogy of History requires the genealogist to inhabit a historical mode of thinking that we have inherited from the nineteenth century without being seduced by the consolations of dialectical History. The genealogist must take up the project of History and transform it from within; it is "only by being seized, dominated, and turned against its birth" that History can become genealogy (NGH, 384). Foucault attempts to undo the dialectical approach to History in the *History of Madness* by writing a history of reason—or, more precisely, of the emergence of our modern form of rationality as it is understood in relation to madness as mental illness—in such a way that makes room for contingent, discontinuous, and fragmented events, all of which resist being reconciled and recuperated within a dialectical conception of history as a process of rationalization. In this way, Foucault's history of madness opens up an internal fracture within the notion of History, a structure of thought that he takes to be definitive for the modern historical a priori.

Hence, even though something called "history" holds a privileged place in Foucault's methodology, unlike Hegel (and also unlike Heidegger and perhaps Derrida as well), Foucault makes no universal, transhistorical claims about the historicity of reason or of philosophy. Rather, as Foucault puts it, "if history possesses a privilege, it would be . . . insofar as it would play the role of an internal ethnology of our culture and our rationality, and consequently would embody the very possibility of any ethnology" (OWWH, 293). That is to say, history is important for Foucault *not* because we are essentially historical beings or because all philosophical knowledge is essentially historically conditioned, *but rather* because History is central to our modern historical a priori, so much so that we might even call our historical a priori the Historical historical a priori. Hence History is something that must be thought through if our modern form of life is to be effectively critiqued.[25]

By transforming History from within and turning dialectics against itself until it becomes genealogy, Foucault is not killing history, as Sartre famously complained, though he is at least attempting to kill what he calls the "philosophical myth" of "History for philosophers," a nineteenth-century myth of continuity, reconciliation, and progressive redemption.[26] However, even if he aims to kill (dialectical) History, this does not mean that Foucault's project should be understood as a story of regress, a romantic *Verfallsgeschichte* in which the moment before the split between reason and madness is presented as the space of freedom. The key to understanding this is the difficult and shifting but crucial distinction between madness and unreason. The Renaissance, according to Foucault, experienced reason and unreason as a unity, as a result of which it embraced what seem to us to be paradoxical notions—that of an unreasonable reason and a reasoned unreason (HM, 47). The classical age broke up this unity of reason and unreason by conquering and confining unreason and defining it in fundamentally moral terms; thus, for the classical age, the category of unreason included not only the mad but also all those whom the bourgeois social order constituted as asocial and undesirable, including libertines, sexual perverts, the unemployed, and criminals. The classical experience of madness came to an end when unreason was distinguished from madness, the latter being understood as a mental illness (which nevertheless retained its moralized connotations) and the former as a deliberate choice of immorality or evil. One of the distinctive characteristics of our modernity, for Foucault, is that it has become impossible to occupy the space of unreason without being forced into madness (see HM, 351). Indeed, this is precisely the lesson that Foucault thinks we can learn from the mad geniuses Nietzsche, Nerval, Artaud, and Van Gogh, whom he continually evokes in the text. The question that is posed by the work of these mad geniuses, however, is not that of the violent exclusion of *madness*. Rather, it is this: "What is this power that petrifies all those who dare look upon [the face of unreason], condemning to *madness* all those who have tried the test of *Unreason*?" (HM, 352). This question, Foucault suggests, somewhat apocalyptically, "concerns the essence of the modern world" (HM, 352).

All of which suggests that *if* there is a romantic idealization of anything in the *History of Madness*, it is not madness, but unreason that is idealized and figured as a space of radical or absolute freedom.[27] *If* there is a lament about how the history of our modern form of rationality has played out, it is a lament about the fact that one cannot be unreasonable without being forced to be mad, and thereby pathologized, medicalized, objectified, and silenced. The gesture toward Nietzsche, Nerval, Artaud, and others isn't a lyrical glorification of their *madness*, for it is precisely their descent into madness that ruptures their philosophical and artistic oeuvres. "*Where there is an oeuvre*," Foucault insists, "*there is no madness*" (HM, 537); madness is the absence of an oeuvre, and these men are geniuses precisely because they were able to create an oeuvre. But they are all unreasonable—indeed, in the modern age, "unreason belongs to all that is most decisive in the modern world in any oeuvre" (HM, 535)—and the tragedy is that they are unable to inhabit the space of unreason without exploding into madness. But this does not lead Foucault to conclude that we should celebrate, much less emulate, madness.

Nor, I think, does it lead him to conclude that we should celebrate or emulate unreason, or claim it as the space of true freedom, although it may be tempting to draw this conclusion, and Foucault's text does seem, at times, to support this romantic reading. Rather, it is through reflection upon the descent of these unreasonable ones into madness that "the world is made aware of its guilt" and "obliged to take part in a process of recognition and reparation, to find an explanation *for* this unreason, and to *explain itself* before it" (HM, 537). Hence, the point of recovering the experience of unreason is not to glorify unreasonableness, but rather to "interrogate [our] culture about its limit-experiences" (HM, xxxix), to make those limit-experiences present to us, and thereby to compel ourselves to reflect on those limits that make thinking, being, and doing possible for us. This is why Foucault keeps coming back to the idea of unreason as untimely, as linked to what he calls the "immobile structures of the tragic" (HM, xxx) and the monotonous "background noise" from which the language of rational thought that "culminates in time" was "extracted" (HM, xxxii).[28] Unlike unreason, madness, from the late eighteenth century onward, was recuperated within the dialectical, developmental structure of reason working itself out in history; it "was intimately connected to history" (HM, 377) and "took shape inside a historical consciousness" (HM, 378). Unreason, by contrast, remained associated with the tragic outside of history and linear temporality, with "a pure plunge into a language that abolished history" (HM, 377); hence unreason resists recuperation within the Hegelian dialectic, and it is precisely this feature of unreason that enables it to open up the possibility of reflection on the limits of our Hegelian, Historical modernity.

So there is a sense in which the experience or figure of unreason is linked, for Foucault, to freedom. But it is not that Foucault views unreason—much less madness—as the space of freedom. Rather, he is arguing that it is only by the illumination provided by the lightning flashes of unreason that we can glimpse the fractures within our own system of thought, and doing this is a necessary condition of freeing ourselves up in relation to that system, so that we might think beyond it. Not only is this not a romanticization of a past experience of madness or unreason or of the moment before the split between reason and unreason that founds modern subjectivity, it is not even an attack on our modern historical a priori, or its conception of reason. If Foucault's histories of the present give the impression that they are polemical attacks on our present, on our way of constituting ourselves as rational, sexually normal, law-abiding, sane subjects, this is simply a function of what is necessary for the very difficult task of problematizing the present. When Foucault attempts to define the classical age, he can do this by contrasting it with the Renaissance, on the one hand, and with the nineteenth century, on the other hand. But when he attempts to define the modern age, he can only do so by contrasting it with the classical age, on the one hand, and our own, still mostly modern era, on the other hand. This project requires, as he says, "pulling oneself free of that modern age," which forms the very conditions of possibility for our own thought and practical activity (OWWH, 293). While the shape and configuration of an age other than our own can be uncovered "through gentle digging," when it comes to articulating the discursive and nondiscursive practices that serve as conditions of possibility for our own form of life, "then archaeology, like Nietzschean philosophy, is forced to work with hammer blows" (OWWH, 293).

So Foucault's historico-philosophical method attempts to move beyond dialectical History by refusing the suprahistorical point of view, and beyond romanticism by refusing nostalgia for the past. Even assuming that such a methodological stance is desirable, that it is useful and worthwhile to write a history of our present while neither presupposing nor lamenting a victory (or the right to a victory) on the part of modernity, (how) can such a stance be maintained? What, in short, is the position of Foucault as archaeologist or genealogist? Does he stand within his own historical a priori or power/knowledge regime or outside of it? If the former, does this vitiate his critical reflections on that historical a priori or undermine his attempt to articulate the limits of his own culture? Does this mean, as Derrida suggests in his famous critique of the *History of Madness*, that "the history of reason cannot be the history of its origin, . . . but must be that of one of its determined figures"?[29] And if the latter, is Foucault guilty of appealing implicitly to a unity of Reason that transcends the specific forms that rationality takes during different historical epochs, thereby, as Derrida also suggests, "confirming metaphysics in its fundamental operation" (CHM, 40)? Foucault seems to have only two options here: either he is stuck within the determined figures of the history of reason, and thus he can't really write the history of the origin of the split between madness and reason that founds that history, or he can write this history, but only by accessing some point of view outside of that history, which could only be a suprahistorical, metaphysical standpoint. As Derrida put it: "Hegel again, always" (CHM, 43).

Derrida is right that Foucault's suspension of "anything that might take on the appearance of an ending, or of rest in truth" seems to require the assumption—or perhaps it would be more accurate to say the *positing*—of something that can be neither fully conceptualized in the language of reason nor reconciled in the dialectical unfolding of History. This something goes by the name of unreason. The assumption that unreason is radically outside of reason and History appears to motivate the recurrent suggestion that unreason escapes language and linear temporality itself, and that this is what the tragic consciousness of madness allows us to glimpse, however fleetingly. But Derrida's charge of metaphysics is not quite on the mark inasmuch as Foucault's aim is neither to describe this unreasonable outside nor to claim that freedom consists in occupying this space. Rather, the figure of the outside, of unreason, represented in language or thought but also in works of art, serves to open up and illuminate lines of gaps and fissures—

what Foucault later calls "lines of fragility" or "kinds of virtual fracture" (CT/IH, 126–127)—in our own historical a priori. These lines of fragility and fracture allow us to see how "that-which-is might no longer be that-which-is" (CT/IH, 126).[30] The function of the figure of unreason, then, is to create some distance between ourselves and our system of thought, our historical a priori; it is this space opened up *within* our historical a priori by the figure of the outside—rather than the space of the outside itself—that is the space of freedom.

Sometimes, in his early work, Foucault suggests that his historical critique is possible because our own historical a priori is in the process of breaking up and transforming into something new. For example, he speaks optimistically of the breaking up of the modern experience of madness and the impending death of "homo dialecticus" (HM, 543): "One day, perhaps, we will no longer know what madness was" (HM, 541); we will be as puzzled by the twentieth century's "deep and pathos filled relationship to mental illness" (HM, 543) as we are by the passage from Borges's Chinese encyclopedia that opens *The Order of Things*. To confront this pathos-filled relationship to mental illness will bring our future selves face to face with the sheer impossibility of thinking *that*. If there is a romanticism to be found in Foucault, this is it, I think. It is not a nostalgic aim of recovering a time or a space—or of achieving a future—in which madness, or, more precisely, unreason, is free and unfettered, but instead a youthful, romantic optimism that our current historical a priori is at the moment undergoing radical transformation, that the ground is crumbling beneath our feet, that we are on the brink of something radically new. Later, Foucault would become more sanguine about what we might call his youthful presentistic exceptionalism.[31]

Not coincidentally, I think, in his later work, Foucault also places more emphasis on the role that critique can and should play in transforming our historical a priori, precisely by revealing it as a contingently emergent way of thinking, experiencing, and acting, in order to open up the space for the possibility of being, doing, and thinking otherwise. The historical task of tracing the contingent emergence of our modern historical a priori—an a priori that is both historical and Historical—is a crucial component of this project of critique. As Foucault puts it:

> What reason perceives as *its* necessity, or rather, what different forms of rationality offer as their necessary being, can perfectly well be shown to have a history; and the network of contingencies from which it emerges can be traced. Which is not to say, however, that these forms of rationality were irrational. It means that they reside on a base of human practice and human history; and that since these things have been made, they can be unmade, as long as we know how it was that they have been made. (CT/IH, 127)

The recurrent glimpses within the modern age of the tragic consciousness of madness in the philosophical and artistic work of such figures as Nietzsche, Artaud, Nerval, and Van Gogh should be understood as examples of how the lines of fragility and virtual fracture within our Historical historical a priori can be illuminated. As Foucault puts it at the end of the final chapter of the *History of Madness*: "By the madness that interrupts it, an oeuvre opens a void, a moment of silence, a question without an answer, opening an unhealable wound that the world is forced to address" (HM, 537). The work of critique is precisely to trace these lines of fragility and fracture, these open wounds, and to use them to open up a difference, a discontinuity, however small, between our historical a priori and ourselves. This opening up generates "a space of concrete freedom, that is of possible transformation" (CT/IH, 127).

The critique of reason elaborated in the *History of Madness* thus does not reject reason or counsel an embrace of either madness or unreason as the space of freedom. Rather, in the *History of Madness*, Foucault implicitly relies on the same conception of critique that he defends more explicitly in his later work, where reason is understood as ambivalently entangled with power relations and where freedom consists in opening up a space between our selves and our historical a priori. In the *History of Madness*, Foucault uses the figure of unreason to open up this space, to reveal the contingency of our Historical historical a priori and the complex social, institutional, and ideological structures out of which our contingent present is constructed.

CRITIQUE AS HISTORICAL PROBLEMATIZATION: ADORNO AND FOUCAULT

Allow me to tie together some of the common threads that have already been implicit in this discussion of the work of Adorno and Foucault; from this discussion, a sketch of their alternative approach to history and its relationship to normativity will emerge.

Reason and Power

Although both Adorno and Foucault are sharply critical of the idea that history is to be understood as the progressive realization of reason, neither endorses a totalizing critique or an abstract negation of enlightenment rationality. For Adorno, "What makes the concept of progress dialectical, in a strictly non-metaphorical sense, is the fact that reason, its organ, is just one thing. That is to say, it does not contain two strata, one that dominates nature and one that conciliates it. Both strata share in all its aspects" (HF, 157). In other words, reason is entangled with power and we cannot, as critical theorists following Habermas have attempted to do, identify a use or a stratum of reason that is not so entangled. And yet Adorno is no advocate of "the denial of reason"; indeed, for him, such a denial would be "certainly not a whit superior to the much derided faith in progress" (HF, 169). Rather, the task for philosophy, as Adorno understands it, is to reflect on its own activity as a rational enterprise and in so doing to attempt to transcend itself (HF, 169–170), to transcend the concept, as he says, "by way of the concept" (ND, 15). This is, as I suggested above, the aim of Adorno's ethics of resistance.

Similarly, for Foucault, although his work starts from the relationship between reason or rationalization and power, he does not conclude from this that reason should be put on trial. "To my mind," he writes, "nothing would be more sterile" (SP, 328). To say that the entanglement of reason with power justifies putting reason on trial is to find oneself trapped into "playing the arbitrary and boring part of either the rationalist or the irrationalist" (SP, 328), a trap that Foucault elsewhere refers to as "the 'blackmail' of the Enlightenment" (WE, 312). To be sure, unlike Adorno, Foucault is skeptical that "'dialectical' nuances" can enable us to escape this trap (WE, 313). Moreover, he suggests that his attempt to "analyze specific rationalities rather than always invoking the progress of rationalization in general" distinguishes his approach to the entanglement of rationalities and power relations from that of the Frankfurt School (SP, 328–29). Nevertheless, like Adorno, he insists that it is the task of philosophy understood as a mode of critical thought to reflect on its own rational activity and its entanglements with dangerous relations of power. As Foucault notes in his essay "What Is Critique?," his approach to the question of Enlightenment is a "way of gaining access, not to the problem of knowledge, but to that of power" (PT, 59).[32]

Utopia and Utopianism

But if the task of philosophy is to reflect on its own rational activity and in so doing to attempt to transcend itself, what sense can be made of this notion of transcendence? If the aim of philosophy is to push beyond itself, then what is meant here by "beyond"? One might think that there is an implicit and abstract conception of utopia in the background here and that as such this view is open to the kind of impotence of the mere ought objection that attracted Habermas and Honneth to Hegel in the first place. Although Adorno is less hostile than Foucault to the concept of utopia—whereas Foucault prefers to speak of heterotopias,[33] Adorno does offer an account of utopia, linked to his notion of reconciliation and defined as "above identity and above contradiction" or as "a togetherness of diversity" (ND, 150)—both are careful to offer only negativistic accounts of utopia or the good life toward which such notions of transcendence might aim.[34] For Adorno, we cannot glimpse the right life from within the wrong one, and the very idea of reconciliation forbids it being posited as a positive concept (ND, 145); this is why utopia can only be glimpsed indirectly and in an anticipatory way through the illumination cast by certain works of modern art.[35] Similarly, for Foucault, we cannot have access to a point of view outside of power relations, which means that any conception of a society that is devoid of power relations will be utopian in the negative sense (ECSPF, 298). Both thinkers are very attuned to the fact that any vision of the good life offered from within a society structured by relations of domination is likely to reproduce those power relations, to be infected by them, so they both eschew utopian speculations about what kind of content "the good life" might have.

However, there is also a sense in which Foucault and Adorno are more radically utopian thinkers than either Habermas or Honneth, for they hold on to the possibility and desirability of radical social change in the direction of an open-ended conception of the future.[36] In other words, Foucault and Adorno envision social transformation not just as the better and fuller realization of our existing normative ideals—for example, a version of liberal democracy that is more transparent and less distorted by power relations, or a recognition order that is more inclusive and egalitarian, or a political system that rests on justifications that cannot be reasonably rejected—but also as the possibility of the radical transformation of those ideals themselves, where that transformation would not necessarily be a regression. The early work of Foucault in particular is filled with thought experiments that pose this possibility: someday we might look back on our present preoccupation with mental illness and wonder what all the fuss was about, and from that point of view our current historical a priori may well seem benighted. Although we can't imagine what it would be like to inhabit that future point of view, there is a critical value for Foucault in being open to this possibility and to the idea that the creatures who inhabit that point of view will inhabit a different historical a priori and hence a different moral universe. In order to be genuinely critical, critical theory has to be open to both kinds of social transformation—not just reformism, whether radical or not, but also radical social change—and it has to be careful not to prejudge the outcome of such radical transformations, for to do so would necessarily be to presuppose that our own historical form of life is not only superior to all that came before it but also unsurpassable, that it constitutes the end point of history. Such a presupposition is, as we have seen throughout this book, both conceptually and politically problematic.

The Historicization of History

Both Adorno and Foucault understood their own critical, historico-philosophical projects as historically situated. In this way, both attempted to think through the logic of the second, historicist Enlightenment, to apply the insights of this historically situated conception of rationality reflexively to the historico-philosophical enterprise itself. As I argued above, this is evident in Foucault's early work when he makes it clear that history is important for him not because historicity is characteristic of our reason or our existence but rather because History—the Hegelian conception of history as the progressive unfolding of a rationalization process—is central to our modern historical a priori, which is thus both historical and Historical. The point of Foucault's historicization of History in the *History of Madness* is to show the historical contingency of this idea of History and to analyze the role that it plays in the exclusion and domination of those who are deemed unreasonable. Similarly, Adorno, in good dialectical fashion, understood his conception of philosophy as historically situated as itself historically situated. In this way, he too historicized his own conception of historicity.[37] Indeed, Adorno is sharply critical of both Heidegger and Hegel on precisely this point, because they fail, in different ways, to historicize their understandings of historicity. Heidegger's is, thus, an "ahistorical concept of history" that, by locating the concept of history in existence, "amounts paradoxically to an ontological inflation that does away with the concept of history by a sort of conjuring trick" (HF, 123).[38] If we are to avoid this "ontological inflation" through which history becomes "mutation as immutability" (HF, 123), we have to locate the concept of history *in history* rather than in existence. Adorno repeats the "mutation as immutability" charge against Hegel, whom he accuses of failing to fully realize his own conception of dialectics by appealing to a timeless, unhistorical conception of history that is both metaphysical and mythological: in this way, history for Hegel "acquires the quality of the unhistoric"

(ND, 356–57). The proper response to this, according to Adorno, is to perform a reverse dialectical "transmutation," this time "of metaphysics into history" (ND, 360). As with Foucault, the historicization of history is both the thread that connects Adorno to Hegel and the gulf that separates them.

Genealogy as Problematization

The historicization of History is closely bound up with its problematization, where this means two things: first, revealing the historical contingency of our own historically situated point of view;[39] second, showing how that point of view has been contingently made up and as such is bound up with particular relations of power.[40] Because our historically situated point of view is inflected with a certain conception of History, effectively problematizing that point of view demands a distinctive way of taking up while radically transforming that conception, which I will characterize as a distinctive kind of genealogical method. Following Colin Koopman, who in turn builds on some insights from Bernard Williams, we can distinguish three different modes of genealogical inquiry: subversive, vindicatory, and problematizing.[41] The common core of these three ways of doing genealogy is their attempt to explicate, as Nietzsche puts it in the preface to *On the Genealogy of Morals*, "a knowledge of a kind that has never yet existed or even been desired," namely, "a knowledge of the conditions and circumstances in which [moral values] grew, under which they evolved and changed."[42] In other words, the common core is a historical approach that asks how specific, contingent historical processes have led human beings to develop and embrace this sort of value or concept.[43] However, each of these three modes of genealogical inquiry uses such knowledge for a different end. The subversive mode of genealogy aims not only to raise the question of the historical emergence of our values, but also to reject them as lacking value in some other, more important sense.[44] Vindicatory genealogy, by contrast, traces the historical emergence of our values with an eye toward showing those values to be justified and reasonable.[45] The third mode of genealogical inquiry has both subversive and vindicatory features insofar as it aims to reveal both the dangers and the promise contained in the values, concepts, or forms of life whose contingent history it traces, but its aim is neither simply subversive nor vindicatory. Rather, its aim is a critical problematization of our historical present.

In a late interview, responding to a question about the difficulty of pinning down his political position, Foucault highlights the importance of problematization for his own practice of critique: "It is true that my attitude isn't a result of the form of critique that claims to be a methodical examination in order to reject all possible solutions except for the valid one. It is more on the order of a 'problematization'—which is to say, the development of a domain of acts, practices, and thoughts that seem to me to pose problems for politics" (PPP, 114). However, the aim of this critical problematization is not, as Foucault's critics have often assumed, to subvert or undermine the acts, practices, and thoughts that are so problematized. Rather, as he put it in an oft-quoted passage from another of his late interviews: "I would like to do the genealogy of problems, of problématiques. My point is not that everything is bad, but that everything is dangerous, which is not exactly the same as bad. If everything is dangerous, then we always have something to do" (OGE, 256).[46] Moreover, although the aim of Foucault's genealogies is clearly not to vindicate our current practices or forms of rationality, there is an important if often underappreciated vindicatory element to his problematizing genealogical method. This element comes out clearly in "What Is Enlightenment?" when Foucault emphasizes "the extent to which a type of philosophical interrogation—one that simultaneously problematizes man's relation to the present, man's historical mode of being, and the constitution of the self as an autonomous subject—is rooted in the Enlightenment" (WE, 312). In other words, Foucault situates his own problematizing critical method within the philosophical ethos of critique that forms the positive normative inheritance of the Enlightenment—an inheritance that demands fidelity not to its doctrinal elements but rather to its critical attitude, an inheritance that involves reaffirming the legacy of the Enlightenment in and through its radical transformation.

Although Adorno does not use the terms "genealogy" or "problematization"—much less "genealogy as problematization" or "problematizing genealogy"—to describe his approach to history, still the outlines of such an approach can be found in his work.[47] One of his major criticisms not only of Hegel but also of Marx and Engels is that they failed to acknowledge that the antagonism that they saw as the fundamental driving force of history was itself historically contingent, that "it need not have been" (ND, 321). Adorno links this recognition to the possibility of a specifically critical social theory: "Only if things might have gone differently; if the totality is recognized as a socially necessary semblance, as the hypostasis of the universal pressed out of individual human beings; if its claim to be absolute is broken—only then will a critical social consciousness retain its freedom to think that things might be different some day" (ND, 323). Moreover, as we saw above, Adorno clearly and emphatically rejects any straightforwardly vindicatory reading of history: "After the catastrophes that have happened, and in view of the catastrophes to come, it would be cynical to say that a plan for a better world is manifested in history and unites it" (ND, 320). However, his aim isn't a straightforward rejection of the values and norms of enlightenment modernity either. For example, although Adorno is highly critical of the entanglement of the modern principle of equality with capitalist mechanisms of exchange and bourgeois coldness and thus with structures of reification and relations of domination, he also regards these principles as important historical achievements that protect individuals from some kinds of injustice. "Anyone who like me has had experience of what the world looks like when this element of formal equality is removed," Adorno writes, "will know from his own experience, or at the very least from his own fear, just how much human value resides in this concept of the formal" (HF, 253). Adorno's position, as Jay Bernstein explains, is that "the ideals of the enlightenment, as they have come down to us, are a mixture of domination and promise: the equality of individuals in the market is also their reduction to their labor power, and the reduction of labor power to labor time; the concepts which enjoin the freedom of the moral law—respect, fear, and so on—are also repressive."[48] Thus the aim of Adorno's philosophy of history, like Foucault's, is to chart the simultaneous historical emergence of both the domination and the promise of the ideals of the Enlightenment, the unity, as he says, of discontinuity and continuity (ND, 320). The method for doing so can be understood as a kind of problematizing genealogy, even if Adorno himself doesn't use this term.

Critical Distance, or, Philosophizing with a Hammer

However, for it to be possible to problematize our own historically situated point of view, our Historical historical a priori, and reflect on its entanglements with power relations, we must be able to get enough critical distance on that historical a priori that we can see it *as* a system of thought. Adorno and Foucault offer us two tools for gaining such critical distance. First, both make use of an image or a figure that cannot be reconciled into the dialectical unfolding of History; by resisting recuperation into the dialectic, this figure reveals the fragmentary nature of and opens up lines of fragility or fracture within our Hegelian Historical modernity, and thus makes possible reflection on it as a historical a priori. This figure of whatever escapes the reconciling, unifying logic of modernity is, for Adorno, the nonidentical and, for Foucault, unreason.[49] Adorno's method for revealing the nonidentical is brought out clearly in "The Essay as Form." For Adorno, the essay is "the critical form par excellence" (EF, 18) precisely because it "allows for the consciousness of nonidentity, without expressing it directly" (EF, 9). Moreover, it is the essay's "fragmentary character" (EF, 9) that enables it to illuminate nonidentity without directly expressing it (and thereby subsuming it under the logic of identity thinking). Moreover, this fragmentary character mirrors the fragmentary and antagonistic nature of the social and cultural reality on which the essay reflects. The essay "thinks in fragments, just as reality is fragmentary, and finds its unity in and through the breaks and not by glossing them over. . . . Discontinuity is essential to the essay; its subject matter is always a conflict brought to a standstill" (EF, 16). Although it might be tempting to see Adorno's negative dialectics as rooted in a metaphysical claim about the nonidentical understood as the ultimate *Ding-an-sich*, negative dialectics is better understood as a historically situated response to a particular form of social organization and its accompanying worldview. As Adorno puts it, "Dialectical reason's own essence has come to be and will pass, like antagonistic society" (ND, 141). In other words, for Adorno, negative dialectics is not a transcendental condition of possibility for thinking but rather a historically situated tool for thinking through our present.[50] It is necessary because of the historically contingent unfolding of the dialectic of enlightenment; it is a method for jump-starting a historical dialectic that has come to a standstill. Similarly, as I argued above, Foucault's invocation of unreason should not be thought of as a metaphysical gesture; rather, for Foucault, it is the figure of unreason that opens up lines of fragility and fracture within our historical a priori and allows us to take up critical distance on that historical a priori. For both Adorno and Foucault, tracing the figure of the nonidentical or of unreason through the fragmentary, nonsystematic, and experimental work of critical thought—or through the anticipatory illumination cast by works of art—serves to reveal the fragmentary, fragile, and internally fractured nature of our present historical situation.

However, since our historical a priori sets the historically specific conditions of possibility for thought for us, it forms the backdrop for what "thought . . . silently thinks," as Foucault once put it (UP, 9). Freeing thought up in relation to what it silently thinks is necessary for enabling it to think differently, but freeing oneself up in this way means pulling oneself free of the very conditions of possibility of one's own thinking and acting. As Martin Saar puts it, the aim of genealogy as a form of critique is that of "telling the subject the story of the powers working on him, telling it the story of its own becoming."[51] Saar argues that this distinctive goal accounts for the hyperbolic and exaggerated nature of genealogical texts; although his focus here is on Nietzsche and Foucault, he also includes *Dialectic of Enlightenment* in this genre.[52] Only stories told through exaggeration and hyperbole, Saar argues, "release the explosive power contained in the revelation of processes of power and forceful construction. In this sense, genealogies are textual shocks and momentous negative world disclosures."[53] While the shape and contours of some prior historical epoch can be uncovered through gentle digging, in order to see one's own historical a priori as historical, one must philosophize with a hammer, as Foucault, following Nietzsche, put it. Or, as Adorno puts it: "The dialectic advances by way of extremes, driving thoughts with the utmost consequentiality to the point where they turn back on themselves, instead of qualifying them" (MM, 86; see also H, 8–9).

Problematization and the Normative Inheritance of Modernity

Finally, and perhaps most importantly, the problematization of our own point of view can and should be understood not as a rejection or abstract negation of the normative inheritance of modernity but rather as a fuller realization of its central value, namely, freedom.[54] Adorno's account of second nature reveals the close link between his philosophy of history and the possibility of freedom. Central to Adorno's complicated account of the relationship between nature and history is the idea that historically constituted objects come, over time, to seem natural and therefore unchangeable (see HF, 115–129). Revealing this "second nature" to be historically contingent and therefore changeable is a crucial task of critical theory for Adorno. As Adorno puts it: "Interpretation . . . is criticism of phenomena that have been brought to a standstill; it consists in revealing the dynamism stored up in them, so that what appears as second nature can be seen to have a history. . . . Criticism ensures that what has evolved loses its appearance as mere existence and stands revealed as the product of history" (HF, 135). This entails uncovering the illusory, congealed history contained within second nature (HF, 136), an illusion that is reinforced by narratives of historical progress. This is very close to Foucault's characterization of genealogy as the attempt to "record the singularity of events outside of any monotonous finality," an attempt that requires us to seek the singularity of events "in the most unpromising places, in what we tend to feel is without history" (NGH, 369).[55] This sort of unmasking of the congealed history contained within what we tend to feel is without history breaks history's illusory and ideological spell, and this is how Adorno understands freedom: "The positive meaning of freedom lies in the potential, in the possibility, of breaking the spell or escaping from it" (HF, 174). Breaking or escaping the spell, freeing thought up from what it silently thinks in order to enable it to think differently—these are both ways of realizing freedom. As Foucault put it, the goal of criticism, understood as "a historical investigation into the events that have led us to constitute ourselves and to recognize ourselves as subjects of what we are doing, thinking, and saying," is that of "seeking to give new impetus, as far and wide as possible, to the undefined work of freedom" (WE, 315–16).

So for both Adorno and Foucault, the problematization of our own point of view has a normative point.[56] It aims at a *fuller realization of a central normative ideal of the Enlightenment: freedom*. But Adorno's work goes further than this, and in this sense goes beyond Foucault, by also suggesting that the problematization of our own point of view not only enhances our freedom in relation to second nature or to our historical a priori; it also is required if we are to do justice to the Other. This idea comes out in the final lecture of Adorno's lectures on moral philosophy. After spending most of the lecture course offering a detailed and devastating critique of Kantian moral philosophy, Adorno argues in his final lecture that moral philosophy can only be possible today as a critique of moral philosophy (PMP, 167). Life under modern capitalism is so deformed and distorted that moral philosophy today cannot provide plans or blueprints for living the good life; as Adorno famously laments, "Wrong life cannot be lived rightly" (MM, 39). Hence, the goal of moral philosophy should be to uncover this situation and to reflect on—rather than obscure, deny, or ignore—the contradictions to which it leads. The most that one can say about the good life under current conditions is that it "would consist in resistance to the forms of the bad life that have been seen through and critically dissected by the most progressive minds. Other than this negative prescription no guidance can really be envisaged" (PMP, 167–168).[57]

Following on from his critique of Kant, Adorno contends that we have to resist the abstract rigorism of Kantian morality but without giving up on notions of conscience and responsibility, without which the idea of the good life is inconceivable. "At this point," Adorno writes, "we find ourselves really and truly in a contradictory situation. We need to hold fast to moral norms, to self-criticism, to the question of right and wrong, and at the same time to a sense of the fallibility of the authority that has the confidence to undertake such self-criticism" (PMP, 169). In other words, we have to hold fast persistently to the norms that we learned from our experience while at the same time engaging in self-criticism of whatever presents itself as "unyielding" and "inexorable" (PMP, 169). This requires an awareness of our own fallibility, but where this fallibilism is both an epistemic stance and a moral one. As Adorno puts it, "The element of self-reflection has today become the true heir to what used to be called moral categories" (PMP, 169). To say that self-reflection is a moral category is to say that it is "by reflecting on our own limitations [that] we can learn to do justice to those who are different" and "that true injustice is always to be found at the precise point where you put yourself in the right and other people in the wrong" (PMP, 169). This is why Adorno claims that if you were to press him into offering a list of cardinal virtues, he "would probably respond cryptically by saying that I could think of nothing except for modesty," by which he means that "we must have a conscience, but may not insist on our own conscience" (PMP, 169–170).[58]

As I have argued throughout this chapter, the best way of achieving the stance of modesty is through a critical, genealogical problematization that combines both vindicatory and subversive, or progressive and regressive, strands, but whose aim is neither simply vindication nor subversion. By allowing us to reflexively critique the social institutions and practices, the patterns of cultural meaning and subject formation, and the normative commitments that have made us who we are, problematizing critique opens up a space of critical distance on those institutions, practices, and so forth, thereby freeing us up in relation to them, and thus also in relation to ourselves.[59] Notice that for Adorno this modest stance is motivated not only by the epistemic point that we have a tendency to go wrong in our normative judgments and thus have a duty to call them into question.[60] Although Adorno was enough of a historicist and a practitioner of immanent critique to agree with Foucault that "we have to give up hope of ever acceding to a point of view that could give us access to any complete and definitive knowledge of what may constitute our historical limits" and thus that, as far as the project of critique goes, "we are always in this position of beginning again" (WE, 316–17),[61] he also makes the further claim that the problematization of one's own point of view is *morally* required if we are to do justice to those who are different from ourselves. In other words, and here is a different way of construing the normative point of the method of problematization, such problematization is motivated not merely by epistemic concerns about our inescapable fallibility given our inability to have access to a God's-eye point of view, but also by our commitment to equal respect for the Other, that is, to justice.

ADORNO, FOUCAULT, AND THE "POSTCOLONIAL"

Adorno and Foucault offer a radically different way of thinking about the backward- and forward-looking conceptions of progress in relation to the project of critical theory. Both reject any vindicatory, backward-looking story of historical progress as a "fact" about what has led up to "us," but they do so not in favor of a romantic story of decline and fall, but rather in service of a critical problematization of the present. Moreover, at least Adorno, if not also Foucault,[62] holds on to the forward-looking conception of progress as a moral-political imperative, though he does reconceive progress negativistically as the avoidance of catastrophe and decouple this forward-looking conception from the backward-looking notion of progress as a historical "fact." In stark contrast to Habermas and Honneth, for whom the backward-looking story of historical learning, social evolution, or progress plays a crucial role in grounding their normative visions of what would count as progress in a forward-looking sense, Adorno claims that calling into question the conception of progress as a historical "fact" is necessary for any kind of future progress to be possible. Thus, even though Adorno doesn't give up on the possibility of progress in the future—in fact, he finds such a resignation to be not only conceptually problematic but also morally repugnant—his understanding of what might count as progress in the future is not rooted in a backward-looking story of progress as what has led up to "us." Progress occurs only where it comes to an end. Although this claim of Adorno's was not motivated by postcolonial concerns, and although his relationship to postcolonial scholarship—like Foucault's—is rather vexed and complicated, it seems to me that this idea is enormously productive for a critical theory that aims to decolonize itself.

Indeed, despite their well-documented and oft-noted Eurocentrism, both Foucault and Adorno have proved to be fruitful resources for postcolonial theorizing. Thus, on the one hand, Foucault has inspired a great deal of work in postcolonial theory, including, but certainly not limited to, the founding text of the field, Said's *Orientalism.*[63] Said productively takes up Foucault's notion of discourse, analyzing Orientalism as a discursive construction that dictated how the West understood the East, as a form of "knowledge" (though largely an ideological fantasy of the Orient that bore little relation to the actual cultures subsumed under that heading) that was also a form of colonial power.[64] This analysis proved so productive for postcolonial studies that Ann Laura Stoler could observe in 1995 that "no single analytic framework has saturated the field of colonial studies so completely over the last decade as that of Foucault."[65] And yet, Foucault's work has also been subjected to harsh critique by postcolonial thinkers—including the later Said, Gayatri Spivak, and Stoler herself.[66] Stoler's important book *Race and the Education of Desire* focuses on Foucault's later work and argues that his historical genealogies of power relations in European modernity systematically ignore issues relating to colonialism, racism, and liberal imperialism. As Stoler puts it, "What is striking is how consistently Foucault's own framing of the European bourgeois order has been exempt from the very sorts of criticism that his insistence on the fused regimes of knowledge/power would seem to encourage and allow."[67] Stoler's critique is motivated by an understandable frustration with Foucault's centrality to postcolonial theorizing despite his own studied ignorance of the problem of colonialism, an ignorance that is all the more galling considering that Foucault could not have been unaware of this problem, given that he lived and taught in Tunisia in the late 1960s and given that no French person of his generation could have been blind to the Algerian question. As Robert Young has argued, Foucault's "virtual silence" on issues of race and colonialism renders his work "so scrupulously Eurocentric that you begin to wonder whether there isn't a deliberate strategy involved"; and yet, Young continues, "the lasting paradox is that despite the absence of explicit discussions of colonialism, Foucault's work has been a central theoretical reference point for postcolonial analysis."[68]

Such issues have played out somewhat differently in the case of Adorno: his oft-noted Eurocentrism makes the usefulness of his work for postcolonial theory seem doubtful, at least at first glance. Thus, Espen Hammer notes that Adorno's "blunt Eurocentrism" is evident in the fact that he was "virtually oblivious to the concerns of postcolonialism, including racism, discrimination, and imperialism,"[69] and the editors of *Adorno: A Critical Reader* acknowledge that he was "deeply Eurocentric" and "possessed no knowledge of a world outside of Austria and Germany, let alone Europe."[70] However, despite this deep and blunt Eurocentrism, in recent years there has been a wave of attempts to claim Adorno as a thinker with substantial resources to offer postcolonial theory, focusing particularly on his conception of negative dialectics.[71] Namita Goswami, for example, offers a "radical postcolonial reading of Adorno," arguing that "Adorno's conception of negative dialectics can be understood as postcolonial in its understanding of difference," where difference for Adorno means non-antagonistic heterogeneity.[72] Goswami also turns to Adorno for the kind of "hopeful despair" that she argues is appropriate to our historical moment, particularly in the face of anthropogenic climate change and its differential effects across the globe.[73]

In light of these complex debates, which I cannot even attempt to settle here, I would like to emphasize that my point is not that postcolonial theory can be understood as a simple or straightforward extension of a certain radical strand of European critical theory represented by the likes of Foucault and Adorno. As Chakrabarty explains, although it is true that Foucault's work, for example, has been highly productive for postcolonial studies, "it would be wrong to think of postcolonial critiques of historicism (or of the political) as simply deriving from critiques already elaborated by postmodern and poststructuralist thinkers of the West. In fact, to think this way would itself be to practice historicism, for such a thought would merely repeat the temporal structure of the statement, 'first in the West, and then elsewhere.' "[74] Nor has it been my aim to show that Foucault and Adorno do in fact offer important resources for postcolonial theorizing—although I think that this may well be the case. Rather, my point is that Adorno and Foucault, for all of their faults and their own tendencies toward Eurocentrism and their blindness to issues of colonialism and imperialism, nevertheless offer important resources within the tradition of critical theory for the crucially important project of decolonizing critical theory. They do so precisely because and to the extent that they enable us to rethink critical theory's commitment to the idea of historical progress, an idea that has been thoroughly implicated in the logic of colonialism and thus subjected to withering critique by post- and decolonial thinkers. By historicizing and critically problematizing the very Hegelian notion of History as the progressive unfolding of a rationalization process on which Habermas and Honneth still implicitly or explicitly rely—even as they seek to recast this idea in more deflationary, pragmatic, and postmetaphysical terms—Adorno and Foucault offer an alternative way of thinking through the relationship between normativity and history. Moving in the opposite direction from Forst's foundationalist, noumenal, neo-Kantian approach to critical theory, and thereby avoiding its problematic methodological implications, Adorno and Foucault offer instead a more radically reflexive and historicized critical methodology that understands critique as the wholly immanent and fragmentary practice of opening up lines of fragility and fracture within the social world. This conception of critique also dovetails in important ways with the recurring image in post- and decolonial theory of colonialism as an open wound or an epistemic fracture,[75] of the subaltern as fracturing History from within,[76] and of decolonial thinking as creating a fracture within imperialist systems of thought.[77]

Moreover, their commitment to what Adorno calls modesty—a stance that is akin to what Mahmood calls humility—leads to a productive inversion of the stance toward subaltern subjects implied by McCarthy's and Habermas's progressive readings of European modernity. As I argued in chapters 1 and 2, the Habermasian theory of modernity compels those of us who are the heirs of the

European Enlightenment tradition to take the stance that we know or at least believe our form of life to be developmentally superior to those that we label pre- or nonmodern, but that we are open to being proved otherwise, albeit in a dialogue to be conducted on our own terms. Such a stance places insuperable cognitive burdens on those who would aspire to engage in genuinely open intercultural dialogue across the colonial divide. The Foucaultian-Adornian position reconstructed in this chapter offers us an alternative way of conceptualizing the relationship between our substantive, first-order normative principles and the metanormative stance we take with respect to them. On this view, we take the position that we are committed at a first-order, substantive level to these normative principles inasmuch as our form of life and sense of ourselves as practical moral agents depend on them, but that we simultaneously acknowledge, at a second-order, metanormative level, that those very ideals themselves demand of us an awareness of the violence inherent in them and also a fundamental modesty or humility regarding their status and authority. But this is just to say that Adorno and Foucault encourage critical theorists to enter into intercultural dialogue with subaltern subjects without presuming that we already know what the outcome of that dialogue should be, that is to say, with an openness to the very real possibility of unlearning. Indeed, both Foucault and Adorno see a kind of unlearning—a critical problematization of our own, historically sedimented point of view that frees us up in relation to it—as the very point of critique. As such, their work makes room for the kind of openness to the other that Chakrabarty has characterized as a "capacity to hear that which one does not already understand."[78] Both Foucault and Adorno allow us to see how we might open ourselves up to postcolonial difference while realizing and accepting that we might be radically transformed in this encounter and that our future selves might well regard that transformation as a kind of progress and we who resisted it as benighted. Moreover, both Foucault and Adorno understand this openness not as a flatfooted rejection of the ideals of European modernity or Enlightenment but rather as a way of taking up this normative inheritance, that is, a way of reaffirming modernity's core notions of freedom and justice to the Other by radically transforming the way that such notions are typically grounded and justified. As such, both thinkers make possible a radical transformation within critical theory itself, an opening up of critical theory to the "postcolonial," a decolonization of critical theory that can enable it to be truly critical of its own ongoing investments in a certain kind of post-Kantian imperialism.

6

Conclusion

"TRUTH," REASON, AND HISTORY

As I have argued in the preceding chapter, even if, as Habermas and Honneth have maintained, we take the ideals of freedom and equal respect as central to "our" Enlightenment inheritance, then what we can learn from Adorno and Foucault is how we might reaffirm these ideals by radically transforming them from within. To inherit the Enlightenment project is to draw on its tradition of critique but to deploy critique in service of criticizing and undermining Enlightenment's own Eurocentrism and thus its ongoing entanglements with the coloniality of power.[1] This requires first and foremost facing up to the ways in which Enlightenment ideals are entangled with relations of colonial domination and epistemic violence, and not just as a function of their application. As Jay Bernstein puts this point, explicating Adorno: "If the ideals of enlightenment are borne by and/or embodied in practices that are dominating, then the ideals must bear in themselves that dominating moment."[2] For example, the realization of freedom requires the uncovering of the conceptual and normative violence implicit in the norm of freedom itself, such as uncovering how the autonomy of the subject depends on the domination of inner nature or the disciplining of the body or the denial of full subjectivity to those who are deemed wholly Other or abject. Thus the realization of the normative inheritance of the Enlightenment necessarily pushes beyond itself. As Christoph

Menke has argued with respect to Adorno, the realization of Enlightenment morality is simultaneously its transcendence, and only by transcending it can Enlightenment morality be fully realized.[3]

There is a fruitful conjuncture here between Foucault's understanding of freedom, where freedom means freeing thought from what it silently thinks and opening up the space for thinking otherwise, and Adorno's understanding of freedom as breaking the spell of what has come to be second nature for us. Both of these conceptions of freedom turn on the thought that we can best realize our existing normative commitment to freedom by opening up our normative commitments to radical questioning.[4] The result is a more radically open-ended, futural conception of freedom, where we leave open the possibility that there may well be some future in which our own normative commitments and ways of thinking and ordering things will have been transcended, and thus will have come to seem impossibly strange. Methodologically, this open-endedness can be achieved through what I called in chapter 5 a problematizing genealogy that strives to reveal the ways in which our normative commitments are entangled with relations of power and domination. Crucially, such a problematizing genealogy is a way of inheriting the normative perspective of the Enlightenment in the dual sense of taking it up while simultaneously problematizing and decentering it, opening up a space for moving beyond it into an unknown and unknowable future. It is precisely this radical openness and open-endedness that make problematizing genealogy ideally suited for the kind of internal decolonization that critical theory sorely needs, Foucault and Adorno's own personal failings and blind spots on that score notwithstanding.

If critical theory starts from the basically Hegelian thought that reason is historically and socially situated, then it follows that critical theory itself, as a rational enterprise, is also so situated. Fully facing up to this insight, however, means following Foucault and Adorno in historicizing the notion of historicity: acknowledging that the very idea that knowledge is historically and socially situated emerges and rises to prominence in a particular philosophical and historical context, and that this context is marked by the convergence of progressive, developmental, Eurocentric theories of history and colonial structures of power. Viewed from this perspective, Fredric Jameson's famous dialectical slogan "Always historicize" becomes curiously problematic.[5] As Chakrabarty argues, however, what is problematic is not the *historicizing* but the *always*, for it is the latter that evinces a failure to acknowledge the extent to which historicization itself remains bound up with History, thus, with Eurocentrism.[6]

However, once we endorse this historicization of historicity and of History, then the best methodology for critical theory cannot be that of a normative or rational reconstruction that aims to vindicate "our" late modern Western point of view. This is so even if we incorporate what Honneth has called a genealogical proviso into our conception of critique, where genealogy is understood as providing a metacritical standpoint that allows us to see how our normative ideals go wrong in practice. Critical theory needs both a different understanding of genealogy and a more robust role for genealogy so conceived: a different understanding from that envisioned by Honneth and McCarthy, both of whom equate genealogy with subversive genealogy, and thus assign it the highly circumscribed role of showing how our normative ideals and principles get entangled with power relations when they are applied in the real world.[7] This latter way of understanding the role of genealogy rests on a problematic normative/empirical or ideal/real dichotomy that presumes that the normative can be purified of power relations. Genealogy is not simply subversive and its role in critical theory should not be confined to the metacritical moment that tells us how our normative ideals go wrong in practice. A more productive conception of genealogy understands it as aiming not at the subversion or the vindication of our normative commitments but rather at their problematization. On this understanding, the reconstruction of the immanent normativity of historically sedimented forms of life and the deconstruction of the power investments—including the imperialist power investments—of those same norms go hand in hand.

The splitting within Habermasian and post-Habermasian critical theory between the ideal, vindicatory, rationally or normatively reconstructive point of view and the nonideal, empirical, power-laden, subversive point of view is tied to another form of splitting, between the first-person and the third-person perspectives. On this view, the first-person perspective and the project of normative reconstruction go hand in hand: when one engages in normative or rational reconstruction, one takes up the perspective of a participant in the normative world, and when one takes up such a perspective, one has to see the normative principles that guide one's actions as valid and as better than what came before, or else one couldn't see them as reasons for one's actions. Similarly, the third-person or observer perspective is connected to the empirical analysis of power relations. On this view, to call attention to the power-ladenness of our normative ideals and practices is necessarily to take up an objectivating, third-person, observer perspective on the normative world, to show that the norms that we adhere to have their roots soaked thoroughly in blood, as Nietzsche would say, and from such a perspective the rational binding force of norms cannot possibly make itself felt. Even as Habermas acknowledges that a complete social theory must encompass both first- and third-person points of view, he gets a lot of mileage out of such splitting, for the structure of his theory struggles to keep the first- and third-person perspectives wholly separate, and this is precisely what enables him to maintain the fiction that the Foucaultian analysis of power has merely empirical and not normative relevance.[8]

Here again the account of genealogy as problematization offered in chapter 5 presents a methodological alternative to this sort of splitting. What is distinctive and innovative about Foucault's genealogical approach in particular is that he employs what we might call a participant-observer methodology, one that aims to bring these two perspectives on our normative lifeworld more closely together, and to draw on both perspectives simultaneously with the aim of conducting what he once called an internal ethnology of Occidental culture and rationality (OWWH, 293). This internal ethnology takes up a participant-observer perspective on our normative world, situating itself within that normative world and drawing on its normative content while simultaneously viewing it with the detached and objectivating glance of the outsider. The point of this internal ethnology is to problematize that normative world or to make it strange for its inhabitants by revealing the entanglement of our normative ideals with relations of power. But the ultimate aim of this ethnology is to enable the fuller realization of one of the central values of "our" normative world, in particular, freedom.

Again, there is a fruitful conjuncture here with Adorno, which comes out in Christoph Menke's perceptive reading of the methodology of his critique of morality. On Menke's reading, the critical questioning of morality, for Adorno, involves the self-questioning of morality, and this involves a combination of "external" and "internal" reflection,[9] that is, a combination of what I am calling observer and participant perspectives. Menke calls this combination of modes of reflection the "negative dialectical constitution of morality" (GC, 302). He further argues that this methodology represents the central point of disagreement between first-generation Frankfurt School thinkers such as Adorno and contemporary critical theorists such as Habermas, since the latter sought to develop a "discursive ethical reasoning of morality" in which "morality was to receive a form which might release it from the negative dialectic of self-questioning and self-limitation" (GC, 302). Moreover, along similar lines to my argument in chapter 5, Menke maintains that Adorno's negative dialectical self-overcoming or self-transcendence of morality, which requires the combination of internal and external modes of reflection, is "necessary precisely for moral purposes involving *others*" (GC, 305) in that it is necessary for the realization of solidarity with their suffering. On Menke's reading of Adorno, fully realizing the fundamental impulse of morality, which is solidarity with the suffering of others, requires us to transcend the formalistic conception of morality that we have inherited from the Enlightenment, for this formalistic conception of morality tends to do violence to the Other. Hence, realizing Enlightenment morality means transcending it, and transcending it means realizing it. The negative dialectical, problematizing critique of morality itself is thus "in itself an act of solidarity with the individuals who suffer from the damage of their lives" (GC, 322). In that sense, it is an attempt to realize justice.

When considered in light of post- and decolonial critiques I have discussed throughout this book, Menke's reading opens up the idea that taking up the inheritance of the Enlightenment by transcending it could itself be seen as a gesture of solidarity with the suffering of the colonized, subaltern subjects who have suffered so much at the hands and in the name of Eurocentric modernity. On this view, the willingness to put "our" Enlightenment inheritance radically into question by interrogating its entanglement with the coloniality of power is a way of taking up this inheritance by decolonizing it, and thus of acting in solidarity with the suffering of the colonized.

UNLEARNING, EPISTEMIC HUMILITY, AND METANORMATIVE CONTEXTUALISM

Central to this attempt to decolonize critical theory as an act of solidarity with the suffering of colonized subjects is the notion of unlearning, which recurs frequently in the literature of post- and decolonial theory. As Walter Mignolo puts it: "The target of epistemic de-colonization is the hidden complicity between the rhetoric of modernity and the logic of coloniality. For critical theory to correspond with decolonization, we need to shift the geography of knowledge and recast it [critical theory] within the frame of geo- and bio-politics of knowledge. Thus, the first step in the grammar of decolonization would be cast . . . [as] *learning to unlearn*."[10] Where Mignolo emphasizes the importance of shifting the geography of knowledge by transplanting theory to the site of the colonial wound, I want to suggest that there are resources immanent to the project of the Enlightenment that, when inherited in a radically transformative way, can be useful for this kind of learning to unlearn. Specifically, as I suggested in the conclusion to chapter 5, the method of problematizing genealogy plays an important role here, by revealing to us the contingency of our beliefs and normative commitments and showing us the ways that those beliefs and commitments have been contingently made up of complex relations of power, domination, and violence.[11] For this kind of unlearning project, the methodologies of normative and rational reconstruction are more hindrance than help, inasmuch as regardless of how willing they may be to acknowledge the contingency of the historical developments that they chart, or the downsides, losses, and regressions that accompany the learning processes that they identify as developmentally progressive, they nevertheless aim at the vindication of our normative point of view. A genuinely open and open-ended dialogue with colonized or subaltern subjects requires a kind of humility or modesty about our normative commitments and ideals that is inconsistent with these vindicatory narratives. Such an openness and open-endedness require what Chakrabarty characterizes as an openness "to the possibility of our thought systems . . . being rendered finite by the presence of the other."[12] This is a kind of humility or modesty that goes beyond Habermasian fallibilism—the acknowledgment of the fact that we may turn out to be wrong—because it entails an active and ongoing problematization of our own point of view and of our belief in its cognitive and moral superiority.

In the background here is the complicated issue of the relationship between metanormative or second-order and substantive or first-order commitments. This issue has come up several times throughout the book, but so far I have deferred discussion of it; now the time has come to tackle it head on. In chapter 2, I mentioned that Habermas does not always clearly differentiate between the metanormative and normative levels of analysis. However, it seems to me that at the metanormative level he defends a strong notion of context-transcendence, since it is only by doing so that he can maintain that the ideals and forms of life that emerge in European modernity may emerge from a particular context but also transcend that context to attain universal significance. This claim, in turn, licenses the inference that premodern or traditional forms of life are developmentally and cognitively inferior to our own, insofar as they haven't learned something that we now know, which is that their worldview is just that, a view of the world, and not the ultimate truth. But then he attempts to combine this second-order or metanormative claim about context-transcendence with a first-order or substantive inclusiveness or openness to learning from those who don't share our worldview. But I don't see how this can possibly work. It is as if we should say, in our substantive intercultural dialogical engagements: I believe my normative principles and procedures to be developmentally superior to yours, but I'm a fallibilist, so I am open to you convincing me otherwise, on discursive terms that are set in accordance with my normative point of view. The problem is that I just don't see how such a stance could possibly frame a genuinely open dialogue across lines of cultural difference.

If we give up the strong metanormative claims that Habermas wants to make—claims that I have argued should be given up since they rest on a problematic developmental reading of history—then we could understand the relationship between our metanormative and our normative commitments differently. We could understand ourselves, at a first-order, substantive normative level, to be committed to the values of freedom, equality, and solidarity with the suffering of others, but understand these commitments, at the metanormative level, to be justified immanently and contextually, via an appeal to specific historical context rather than via an appeal to their putatively context-transcendent character. Such a metanormative contextualism offers a better way of instantiating the virtues of humility and modesty that are required for a genuine openness to otherness. As Judith Butler puts it, glossing Adorno, "If the human is anything, it seems to be a double movement, one in which we assert moral norms at the same time as we question the authority by which we make that assertion."[13] In other words, we advance our normative commitments with a fundamental modesty or humility about the justificatory status of those commitments; we recognize that such modesty or humility is necessary for realizing those very commitments, that is, for the possibility of finally becoming human. Indeed, Adorno understood the possibility of progress in the future in precisely these terms: "Progress would be the very establishment of humanity in the first place, whose prospect opens up in the face of its extinction" (P, 145).

As I have argued in chapters 2 and 4, critical theorists such as Habermas and Forst mightily resist this sort of metanormative contextualism about the justification of our normative principles. Even though Forst describes his view as a contextualist universalism, he makes it clear that the theory of practical reason on which his moral theory rests is not a contextualist one, and that his contextualism is confined to the contexts of application of the basic right to justification. I suspect that Habermas and Forst resist contextualism so strenuously because they think that contextualism about normative justification necessarily devolves or collapses into first-order moral relativism. In other words, they are worried that holding a contextualist account of normative justification requires me to undermine or qualify all of my normative claims as soon as I utter them—to add "but that's just for me" on to every normative validity claim I utter—and thus undermines the very idea of engaging in a discursive assessment of validity claims. But I don't think that this is the case. The key to understanding why not lies in the distinction between the metanormative or second-order and substantive or first-order normative levels, a distinction that is implicit, but only implicit, in the work of Butler, Adorno, and Foucault. Once we draw out this distinction, it will become clear that contextualism at a metanormative or second-order level—that is, contextualism about normative justification, contextualism as a position in moral epistemology—need not entail relativism at the level of our first-order substantive normative commitments.

In order to see why this is the case I think we can usefully draw on some insights from contextualist epistemology, as developed in the work of Michael Williams and Linda Martín Alcoff.[14] In his book *Unnatural Doubts*, Williams develops a form of epistemological contextualism that holds that propositions and statements only have an epistemic status at all in relation to situational and contextually variable factors.[15] Epistemic contexts are differentiated from one another by what Williams calls their inferential structure—namely, what stands fast relative to what, or which propositions are taken to be basic or indubitable within that context. Drawing on Wittgenstein and Rorty, Williams adds the further idea that there is no hierarchical array of contexts and there is no context-independent standard or manner of evaluating the relative merits of different contextual standards. The objects of epistemic inquiry, for Williams, have no inherent, context-independent structure, and to think that they do is to assume epistemological realism. Contra epistemological realism, Williams's inferential contextualism holds that "the epistemic status of a given proposition is liable to shift with situational, disciplinary and other contextually variable factors," and that "independently of such influences, a proposition has no epistemic status whatsoever."[16] Thus, Williams defends the radical view that there are no context-independent or context-transcendent means by which we can evaluate different contextual epistemic standards, but he also maintains that this does not lead to the skeptical conclusion that we cannot have knowledge. Rather, it leads to a deflationary conception of knowledge according to which even though there may be no context-transcendent conception of human knowledge as such that ties all instances of knowledge together, nevertheless the word "know" can be "embedded in a teachable and useful linguistic practice."[17]

Like Williams, Alcoff develops a, broadly speaking, contextualist account of epistemology but, unlike Williams's, her project is motivated by explicitly political concerns. Alcoff argues that the Hegelian strategy for avoiding foundationalism—a commitment that, as I have argued, both Habermas and Honneth share—doesn't necessarily avoid the problematic authoritarianism of foundationalism if it hews too closely to Hegelian ideas about the superiority of the European perspective. As she puts it, Hegelian epistemology constitutes a laudable attempt to "come to grips with the implications of the historical and social locatedness of knowledge,"[18] but in Hegel's system, all knowledge may be perspectival, but "all perspectives are not equal, and thus Hegelian epistemology instantiates once again the authoritarian perspective characteristic of the Enlightenment" (RK, 206). Thus Hegel's legacy leads to an "epistemology of imperialism" and as such is "only partially trustworthy" (RK, 206). What is needed is a way of coming to grips with the historical and social locatedness of knowledge that disentangles that conception of knowledge from Eurocentric imperialism. Alcoff finds Foucault's account of power/knowledge useful for this task inasmuch as it takes a long list of "discursive and nondiscursive elements—including subject-positions, institutional practices, systems of exclusion, epistemes, and so forth"—to be "operative in the production of knowledge" and thus understands them as relevant parts of our web of belief (RK, 207). Moreover, Foucault does this without ceding the possibility of justification; rather, he understands justification as always "indexed to a context made up of very particular elements" (207–08). Thus, Alcoff roots her account of epistemic justification in particular historical and social contexts but without buying into the pernicious Hegelian fiction that a particular context—namely, the context of European modernity or Enlightenment—transcends its contextual beginnings and thus constitutes the overarching context against which or in terms of which other contextually rooted standards of justification can be measured.

To be sure, Alcoff's account differs from that of Williams in that she argues for a coherentist epistemology, whereas he contends that coherence epistemologies tend to collapse back into versions of epistemological realism because of their underlying drive toward unifying all contexts into one coherent picture of the world. Some of this disagreement can be chalked up to differences in how each of them understands the term "coherence." For Alcoff, coherence theory does imply an impulse toward unification but, on her version, the drive for unifying our web of beliefs and for eliminating contradictions is not paramount. Rather, on her view, "the need for resolutions is more realistically understood as contextual, arising from specific problems in specific contexts" (RK, 224). That is to say, some contradictions need to be resolved and others don't; some contradictory beliefs can coexist peacefully with one another and others can't; and which ones are which will depend on contextually specific features of the situation. Thus, on her view, we can't know in advance what the limits are on the scope of elements that must be made to cohere with one another within one's web of belief, and even "the claim to have achieved coherence is itself subject to contextual, and therefore coherentist, constraints" (RK, 225). Therefore, Alcoff's coherentist epistemology could justifiably be characterized as a contextualist coherentism.

More important for my purposes than the differences between Alcoff's coherentism and Williams's contextualism are the following points: both views tie justification and knowledge to specific contexts; both encompass not just beliefs and statements but also historically specific, social, cultural, and material conditions and even, for Alcoff, power relations in the scope of relevant elements involved in knowledge; and, for both, knowledge is only possible within a context, and what makes knowledge possible within that context is coherence with other beliefs. For Williams, some basic commitments are held fast and others are made to rest on that contextually specific foundation; for Alcoff, commitments have to be supported by relations of inference, correlation, or analogy by other elements of the web of belief. But the crucial point here is that knowledge is still possible within these contextualist epistemological frameworks; contextualism about epistemic justification does not entail skepticism or relativism. Both of these views thus contend that a thoroughly immanent and contextualist account of epistemic justification can still yield justified knowledge claims within particular epistemic contexts. In other words, they show, as Alcoff puts it, how one can "account for the historical and social embeddedness of all truth-claims without lapsing into epistemological nihilism" (RK, 13).[19]

Borrowing from and building on these efforts in contextualist epistemology, we can get an idea of how one can be a contextualist about normative justification—that is, how one can accept contextualism at a metanormative level, as a claim about moral epistemology—without thereby undercutting the possibility of normative validity at the first-order normative level and thus collapsing into moral relativism or nihilism.[20] Metanormative contextualism or contextualism about normative validity consists in two claims: First, moral principles or normative ideals are always justified relative to a set of contextually salient values, conceptions of the good life, or normative horizons—roughly speaking, forms of life or lifeworlds. Second, there is no über-context, no context-free or transcendent point of view from which we can adjudicate which contexts are ultimately correct or even in a position of hierarchical superiority over which others. On this view, our normative principles can be justified relative to a set of basic normative commitments that stand fast in relation to them, but because there is no context-transcendent point of view from which we can determine which contexts are superior to which others, those basic normative commitments must be understood as contingent foundations.[21]

Here again we might fruitfully turn to Adorno, who, like Alcoff, links the very idea of a transcendent point of view to authoritarianism.[22] As Adorno puts it: "Transcendent critique sympathizes with authority in its very form, even before expressing any content; there is a moment of content to the form itself. . . . Anyone who judges something that has been articulated and elaborated—art or philosophy—by presuppositions that do not hold within it is behaving in a reactionary manner, even when he swears by progressive slogans" (PMP, 146). Thus, for Adorno, resisting the pull of the transcendent is itself a moral imperative: "Whenever anyone expects you to deal with something intellectually uncomfortable by asking you to 'transcend' it, just pause and ask by what authority you should do so. If you were to do that, I think that would be an instance of a right action in a wrong life" (PMP, 174–75). Adorno, however, also makes clear that the refusal of the point of view of transcendence does not lead to relativism. In fact, for him, relativism is a pseudoproblem:

> For the positive nature of beliefs, of ideologies, that prevail here and now is not relative at all. They confront us at every moment as binding and absolute. And the criticism of these false absolutes . . . is much more urgent than the quest for some absolute values or other, fixed in eternity and hanging from the ceiling like herrings, which would enable us to transcend this relativism with which, as real living people who are attempting to live decent lives, we have absolutely nothing to do. On the other hand, however, the postulates and values that surface wherever people imagine that they have to overcome relativism are the products of arbitrary acts, things that are freely posited, that are created and not natural, and thus they necessarily always succumb to the relativism they denounce.
>
> (PMP, 175)

Relativism and absolutism are thus correlates, and "dialectical thinking . . . is a kind of thinking that, to express it in Nietzschean terms, would persist beyond that alternative" (PMP, 175). I submit that the kind of metanormative contextualism that I have been sketching here is an example of a point of view that is beyond the alternatives of relativism and absolutism. Embracing this as a view about moral epistemology or metanormative justification is perfectly consistent with endorsing first-order substantive normative principles such as mutual respect, egalitarian reciprocity, openness to the other, inclusiveness, and so forth. It is even compatible with regarding these principles as universal in the scope of their application, so long as we don't understand these principles, from a metanormative perspective, as justified insofar as they are absolute values that are "fixed in eternity and hanging from the ceiling like herrings."[23] This is why even Adorno's new categorical imperative is a historically indexed claim: it arises out of a particular historical situation, namely, the horror of Auschwitz, and it holds for us in light of that historical situation.[24] Hence, Adorno follows up his critique of metaethical absolutism by saying: "We may not know what absolute good is or the absolute norm, we may not even know what man is or the human or humanity—but what the inhuman is we know very well indeed. I would say that the place of moral philosophy today lies . . . in the concrete denunciation of the inhuman" (PMP, 175). And when he says this, it is significant that he does not say that we know very well what the *absolutely* inhuman is. In other words, what we know very well is not some absolute—objective or morally realist—negativistic ground, but rather a concrete, historically situated, and in that sense contingent experience of inhumanity and suffering.[25] For Adorno, just as for Hegel, there is no unmediated access to things in themselves; rather, our access is always mediated through concepts, which themselves contain the sedimentations of history, social practices, and culture. So Adorno's appeal here to the reality of suffering cannot be indicative of a naïve or straightforward realism or objectivism about moral truths or values. In fact, Adorno appeals to the reality of suffering precisely because the moral impulse of solidarity with suffering is what has been both presupposed and suppressed within the Kantian conception of morality that he takes to be predominant in modernity. In other words, the appeal to suffering or concrete inhumanity as a ground for our negatively framed moral judgments is an appeal not to a set of objective moral facts but rather to the suppressed moment within our own historically conditioned way of experiencing the normative world.

But if we ask the further question of what makes the lifeworld horizon that forms the social and historical context for our normative commitments and principles deserving of our support, and if we have given up the possibility of a context that transcends all contexts, and if we have problematized the idea that "our" lifeworld horizon is developmentally or cognitively superior to others, then our answer to this question will have to acknowledge that our normative principles and commitments themselves rest on a contingent foundation. There are, however, two important features of the normative horizon of Enlightenment modernity that mitigate against what might seem like the arbitrariness implied by this picture: first, like all horizons, this normative horizon is open and not closed, permeated by and formed in interaction with other normative horizons; second, it takes openness to criticism and reflexivity as normative goals, and hence as a form of life it requires me to be open to being changed, including when that means learning to unlearn. The first feature means that the critical resources of one normative horizon can be and quite often are brought to bear on those of another. Thus, we are not limited to a choice between wholly internal forms of critique in which existing social practices or institutions are measured against the normative ideals internal to the social worlds in which they are situated, on the one hand, and transcendent critique based on context-transcendent standards of justification, on the other. Rather, we can envision "external" modes of critique in which justificatory standards that are held fast in one context are brought to bear on those of another, and vice versa. These "external" modes would be more radical than wholly internal critiques but without appealing to potentially authoritarian notions of context-transcendence as a way of securing their radicality.[26] The second feature means that even when I acknowledge that my first-order normative commitments rest on contingent foundations, this does not lead me to embrace them dogmatically or ethnocentrically because those very commitments require me to be open to coming to see—whether through rational argument or through expressive/hermeneutic insight or through experiences of aesthetic world disclosure—that parts of my normative horizon are flawed or limited in some way. Thus, my first-order normative commitments require—in a further reflexive turn—a metanormative or second-order reflexivity about the status of my own normative horizon.[27] This is, I think, very close to the kind of openness that Chakrabarty invokes when he talks about being open to hearing what we do not already understand and to having our systems of thought be rendered finite by the encounter with the subaltern.[28]

THE IMPURITY OF PRACTICAL REASON (REPRISE)

Both Habermas and Honneth link the idea of historical progress to the progressive purification of reason from power relations. For Habermas, the progressive rationalization of the lifeworld goes hand in hand with the overcoming of power-laden, systematically distorted relations of communication; despite Honneth's critique of Habermas's account of societal rationalization as having too little to say about the role of social actors in that process, he accepts this basic picture of progress as the process whereby a socially instantiated reason is progressively purified of power relations. In both cases, then, moral-practical progress consists in a socially instantiated reason working itself free of its entanglement with power relations. Although Forst does not present such a historically inflected account of the relations between practical reason and power, he too presupposes the possibility of a practical reason that is disentangled from power relations, and this despite his commitment to viewing practical reason as an actual social practice and his attempt to put first things—that is, the question of power—first.

As we saw in chapter 5, Foucault and Adorno offer a very different account of practical reason and its relationship to power. As Adorno points out, reason is just one thing, such that if reason serves as a medium for domination, then this cannot be neatly cordoned off into a separate strata—the ways in which the ideal of reason goes wrong in practice—but rather must be regarded as an aspect of reason itself. Similarly, for Foucault, the task of critical thought is to accept and to interrogate the spiral formed by the entanglement of power and reason, by the fact that we are fortunately committed to a form of rationality that is unfortunately crisscrossed by relations of power and domination. However, for both Adorno and Foucault, these claims are not about practical reason as such, for both of them doubt that it makes much sense to talk about such a thing. As Foucault put it: "The word 'rationalization' is dangerous. What we have to do is analyze specific rationalities rather than always invoking the progress of rationalization in general" (SP, 329). Similarly, Adorno endorses what he claims is the "mainspring of Hegel's thought," namely, that "the a priori is also the a posteriori" (H, 3). In other words, the a priori is a historical a priori, and all of our thought forms, including our conceptions of reason, are a posteriori, that is, socially and historically conditioned.[29] This holds not only for what Adorno calls identity thinking, which is a specific mode of reasoning that emerges in its fullest articulation in the Enlightenment, but also for negative dialectics, which offers not an alternative conception of practical reason as such but rather a historically specific mode of resistance to identity thinking—the mode of rationality that predominates in modernity—and to the social and institutional structures that correspond to and reinforce it—the reified social structures characteristic of late capitalism, the culture industry, and so forth. Moreover, since Adorno and Foucault also reject the story of progress as a historical "fact" that has led up to us, they rule out the consoling story that might reassure us that our current conception of practical reason is less entangled with relations of power and domination than what came before—but they do so without, as I have argued throughout, offering an alternative story of decline and fall, according to which reason was purer and less entangled with domination in some mythical past.

These ways of thinking about the relationship between power and reason give us some idea of how to conceptualize practical reason in a way that is attentive to its impurities, its entanglements with power relations, without thereby sliding into irrationalism. The conception of reason that I have in mind can be further elaborated by considering the thoroughly practical and resolutely antifoundationalist account of reasoning as a social practice recently advocated by Anthony Laden.[30] As Laden describes it, reasoning is not the work of deducing conclusions from a set of premises, nor does it involve convincing an interlocutor by means of the unforced force of the better argument; rather, on his view, reasoning is "the responsive engagement with others as we attune ourselves to one another and the world around us" (RASP, 8). Laden understands reasoning as a species of casual conversation, which makes his conception of reasoning thoroughly open-ended; like casual conversation, reasoning has no end both in the sense that it has no goal and in the sense that it has no end point (RASP, 82). Rather, it is an open-ended, ongoing practice of mutual and reciprocal attunement through which shared spaces of reasons are constructed and mapped. On this account, to reason with others is to issue invitations to take the things that we say as speaking for all of us, as correctly mapping the bounds of our shared space of reasons: "The activity of reasoning is the activity of sharing the world, of attuning ourselves to others within reciprocal relationships" (RASP, 46).

Because Laden construes reasoning as involving the issuing of invitations—as co-constructing and inhabiting a shared space of reasons—rather than the issuing of commands, his account of reason differs markedly from the authoritarian conception of reason defended by Kant and Forst and criticized by Adorno. For Laden, as for Forst, reasoning is a "norm-governed, reciprocal, and revisable activity" (RASP, 77), but reason's authority lies not in its capacity to issue legitimate commands but rather in its capacity for the parties who are reasoning together to remain connected to one another (RASP, 63). By understanding reason's authority in terms of its ability to connect rather than to command, Laden's account "recognizes and respects those with whom we talk and argue in a way that arguing from already established philosophical foundations does not."[31] Thus Laden shows how one might take on board Adorno's critique of the authoritarianism of the Kantian conception of reason while still making sense of Adorno's commitment to reason and to conducting a rational critique of reason. Laden's emphasis on reciprocity, mutuality, and attunement as the point of reasoning as a shared social practice also resonates with Adorno's notion of reconciliation as the nontotalizing, open-ended togetherness of diversity.

Laden's conversation-based account of reasoning can also be connected to the postcolonial critique of the idea of speaking for others that surfaced in my discussion of McCarthy in chapter 1 and to the Foucaultian critique of Forst's account of the space of reasons that I offered in chapter 4. Because Laden's account views reasoning as a species of conversation, it models reasoning as a practice of speaking *with* others in mutual, reciprocal, and open-ended ways. Although he does describe this as a kind of speaking for others, what Laden means by this is only that through speaking, I am including them in a "we" on behalf of which I speak, and that in so doing I am not only inviting them to accept or reject my claims but also inviting them to speak for me as well. As he puts it: "Acceptance of a reason, then, involves an acknowledgment that we share some, perhaps small, space of reasons. Sharing such a space, however, makes it possible for either of us to speak for both of us, and so we can describe the invitation the reason proffers as an invitation to take another's words as speaking for us as well" (RASP, 15–16). Laden's is thus a fully open-ended, mutual, and reciprocal conception of speaking for, in which "I speak for you by speaking for an us of which we are both members, by saying what I take it we would say" (RASP, 41). Such a stance does not involve treating those for whom one speaks as inferior or incapable of representing their own interests (RASP, 40); to the contrary, it demands a high degree of vulnerability on the part of the speaker, inasmuch as it requires me to allow that "my position within what I take to be a space of reasons can change as a result of our interaction" (RASP, 41).

If reasoning is a social practice, and if our social practices and institutions are structured by relations of power, domination, and oppression, reason will necessarily be entangled with power. To his credit, Laden does not shy away from this implication; in fact, he acknowledges its full force but also shows compellingly how his open-ended, non-authoritarian, non-foundationalist conception of reason can provide a way of thinking through reason's entanglements with power without rejecting reason or putting it on trial. He maintains that we have to take seriously the claims of oppressed or marginalized groups that they are excluded from the norms of reason—the kinds of postcolonial, queer, and feminist critiques of reason that I discussed in chapter 4—inasmuch as such claims make visible how "the very terms in which a conversation proceeds" are "themselves set and structured by inequalities of power, and thus unable on their own to make those inequalities visible and thus to challenge them" (RASP, 128). Here Laden's account is highly attentive not only to how power enables and constrains certain moves within an existing space of reasons, but also to how reasoning practices serve to construct and modify those spaces in an ongoing way (RASP, 33). Thus, his view goes beyond Forst's in that it enables us to see how power works not only *in* the space of reasons but also *through* its very constitution. However, acknowledging that power works through the constitution of spaces of reasons does not lead Laden to conclude that we cannot or should not reason. Rather, Laden argues, the very claim that the terms of a particular conversation structurally exclude or marginalize some individuals is itself a move within a conversation; thus, a conversation-based conception of reason must find a way to remain perpetually open to such challenges, rather than rejecting them as confused or performatively contradictory. This means that reasoning well demands a particular set of virtues: not only a willingness to make oneself vulnerable and an openness to change, but also a "receptivity to unfamiliar lines of criticism, especially those that may initially seem as if they are themselves incoherent or conceptually confused because they challenge the basis of one's conceptual map" (RASP, 129). Only this kind of radical openness and receptivity can enable reason to ameliorate the distorting and exclusionary effects of domination and oppression. Moreover, precisely because domination, when viewed from above, so often looks like equality, "it is particularly important that those who are privileged by inequalities of power possess and deploy" these virtues of vulnerability, openness, and receptivity (RASP, 129).

Although this way of thinking about practical reason does leave us unable to claim a context-transcendent ground for our normative point of view, it does not leave us with nothing to say when we are faced with those who reject that point of view. Rather, Laden argues that a non-foundationalist account of reasoning as a social practice should rest content with describing our normative commitments not as necessary preconditions that we are forced to accept on pain of being deemed unreasonable but rather as attractive ideals toward which we might aspire (RASP, 44). This is the main difference between Laden's practice-based conception of reasoning and Forst's neo-Kantian conception of practical reason. Laden acknowledges that "to those used to normative arguments that attempt to ground norms on undeniable or unavoidable foundations, the invitation to consider an ideal and find it attractive will seem hopelessly weak and underwhelming" (RASP, 44), but his account of reasoning as a social practice shows compellingly how we might move beyond the problematic idea of practical reason as such without thereby giving up on reason altogether. And by showing how reasoning can be understood as a radically open-ended practice whose principal virtues are vulnerability, receptivity, and openness to change, he offers an account of rationality capable of facing up to the fact that our form of rationality—like all forms, rooted as they are in social practices and cultural forms of life that are structured by relations of power—is crisscrossed with inherent dangers.

Laden's social picture of reasoning also shows how we might avoid the self-congratulatory temptation to prejudge ourselves as cognitively or developmentally superior to "nonmodern" or "premodern" cultures or forms of life—for example, to African cultures who practice various forms of magic or witchcraft or to Indigenous legal practices—while simultaneously avoiding the slide into relativism. As Laden argues, to take the stance that we are developmentally superior, that "we" now know something that "they" have not yet learned, is to insist that other cultures can only count as reasoning insofar as "there is a way to fit their activities into ours" (RASP, 155). But this way of thinking "is to prepare the way for arguments for assimilating them to our way of doing things, bringing them to reason, civilizing them" (RASP, 156). If, on the other hand, we reject this move, then it looks like we are left with a kind of relativism "that devalues both ways of thinking or doing things: just what we do around here" (RASP, 156). Laden argues that this double bind is itself an artifact of a problematic way of conceptualizing reason as resting on a strong, philosophical foundation or ground, what he calls the standard picture of reason. The trick is to stop thinking of ourselves as developmentally or cognitively superior or capable of reasoning better than those whom we deem to be "nonmodern" or "premodern," and to understand the participants in this kind of intercultural dialogue instead as "two groups, each of which has practices that allow them to share normative spaces within their group, but neither of which yet has the means to reason with the other" (RASP, 156). And the key to learning how to reason across such divides is to adopt the kind of open, vulnerable, receptive, and, I would also say, modest and humble stance toward our own reasoning practices described above. Importantly, this does not mean that we thereby give up the ability to criticize practices or institutions. As I have argued above, it is one thing to say that someone else is wrong, and another to say that they are backward or primitive; the former claim is compatible with treating the other as a moral contemporary, while the latter is not.[32] As Laden puts it, "Coming to recognize the practices of another group as a form of reasoning is precisely not to foreclose the possibility of criticizing them. It is to recognize the work that may need to be done in order to be able to properly articulate and formulate criticisms, as well as to simultaneously recognize that they can criticize our practices" (RASP, 157).[33]

Laden's anti-foundationalist conception of reason as a social practice that demands openness, vulnerability, and humility finds an echo in the epilogue to Dipesh Chakrabarty's *Provincializing Europe*. There, Chakrabarty argues that the "tendency to identify reason and rational argumentation as a modernist weapon against 'premodern' superstition ends up overdrawing the boundary between the modern and the premodern" (PE, 238). Chakrabarty's point is not that reason as such is elitist. Rather, his point is that it is elitist to equate the "premodern" with unreason and superstition, to fail to see the practices that we deem to be superstitious as themselves instantiating a form of rationality. As he puts it, "Reason becomes elitist whenever we allow unreason and superstition to stand in for backwardness, that is to say, when reason colludes with the logic of historicist thought. For then we see our 'superstitious' contemporaries as examples of an 'earlier type,' as human embodiments of the principle of anachronism" (PE, 238). The challenge that Chakrabarty's work poses is that of thinking beyond historicism without rejecting reason (PE, 249); Laden's nonfoundationalist, open-ended, and pluralistic conception of reasoning as a social practice helps us to meet this challenge.[34]

PROGRESS, IN HISTORY

Finally, we can now ask what, if anything, remains of the idea of progress, especially once we have taken on board the contextualist conception of normative justification and the practical conception of practical reason that I have outlined? Throughout this book, I've attempted to delineate two different conceptions of normative progress—the backward-looking conception of history as a progressive, developmental story that leads up to "us" and the forward-looking conception of the possibility of achieving a more just or less oppressive social world. Taking inspiration from Adorno, I've argued that forward-looking progress with respect to the decolonization of the normative foundations of critical theory can take place only if we abandon the backward-looking story that positions European modernity as the outcome of a historical learning process. In this sense, progress occurs where it comes to an end. At the same time, again following Adorno, there is no inference from the lack of progress in the past to its impossibility in the future; this means that letting go of the backward-looking story about historical progress as a "fact" need not compel us to give up on the hope for progress in the future, though it may well change how we think about what that might mean. In other words, it may be the case, as McCarthy argues, that our politics cannot be truly progressive unless we have some way of conceptualizing what would count as progress in a forward-looking sense, as a moral-political imperative, but it is also the case that our politics cannot be truly progressive if our conception of progress as an imperative rests on a self-congratulatory, Eurocentric story about historical progress as a "fact." Moreover, for the project of decoupling progress as an imperative from progress as a "fact," it isn't sufficient to lace our vindicatory or rationally reconstructive story with an acknowledgment of the downsides, losses, and regressions that have accompanied our historical learning process. Rather, we need to go further and actively problematize our own normative point of view.

To be sure, both of these conceptions of progress, the forward-looking and the backward-looking, rest on normative principles. This follows from the claim that the very concept of progress does not make sense without some conception of a goal or benchmark against which progress can be measured; normative progress, then, can only be measured with respect to some sort of normative benchmark. Thus, whether we identify increases in autonomy or social freedom as gains that mark modernity as developmentally superior to premodern forms of life or as normative potentials in the present the full realization of which we should strive to attain in the future, we are identifying them as the normative benchmarks against which claims about progress, whether backward- or forward-looking, should be measured. In this sense, the backward- and forward-looking conceptions of progress could be seen as distinguishable only inasmuch as they are distinct temporal references that are indexed to a common set of normative assumptions. If that's right, then one might wonder how much work this distinction between forward- and backward-looking conceptions of progress really does. One might also ask whether my aim is really to disentangle the former from the latter, or rather to undercut the whole idea of normativity that runs through both conceptions or temporal dimensions of progress?[35]

In response to this last question, I want to say: both. As I have argued in chapters 1 through 3, one can distinguish between backward-looking and forward-looking conceptions of progress in the work of McCarthy, Habermas, and Honneth, and, more important, these conceptions hang together in a particular way, such that the backward-looking story about modernity as the result of a historical learning process undergirds forward-looking claims about what would count as moral-political progress in the future. This strategy for grounding normativity emerges from a desire to avoid foundationalism—by refraining from appealing to a transhistorical normative standard or conception of rationality—while also avoiding historical relativism—by identifying a historically emergent but still developmentally superior set of normative standards. It is also rooted in a desire to avoid problematic forms of utopianism, as evidenced by Habermas's critical remarks about utopian socialism and Honneth's appeal to the impotence of the mere ought objection to Kantian morality. The thought here is that critical theory runs the risk of becoming overly utopian unless it identifies normative potentials that are present in existing social reality, potentials on which we can build in order to make progress in the future. But, again, if we are to avoid historical relativism, we have to have some reason to think that those normative potentials are themselves worthy of being built upon, and the backward-looking story of historical progress as a "fact" steps in to play this role. In this respect, McCarthy's, Habermas's, and Honneth's positions are distinct from Forst's, since he identifies a normative foundation—the basic right to justification, which is rooted in his conception of practical reason—that can justify both forward- and backward-looking conceptions of progress. As I have argued throughout this book, both of these strategies are problematic from the point of view of post- and decolonial theory, though in somewhat different ways, and my argument is designed to challenge both. The combination of problematizing genealogy as central to the methodology of critical theory and the related metanormative contextualism that I advocate undercuts any sort of normative foundationalism and replaces it with a contingent, context-immanent normativity; in that sense it should undermine our faith in certain kinds of strong claims about progress, whether backward- or forward-looking. This means that if we are to hold on to the idea of progress as a forward-looking moral-political imperative, that commitment will have to go together with a relentless and ongoing problematization not only of any and all judgments about what would constitute progress but also of the normative standards by which such progress could be measured.

The same goes for the distinction that I made in the first chapter between historical progress and progress in history, which is also bound up with the question of normativity in complicated ways. As I have used these terms, "historical progress" refers to a transhistorical claim according to which the transitions between different historical epochs or time periods can be understood on a model of sociocultural learning or progressive development. In its strong form, this notion appeals, explicitly or implicitly, to an ahistorical normative standard against which transhistorical claims about progress can be measured. Thus, the strong version brings us back to the problem of normative foundationalism, discussed above. "Progress in history," by contrast, refers to improvements within a specific domain and measures those improvements by appealing to standards that are themselves historically and contextually grounded. In chapter 3, this distinction was further complicated through my discussion of Honneth, who can be interpreted as defending a medium-strength account of something like historical progress "for us," where the claim about historical learning or progress across different historical epochs is indexed not to an ahistorical normative standard but rather to a set of contextually grounded normative commitments. As I argued in chapter 3, although this conception of historical progress is conceptually coherent, it cannot do the kind of metanormative work that Honneth needs for it to do, and it also remains vulnerable to the political objections raised by post- and decolonial theorists.

So, this leaves us with progress in history. As I have said before, in order to make judgments about progress, all that we need is some sort of benchmark or standard against which progress can be measured. Thus, my contextualist conception of normativity not only leaves room for progress as a forward-looking moral-political imperative; insofar as it articulates normative standards at all, it makes possible backward-looking claims about progress as well. In that sense, the backward- and the forward-looking conceptions of progress can never be fully disentangled, for as soon as one articulates a normative standard of any sort, one can use it to make judgments about what has constituted progress up to now and what would constitute progress in the future. This means that my view would allow one to say, for example, that the expansion of gay rights in the latter half of the twentieth and first part of the twenty-first centuries in Western, postindustrial democracies constitutes progress in history, where progress is understood in terms of the fuller realization of certain normative commitments that we take to be fundamental—for example, equality—and is not linked to any sort of claim about whether the historical form of life in which such normative commitments are embedded is developmentally superior to pre- or nonmodern forms of life. Still, as my discussion in chapter 3 of gay marriage shows, we have to be very cautious even about such locally and contextually grounded judgments about progress in history, precisely because the tendency to self-congratulation can be so seductive and so dangerous for a critical theory that aims to reflect on its own investments in relations of power. Thus, even our local and contextual judgments about progress in history, whenever we feel compelled to make them, must be ongoingly and relentlessly problematized.[36]

CODA: CRITICALIZING POSTCOLONIAL THEORY

The charge that postcolonial theory is unable to ground its own critical perspective because it remains mired in irrationalism and relativism is by now a familiar complaint.[37] Indeed, given post-colonial theory's intellectual roots in postmodernist or poststructuralist theory, this charge should not be at all surprising, since it is a charge frequently leveled against postmodern theorists as well.[38] In closing, let me say a few words about how the approach laid out in this book and particularly in these last two chapters might be useful for responding to such charges. The metanormative contextualism that I have defended shows how postcolonial theory could be grounded in a thoroughly immanent normativity that enables its capacity as critique, thus allowing it to avoid relativism, without appealing to developmental readings of history, which would endorse Eurocentrism, or to strong foundationalist conceptions of normativity, which would end up in authoritarianism or informal imperialism. The anti-foundationalist, open-ended, and pluralistic conception of practical reason discussed above shows how postcolonial theory can reject the notion of practical reason as such as overly abstract and formal—thus, again, as imperialist in its very form—but without opening itself up to the charge of lapsing into a romantic over-valorization of superstition, magic, and myth.[39] Finally, the local and contextual account of progress in history shows how postcolonial theory might articulate some sort of normative benchmark for what might count as progress in the future—thus accepting a version of Forst's claim that one can be against progress only by being for it—but without appealing to the problematic readings of history or abstract conceptions of normativity that the theory rigorously criticizes. In these three ways, I hope that this book shows what postcolonial theorists might stand to gain from the kind of encounter with the Frankfurt School tradition of critical theory that this book attempts to make possible. That is to say, I hope not only to have showed how critical theory can and must be decolonized, but also to have given some indications of how postcolonial theory could be criticalized.

NOTES

PREFACE AND ACKNOWLEDGMENTS

1. Horkheimer, *Critical Theory*, 209.
2. Horkheimer himself isn't, in my view, entirely successful in holding open this tension, at least not in this early essay, but he does offer an important and instructive articulation of the tension.
3. Horkheimer, *Critical Theory*, 246.
4. Allen, "Emancipation Without Utopia."
5. Thomas McCarthy's important book *Race, Empire, and the Idea of Human Development* is a prominent exception to this general lack of engagement, one that I will discuss in more detail in chapter 1. In many ways my book should be read as a response to his.

1. CRITICAL THEORY AND THE IDEA OF PROGRESS

1. Said, *Culture and Imperialism*, 278.
2. Ibid., 279.
3. To be sure, in his recent work, Habermas has drawn on the multiple modernities literature to rethink his account of modernity; I discuss this aspect of his recent work in chapter 2. Honneth, unlike Habermas, has mostly refrained from discussing how his recognition theory might apply in a global context. An exception is his essay "Recognition between States."
4. Habermas's sharp criticisms of George W. Bush's foreign policy notwithstanding, his faith in existing international institutions and his hopes for the constitutionalization of international law can be seen as indications of failure to appreciate the full complexity of the structures of informal

imperialism or neocolonialism that have persisted in the wake of formal decolonization. On this point, see Tully, "On Law, Democracy and Imperialism."

5. Perhaps the most prominent exception, which will be discussed in more detail in this chapter, is McCarthy's important recent book *Race, Empire, and the Idea of Human Development*.
6. See, for example, Cornell, *Moral Images of Freedom*; Marasco, *The Highway of Despair*; Willett, *The Soul of Justice*.
7. On the importance of the idea of progress for normativity in Habermas's work, see Owen, *Between Reason and History*; in Habermas's and Honneth's work, see Iser, *Empörung und Fortschritt*.
8. The literature here is too vast to cite in a single note. For an incisive and influential overview of postcolonial theory, focusing on the relationship between Eurocentrism and the philosophy of history, see Young, *White Mythologies*.
9. James Tully, personal communication.
10. Fraser, "What's Critical About Critical Theory?," 113.
11. In saying this, I am assuming that the waves of formal decolonization that have run through Africa, India, and other parts of Asia in the wake of World War II and the resulting neocolonial and informally imperialist world order that has been in place at least since 1970 constitute and are the loci of some of the most significant social and political struggles and wishes of our age. Of course, I realize that many anticolonial struggles predate this time period—including the American Revolution, the Haitian Revolution, and the formal decolonization of Latin America—and that a very wide variety of historical, social, and political phenomena fall under the heading of decolonization. The important point here is that the most recent wave of decolonization is greatly implicated in the creation of the so-called Third World and thus in some of the major sources of global economic and social injustice today.
12. On this point, see Mignolo, "Delinking," 449–450.
13. Benjamin, *Illuminations*, 257–258. For an astute account of the differences between Adorno's and Benjamin's philosophies of history, see Vázquez-Arroyo, "Universal History Disavowed."
14. Pensky, "Contributions Toward a Theory of Storms," 170.
15. See Young, *White Mythologies*, 1–31. Although Young does mention the Frankfurt School occasionally, his main target is British Marxist literary critics, not German social and political theorists. Thus the question of the relationship between the theory of history and the problem of the normative foundations of critique—a primary focus of this book—is not a central concern for Young. I also follow Young by relying heavily on Foucault's radical critique of the Hegelian notion of history, though unlike Young, I see Adorno's philosophy of history as working in the

same vein. For Young's critique of Adorno, see Young, *White Mythologies*, 39–40.

16. I am well aware of the important differences between postcolonial and decolonial approaches and of the charge that the former, insofar as it relies heavily on the theoretical edifice of European philosophy, constitutes a Eurocentric critique of Eurocentrism. Following Walter Mignolo, I would say that although the Eurocentric critique of Eurocentrism may well be insufficient for the project of fully decolonizing critical theory, this does not mean that it is unnecessary. Moreover, I see post- and decolonial theory as allied critical projects with distinct genealogies, and I draw throughout this book on both. However, insofar as my primary aim is to conduct an internal critique of the critical theory tradition, to work through a particular genealogy of European critical theory in an attempt to open that project up to post- and decolonial concerns from within, this book may well be particularly vulnerable to the Eurocentric critique of Eurocentrism charge. In response, I would point out that although an internal critique of European critical theory has to move largely within that horizon, the impetus for such a critique is the desire to push critical theory in a new direction, to compel it to decenter its own critical perspective, and, in so doing, to enable it to become something else.
17. Koselleck, "'Progress' and 'Decline,'" 221. Henceforth cited parenthetically in the text as PD.
18. I am grateful to Max Pensky for pressing me to think through this issue more carefully, and to Colleen Boggs for suggesting that I use Latour's work to do it.
19. Latour, *We Have Never Been Modern*.
20. For Latour's critique of Habermas, see ibid., 59–61.
21. Ibid., 99.
22. McCarthy, *Race, Empire and the Idea of Human Development*, 240.
23. On this point, see Iser, *Empörung und Fortschritt*.
24. On this point, with respect to Habermas in particular, see Owen, *Between Reason and History*.
25. For Honneth's statement of this commitment, see SDD, 66. For an insightful discussion of this aspect of Habermas's work, see Stahl, "Habermas and the Project of Immanent Critique."
26. See also Habermas's response to the charge of foundationalism in TCA2, 399–403.
27. I want to emphasize that by calling this a Hegelian strategy, I am not suggesting that the position I am imputing to Habermas and Honneth represents the correct interpretation of Hegel's position. I am well aware that there is a lively, ongoing debate between metaphysical, pragmatist, and deconstructive interpreters of Hegel over whether Hegel himself

was in fact committed to the kind of progressive reading of history that I am attributing to Habermas and Honneth. Further complicating this discussion is the apparent shift in Hegel's own views on this point from the time that he wrote the *Phenomenology* to the later *Philosophy of Right* and the posthumously published *Lectures on the Philosophy of History*. (Still further complications are raised by the status of the latter text, as a set of notes compiled and edited by Hegel's students.) I cannot take on these debates here, but luckily I don't think I need to, since this is not a book about Hegel but rather a book about how a certain version of left-Hegelianism has informed contemporary critical theory. If one wanted to argue that there are resources within Hegel's own work that provide an alternative to the account of the relationship between history and normativity found in Habermas and Honneth, then, to my mind, that would be all to the good (though that is not the strategy that I will pursue here). For a compelling argument to this effect, see Marasco, *The Highway of Despair*. However that interpretive question gets decided, I think it is clear that neither Habermas nor Honneth accepts the deconstructive reading of Hegel; their reading is much closer to the pragmatist reading that remains committed to the idea of historical progress (though it understands this in a post- or nonmetaphysical way). On this point, see Pippin, "Hegel, Modernity, and Habermas."

28. On this point, see Iser, *Empörung und Fortschritt*.

29. For contrasting readings of Habermas's normative strategy, which argue, in different ways, that his view of legitimacy is fundamentally forward-looking or futural, see Honig, "Dead Rights, Live Futures"; and Olson, "Paradoxes of Constitutional Democracy." Honig is highly critical of what she sees as Habermas's future-oriented conception of normativity because of its reliance on a teleological conception of progress as a "self-correcting learning process" (see CD, 774). Olson, by contrast, defends the dynamic constitutionalism that he sees as implicit in Habermas's work and argues that his reading shows that Habermas "need not resort to a complex theory of cultural progress to resolve the paradoxes" of constitutional democracy (Olson, "Paradoxes of Constitutional Democracy," 342). Although these readings seem at odds with my thesis that Habermas's conception of normativity depends on his backward-looking reading of history as a progressive story of sociocultural development and historical learning, I think that this discrepancy can be accounted for by the fact that both Honig and Olson are exclusively concerned with Habermas's work in political theory, specifically with his attempt to address the paradox of the founding in constitutional democracies. As I see it, this is a separate question from the broader and also ultimately (for Habermas, at least) more basic question of the grounding of normativity per se. As I read him, his work in political

theory does not introduce a wholly new conception of normativity but rather is meant to fit within the broader structure of his overall normative theory, which rests, at least in part, on his theories of social evolution and modernity—or at least so I will argue in chapter 2. As a result, I mostly leave Habermas's work in political theory aside, though I have discussed it in greater detail in Allen, "The Unforced Force of the Better Argument."

30. I shall not attempt to do justice to the whole of post- or decolonial theory here, nor do I assume that there is some unified post- or decolonial perspective, let alone one that unites both approaches. Still, I think it is fair to say that the critique of the developmental reading of history—particularly when that history is taken to culminate in the emergence of modern Europe—is central to both critical projects.
31. Tully helpfully describes the informal imperialism that persists in the wake of decolonization as consisting in "rule over another people or peoples by means of military threats and military intervention, the imposition of global markets dominated by the great powers, a dependent local governing class, and a host of other informal techniques of indirect legal, political, educational and cultural rule, such as spheres of influence and protectorates, with or without the imposition of formal colonial rule." Tully, "On Law, Democracy and Imperialism," 132.
32. For a related account, though one that culminates in a different assessment of the usefulness of Kant's philosophy of history for contemporary critical theory, see ibid., 143–149.
33. McCarthy, *Race, Empire, and the Idea of Human Development*, 67.
34. Ibid.
35. To be sure, Kant, like other Enlightenment thinkers, can also be read as an anti-imperialist. On this point, see Muthu, *Enlightenment Against Empire*. Moreover, there are lively and ongoing debates among Kant scholars about the centrality of racism to Kant's thinking. I won't attempt to settle questions of Kant interpretation here.
36. See Wallerstein, *World-Systems Analysis*, chap. 3.
37. Fanon, *The Wretched of the Earth*, 102.
38. Quijano, "Coloniality of Power," 552.
39. See Hesse, "Racialized Modernity," 647–648.
40. Said, *Orientalism*, 7. See also Mitchell, "The Stage of Modernity."
41. Buck-Morss, *Hegel, Haiti, and Universal History*, 21.
42. See Hesse, "Racialized Modernity."
43. Larmore, "History and Truth," 47. To be sure, Larmore goes on to defend the idea of progress against this charge.
44. Bhambra, *Rethinking Modernity*, 37.
45. Ibid., quoting Locke's *Two Treatises of Government*.
46. Ibid., 45.

47. Quijano, "Coloniality of Power," 541.
48. Ibid.
49. Ibid., 552.
50. Ibid., 556.
51. Bhambra, *Rethinking Modernity*, 45.
52. For a related critique of modernization theory, see McCarthy, *Race, Empire, and the Idea of Human Development*, chap. 7.
53. Ibid., 131ff.
54. On this point, see Owen, *Between Reason and History*, 29.
55. Indeed, this was one of the central arguments of Said's *Orientalism*. See especially 1–28.
56. Quijano, "Coloniality of Power," 550. For further discussion, see Mignolo, "The Geopolitics of Knowledge and the Colonial Difference" and "Delinking."
57. Chakrabarty, *Habitations of Modernity*, xix.
58. Eagleton, "Postcolonialism and 'Postcolonialism.'"
59. See Harvey, *Spaces of Capital*.
60. For a critique of the cultural turn in critical theory in light of the "post-socialist" condition of the latter decades of the twentieth century, see Fraser, *Justice Interruptus*.
61. www.youtube.com/watch?v=xbM8HJrxSJ4. The context for the debate was a discussion of Chibber's vehement Marxist critique of "postcolonialism" in his book *Postcolonial Theory and the Specter of Capital*; Chatterjee's equally impassioned response was published as "Subaltern Studies and *Capital*."
62. Young, *White Mythologies*, 1–31.
63. Ibid., 5. Said emphasizes the extent to which the crisis of modernism that gave rise to postmodernism or poststructuralism was occasioned by the disruptions and dislocations caused by formal de-colonization, even if most accounts of postmodernism, including Lyotard's, have failed to appreciate this connection. See Said, "Representing the Colonized."
64. Young, *White Mythologies*, 33.
65. To be sure, Adorno is, in some sense, a Western Marxist, but, as I shall discuss further in chapter 5, his work provides a thorough and radical critique and rethinking of the Hegelian conception of history.
66. For an argument to this effect with respect to Habermas, see Hesse, "Racialized Modernity."
67. McCarthy, *Race, Empire, and the Idea of Human Development*, 18. Henceforth cited parenthetically in the text as RED.
68. I return to this issue in chapter 3.
69. Tully, "On Law, Democracy and Imperialism," 149.
70. Marx, "The Eighteenth Brumaire of Louis Bonaparte," 608. This claim has sparked a great deal of commentary in postcolonial theory, starting

with Said, *Orientalism*, and including Spivak, *A Critique of Postcolonial Reason*, 257–264.

71. Bhambra, *Rethinking Modernity*, 75.
72. See Tully, "Political Philosophy as a Critical Activity." Tully, in turn, borrows this phrase from Foucault (PPP, 111).
73. Scott, "The Traditions of Historical Others," 6.
74. Koopman, *Genealogy as Critique*, chap. 2.
75. As I'll discuss further in chapter 3, Honneth offers a similar conception of the role of genealogy within critical theory.
76. Moyn, "The Continuing Perplexities of Human Rights."
77. Again, Forst's approach is an alternative here that moves in the opposite direction. I discuss this aspect of Forst's work in more detail in chapter 4.

2. FROM SOCIAL EVOLUTION TO MULTIPLE MODERNITIES: HISTORY AND NORMATIVITY IN HABERMAS

1. On TCA specifically, see the essays by Schnädelbach and Taylor in Honneth and Joas, *Communicative Action*. For more recent assessments, see Stahl, "Habermas and the Project of Immanent Critique"; and Finlayson, "The Persistence of Normative Questions." On Habermas's strategy for grounding normativity more generally, see Baynes, *The Normative Grounds of Social Criticism*; Benhabib, *Critique, Norm, and Utopia*; and Honneth, CP.
2. Benhabib, review of Matthew Specter, *Habermas*, 591.
3. This is closely related to, though not quite the same as, the question of whether Habermas is engaging in a form of transcendent critique—with formal pragmatics providing the universal, context-transcendent normative standard for critique—or a form of immanent critique—one that draws its normativity from the normative inheritance of the Enlightenment. For the former sort of reading, see Ingram, *Habermas*, chap. 1; for the latter, see Stahl, "Habermas and the Project of Immanent Critique"; and Finlayson, "The Persistence of Normative Questions."
4. McCormick, *Weber, Habermas, and the Transformations of the European State*, 52. McCormick argues that Habermas continues to operate with an implicit philosophy of history, and a deficient one at that. While I agree with much of McCormick's critique of Habermas's conception of history, especially his worries about its potentially ideological character and its closed conception of the future, I think that McCormick takes some of Habermas's rejections of the philosophy of history too much at face value and thus doesn't appreciate the extent to which he relies on a reformulated—postmetaphysical, deflationary, empirical—philosophy of history. See ibid., 52–56.

5. See, for example, McCarthy, *The Critical Theory of Jürgen Habermas*, chap. 3; Owen, *Between Reason and History*; and Iser, *Empörung und Fortschritt*.
6. See Eisenstadt, "Multiple Modernities" and "Multiple Modernities in an Age of Globalization."
7. See, for example, Dussel, "Eurocentrism and Modernity"; Hesse, "Racialized Modernity"; Said, *Culture and Imperialism*, 278; Spivak, *In Other Worlds*, 173 and 275; and Tully, "On Law, Democracy, and Imperialism."
8. See, for example, Baynes, *The Normative Grounds of Social Criticism*.
9. Specter, *Habermas*, 182. Quoting Habermas, "Concluding Remarks," 469.
10. See Azmanova, *The Scandal of Reason*, chap. 2; and Fraser in RR2.
11. For a portrait of Habermas as a radical reformist, see Specter, *Habermas*, 116.
12. Scheuerman, "Between Radicalism and Resignation." For a defense of Habermas against these charges, see Specter, *Habermas*.
13. See BFN for a full articulation of this position.
14. His response begins: "I'll have to get over the shock to answer such a question. . . . As I understand you, you are saying, Let's try to be early socialists, political socialists, utopian socialists, and then say what we think the design should be." Habermas, "Concluding Remarks," 469.
15. See, for example, Marx and Engels, "Manifesto of the Communist Party," section 3.3.
16. For a compelling discussion of this aspect of Habermas's work that is critical of Habermas's later work for straying too far from the methodology of STPS, see McCormick, *Weber, Habermas, and the Transformations of the European State*.
17. On the centrality of the reconstruction of historical materialism for Habermas's intellectual project, see Specter, *Habermas*, 121ff.
18. Note that this is distinct from the project of rational reconstruction, which involves the quasi-transcendental reconstruction of species competences and of the developmental sequence that leads to their achievement. The project of rational reconstruction is very closely tied to Habermas's theory of social evolution, which will be discussed in much greater detail below; indeed, the theory of social evolution is perhaps best understood as an instance of rational reconstruction applied to the question of sociocultural development. On this point, see McCarthy, *The Critical Theory of Jürgen Habermas*, 264.
19. For a contrary view, which takes Habermas's understanding of history after STPS to be more Weberian than Marxist, see McCormick, *Weber, Habermas, and the Transformations of the European State*.
20. In this sense, Marx's philosophy of history could be understood as closer to Kant's philosophy of history than to Hegel's, and the same

could be said of Habermas's own empirical philosophy of history with practical intent. As I see it, the fact that Habermas's philosophy of history is closer to Kant than to Hegel is compatible with the claim that his strategy for grounding normativity is closer to Hegel than to Kant. The reasons for this will become clear later on, as I discuss Habermas's critique of Marx's philosophy of history. I am grateful to Max Pensky for pushing me to clarify this point.

21. Interestingly, although Habermas notes the rootedness of the idea of universal history in European colonialism and imperialism, he does not see this as a reason for calling Marx's philosophy of history into question. As I discussed in the previous chapter, precisely this point has been central to the postcolonial critique of Marxist thought.
22. To be sure, the idea that the capacity to make history is a product of the European Enlightenment is itself problematic from the postcolonial point of view insofar as it implicitly positions all pre- or nonmodern peoples as "people without history." On this point, see Wolf, *Europe and the People Without History*.
23. Indeed, at this point, Habermas defends the strong claim that moral-practical development is the "pacemaker" of social evolution. CES, 120; see also TCA2, 174–180.
24. On the importance of this move for understanding Habermas's theory of social evolution, see Owen, *Between Reason and History*; and Zurn, "Jürgen Habermas," 209–210. For a critique of this move, see Bernstein, *Recovering Ethical Life*, 159–196.
25. Drawing on Marx's notebooks and the French edition of volume 1 of *Capital*, Kevin Anderson argues that Marx's late work actually offers a multilinear rather than a unilinear conception of history. See Anderson, *Marx at the Margins*.
26. In that sense I agree with Finlayson that "according to the original programme of Discourse Ethics a normative moral theory falls out of a pragmatic theory of the meaning of utterances." Finlayson, "Modernity and Morality," 320.
27. Schnädelbach, "The Transformation of Critical Theory," 16. Schnädelbach argues that Habermas fails to establish this link and therefore fails in his attempt to provide normative grounds for critical theory.
28. For a similar claim with respect to his reconstructive sociology of democratic law, see BFN, 287–288.
29. Stahl, "Habermas and the Project of Immanent Critique," 538.
30. For helpful discussion of this point with respect to Hegel's philosophy of history, see Beiser, *Hegel*, 264ff. McCarthy notes that Habermas's universalism is "Hegelian rather than Kantian in form, empirical rather than transcendental or ontological in intention." TCA1, 403n7.
31. McCarthy, *Ideals and Illusions*, 145.

32. See, for example, CES, xvii.
33. I leave aside here the important but also complicated issue of what Habermas says about aesthetic or therapeutic discourses as spaces for adjudicating expressive claims. For illuminating discussion of Habermas's treatment of aesthetic discourse, see Bernstein, *Recovering Ethical Life*; and Kompridis, *Critique and Disclosure*. Habermas defines discourse as a situation in which "the meaning of the problematic validity claim conceptually forces participants to suppose that a rationally motivated agreement could in principle be achieved, whereby the phrase 'in principle' expresses the idealizing proviso: if only the argumentation could be conducted openly enough and continued long enough" (TCA1, 42).
34. These debates were sparked in large part by the publication of Peter Winch's controversial *The Idea of a Social Science and Its Relation to Philosophy*. For an overview of the main positions in the debate, see Wilson, *Rationality*.
35. For an overlapping but slightly different list of criteria for the rationality of a lifeworld or cultural tradition, see TCA1, 71–72.
36. Note that this is a further development of the idea, discussed above, that Marx's account of social evolution needed to be expanded to encompass not only development of the forces of production but also moral-practical development. "The rationalization of the lifeworld" is the term that Habermas uses to characterize moral-practical development in his mature work.
37. Bhambra, "Historical Sociology, Modernity, and Postcolonial Critique," 656.
38. Finlayson, "The Persistence of Normative Questions."
39. For a more recent reformulation of U, see IO, 42.
40. Finlayson is also worried about Habermas's inability to successfully derive (U) from (D); see Finlayson, "The Persistence of Normative Questions," 523–524. The question of the precise relationship between (U) and (D) is complicated and the discussions on this point are rather technical; since my main concern is not the internal coherence of discourse ethics but rather the relationship between discourse ethics as a program of normative justification and Habermas's theory of modernity, I shall sidestep these questions here. But for helpful discussion, see Baynes, "Democracy and the Rechtstaat"; Finlayson, "The Persistence of Normative Questions"; Finlayson, "Modernity and Morality"; and Lafont, *The Linguistic Turn in Hermeneutic Philosophy*, chap. 7.
41. Finlayson, "The Persistence of Normative Questions," 525.
42. I will return to this issue in chapter 4 in my discussion of Rainer Forst's work.
43. Finlayson, "The Persistence of Normative Questions," 523.
44. Finlayson, "Modernity and Morality," 319.

45. On this point, see also Benhabib, *Situating the Self*, 68–88; and Rehg, *Insight and Solidarity*, 65ff.
46. This leaves open the possibility that the two elements of Habermas's theory, his discourse ethics and his theory of modernity, provide justificatory support for each other, in a coherentist fashion. I consider this possibility in further detail below.
47. I discuss this aspect of Habermas's defense of discourse ethics in Allen, "Discourse, Power, and Subjectivation."
48. On this point, see also Stahl, "Habermas and the Project of Immanent Critique."
49. Finlayson, "Modernity and Morality," 321, 337.
50. Ibid., 335.
51. I discuss the issue of contextualism in relation to the tension between facticity and validity in more detail in Allen, "The Unforced Force of the Better Argument."
52. I discuss the issue of contextualism in relation to Habermas's recent work on religion in more detail in Allen, "Having One's Cake and Eating It, Too."
53. For a representative sample, see Passerin d'Entreves and Benhabib, *Habermas and the Unfinished Project of Modernity*.
54. Dussel, "Eurocentrism and Modernity," 65.
55. Ibid., 74. See also Habermas, PDM, 23–44.
56. Note that in his later reflections on discourse ethics, Habermas retreats a bit and admits that while (U) might be thought to have smuggled in some ethnocentric assumptions, "it would be difficult to dispute the neutrality of the discourse principle (D)" since "the practice of deliberation and justification we call 'argumentation' is to be found in all cultures and societies (if not in institutionalized form, then at least as an informal practice) and that there is no functionally equivalent alternative to this mode of problem solving" (IO, 43).
57. See note 6.
58. For a related attempt to distinguish modernization from Westernization, see Heath, "Liberalization, modernization, westernization."
59. On this point, see also Chibber, *Postcolonial Theory and the Specter of Capital*, chap. 5.
60. See Amin, *Eurocentrism*, 71–86.
61. Ibid., 89.
62. Ibid., 185.
63. Bhambra, "Historical Sociology, Modernity, and Postcolonial Critique," 655.
64. Ibid.
65. For discussion of this aspect of Habermas's recent work, see Calhoun, Mendieta, and VanAntwerpen, *Habermas and Religion*.

66. Though Habermas now suggests that his earlier understanding of social evolution is too narrow (EFK, 25n51).
67. For an analogous point about the insuperable cognitive obstacles placed on the "well-intentioned hegemon" who attempts to bypass actual practical discourses and to substitute hegemonic liberalism for the constitutionalization of international law, see DW, 184–185.
68. Chakrabarty, *Provincializing Europe*, 238.
69. Chakrabarty, *Habitations of Modernity*, 33–34.
70. Ibid., 36.
71. Ibid.
72. Mahmood, *Politics of Piety*, 197–198.
73. Ibid., 199.
74. See Finlayson, "Modernity and Morality."
75. Chakrabarty, *Habitations of Modernity*, xix.

3. THE INELIMINABILITY OF PROGRESS? HONNETH'S HEGELIAN CONTEXTUALISM

1. For related reasons, Honneth also questions certain features of Habermas's theory of social evolution and of modernity, specifically, that theory's tendency to press its critical diagnosis of the times "into the narrow scheme of a theory of rationality" (SDD, 74). However, one shouldn't mis- or overinterpret Honneth's critique here. His point is not that Habermas is mistaken for leaning on a progressive, developmentalist reading of history, but merely that Habermas's account fails to appreciate the important role that social groups struggling for recognition play in social learning processes (see SDD, 77, and CP, 284). In effect, Honneth seems to understand Habermas's view of social evolution as too close to the kind of objective teleology that he associates with Hegel's philosophy of history—an objective teleology that Habermas claims to reject in his reconstruction of Marx's historical materialism in the 1970s.
2. Zurn, "Anthropology and Normativity," 119.
3. Ibid., 120–122.
4. For Honneth's critique of constructivism, see FR, 1–14.
5. Zurn, *Axel Honneth*, 226n16.
6. In this chapter, I will use the terms "ineliminable" and "ineliminability" because I think that they are better translations of Honneth's "unhintergebar" and "unhintergebarkeit," which his translator renders as "irreducible" and "irreduciblility" (see IP).
7. I am grateful to Jörg Schaub for pushing me to articulate the difference between these two kinds of necessity claims more clearly.

8. For a judicious formulation of this point, see Zurn, *Axel Honneth*, 192–194.
9. Kant, "Idea for a Universal History"; and Kant, *Critique of the Power of Judgment*, section 83.
10. Kant, "Idea for a Universal History," 424.
11. See, especially, Kant's "On the Common Saying: 'This May Be True in Theory but It Does Not Apply in Practice,'" and "Perpetual Peace." For insightful discussion and limited defense of Kant's views, see Kleingeld, "Kant, History, and the Idea of Moral Development."
12. See Kant, "The Contest of the Faculties" and "What Is Enlightenment?" For a compelling alternative account of Kant's philosophy of history in "The Contest of the Faculties," see Pensky, "Contributions Toward a Theory of Storms," 159–165.
13. For a contrary view, see Kleingeld, "Kant, History, and the Idea of Moral Development."
14. This is a debatable assumption as far as Hegel interpretation goes, but I will not explore this issue here, since whether or not Honneth has got Hegel right on this score does not affect my critique of his position. For a helpful overview of the issues, see Dudley, *Hegel and History*.
15. Kant, "What Is Enlightenment?," 462.
16. See CES, 119–120. For my discussion of this point in Habermas, see page 46.
17. See Kant, "Idea for a Universal History," second thesis.
18. See, for example, Brown, *Edgework*; Edelman, *No Future*; Eng, *The Feeling of Kinship*; and Warner, *The Trouble with Normal*. Thanks to Mari Ruti for suggesting that I clarify this point.
19. See, for example, Geuss, *Philosophy and Real Politics*; and Williams, *In the Beginning Was the Deed*.
20. Compare Habermas's related critique of utopian socialism, discussed in chapter 2.
21. But note that, as I argued in chapter 2, there is a distinctively Hegelian sense of "universal" at play in Habermas's work, inasmuch as the competence that is being reconstructed is attained only by certain individuals, namely, postconventional members of posttraditional societies. Taking this point into account, one might say that the difference between Habermasian rational reconstruction and Honneth's normative reconstruction is that the latter is more explicitly and avowedly historically indexed than the former. Hence it is a difference not in kind but in degree. For a different perspective on these two methods, see Gaus, "Rational Reconstruction as a Method."
22. Moreover, Honneth endorses a strong ontological version of this thesis, as opposed to a weaker version that merely asserts that our understandings of autonomy and freedom remain incomplete and unfulfilled

so long as we do not also pay attention to the social resources that are needed to realize them.

23. Thanks to Jörg Schaub for this point.
24. For criticisms of Honneth's rather optimistic reading of the historical trajectory of marriage and the family, see McNay, "Social Freedom in the Family"; and Zurn, *Axel Honneth*, 193 and 225n14.
25. See Duggan, "The New Homonormativity."
26. Honneth could attempt to avoid this criticism by restricting the scope of his claims about progress to European societies alone; I will discuss the problems with this potential response below.
27. Puar, *Terrorist Assemblages*, xvi.
28. Ibid., 5.
29. Puar's critique thus echoes the feminist critique of the kind of gender exceptionalism that was used, for example, by the Bush administration to justify the war in Afghanistan as necessary for saving women from the Taliban. For a recent critical discussion of such deployments of gender exceptionalism, see Abu-Lughod, *Do Muslim Women Need Saving?*
30. Puar, *Terrorist Assemblages*, 9.
31. Ibid., 38–39. Cf. Duggan, "The New Homonormativity"; on the relationship between homonormativity and "reproductive futurity," see Edelman, *No Future*.
32. Puar, *Terrorist Assemblages*, 20.
33. Ibid., 95.
34. Ibid., 78.
35. For further discussion, see below, 116–117.
36. Williams, *In the Beginning Was the Deed*, 22.
37. I'm grateful to Mari Ruti for this point. For an insightful critique of strong and weak readings of this version of Honneth's transcendental argument, see Schaub, "Misdevelopments, Pathologies, and Normative Revolutions."
38. See Butler, *Psychic Life of Power*. Thanks to Eva von Redecker for suggesting the connection to Butler here.
39. For Honneth's discussion and critique of Foucault's conception of power, see Honneth, CP.
40. Williams, *In the Beginning Was the Deed*, 6.
41. See Geuss, *The Idea of a Critical Theory*. Thanks to Jörg Schaub for reminding me of this connection.
42. On this view, Foucault can offer only empirical but never normative insights, and to think that Foucault's analysis of disciplinary power is relevant for our normative conception of autonomy is to succumb to a normative confusion. For the classic statement of this position, see Fraser, "Foucault on Modern Power."

43. I discuss this issue in relation to Habermas's work in Allen, "The Unforced Force of the Better Argument."
44. This way of putting it suggests that Honneth thinks that the two kinds of necessity claims that he raises on behalf of the idea of historical progress—the claim that belief in it is necessary to avoid sliding into relativism and that it is a transcendental-practical necessity for anyone doing critical theory—are related, in the following way: the fact that we are necessarily committed to viewing our own society as an intermediary stage in a directed process of historical development somehow justifies the norms that are embedded in our social world. I'm not convinced that Honneth does hold this view, but if he does, it seems quite obviously flawed. Even if it were the case that we were committed to the idea of historical progress by virtue of some other commitments that we hold, this does not in any way show that we are justified in making such a commitment. Engaging in the act of praying may well commit one to a belief in the existence of God, but this transcendental-practical argument does not show that the belief in God is itself justified. I'm grateful to Jörg Schaub for this point and this analogy.
45. Although, as I argued in the previous chapter, Habermas's position is probably best understood as a quasi-Hegelian coherentist one, in which the theory of modernity and the theory of formal pragmatics—the Hegelian and Kantian aspects of the theory—provide mutual support for each other.
46. Hence in this paper, Honneth attempts to respond to the charge that his critical theory is not open to the possibility of radical, revolutionary social change. For a version of this criticism, see Schaub, "Misdevelopments, Pathologies, and Normative Revolutions."
47. Thanks to Eva von Redecker for this point.
48. Chakrabarty, *Provincializing Europe*, 23.
49. Ibid., 8.
50. On this point, see Zurn, *Axel Honneth*, 194.
51. On this point, see René Gabriëls, "There Must Be Some Way out of Here."
52. A third option might be for Honneth to appeal to the notion of entangled modernities. This would allow him to avoid claiming that he could tell the story of European history without also telling the story of colonialism, as it would also allow him to decenter the Eurocentric conception of modernity. On this point, see Therborn, "Entangled Modernities." It is difficult to see how Honneth could take on board this idea, however, without radically changing his strategy for grounding normativity. Thanks to Eva von Redecker for this suggestion.
53. On this point, see Beiser, *Hegel*.

54. See Petherbridge, *The Critical Theory of Axel Honneth*; and Lear, "The Slippery Middle."
55. I'm grateful to Robert Pippin and to Christopher Zurn for suggesting this possibility.
56. For a related critique, see Schaub, "Misdevelopments, Pathologies, and Normative Revolutions."

4. FROM HEGELIAN RECONSTRUCTIVISM TO KANTIAN CONSTRUCTIVISM: FORST'S THEORY OF JUSTIFICATION

An earlier and shorter version of this chapter was published as "The Power of Justification."

1. For an interesting critique of theories of democratic self-determination on the grounds that they do not necessarily get a good critical grip on structures of informal imperialism, see Tully, "On Law, Democracy and Imperialism," 152–158.
2. Note that since Forst grounds political norms in a constructivist account of the validity of moral norms, his version of constructivism is more Kantian than Rawlsian. Compare Rawls's classic statement of constructivism, which is limited to a political conception of justice, in Rawls, "Kantian Constructivism in Moral Theory." For Forst's account of the differences between his constructivism and Rawls's, see RJ, 111ff.
3. In line with Habermas's discourse ethics, Forst focuses on the validity of moral norms rather than their truth. For Habermas's argument that normative validity is analogous to but not a species of truth, see Habermas, DE.
4. Note that Forst distinguishes his account of practical reason from Kant's because he takes Kant to fail to appreciate the intersubjective nature of morality's demands; see RJ, chap. 2, sec. 13.
5. Bagnoli, "Constructivism in Metaethics."
6. See, for example, RJ, chap. 2, esp. sec. 19, where Forst responds to Charles Larmore.
7. The qualifier "reasonably" is significant here inasmuch as it indicates that Forst's view aims not at de facto rejection (or acceptance) of a validity claim but rather at idealized acceptability. In other words, the relevant metric here is not whether as a matter of fact individuals do reject a certain validity claim as insufficiently reciprocal or general but rather whether they could or would do so. See RJ, 21–22. For insightful discussion of this point and an interesting attempt to push Forst's theory in a more pragmatic direction, see Laden, "The Practice of Equality," 121–123. For Forst's reply, see JJ, 193–199.
8. Compare Habermas's essay "On the Pragmatic, the Ethical, and the Moral Employments of Practical Reason," in JA, which offers a pro-

grammatic sketch of the framework that Forst's book works out in much greater detail.

9. Here Forst parts company with Habermas's position as it is articulated in *Between Facts and Norms*, where Habermas attempts to derive his system of political rights from a combination of the discourse principle and the legal form, leaving specifically moral considerations aside (see Habermas, BFN, 118–131). Forst regards this strategy as "overly immanent to law" (RJ, 109) and argues instead for an integrated, two-stage moral and political constructivism in which "moral justification (according to the strict criteria of reciprocity and generality)" forms "the core of every fundamental political legitimation" (RJ, 110).
10. The overarching role played by moral contexts of justification is the key to the difference between Forst's account and the alternative approach offered in Boltanski and Thévenot, *On Justification*. Like Forst, Boltanski and Thévenot analyze society as an ensemble of practices of justification, but they refrain from positing an overarching logic of justification that transcends the specific orders of justification, or *cités*, that they delineate. See Forst, JC, 5n7.
11. On this point, see Bagnoli, "Constructivism in Metaethics"; and Street's discussion of restricted constructivism in "Constructivism About Reasons."
12. On this point, see Laden, "The Practice of Equality."
13. On the distinction between philosophical and political justifications of normativity, see Laden, "The Justice of Justification." I will come back to this issue in chapter 6.
14. In feminist theory, the locus classicus of such discussion is Lloyd, *The Man of Reason*; in critical race and postcolonial theory, the central text is Fanon, *Black Skin, White Masks*, but a more recent postcolonial feminist articulation can be found in Spivak, *A Critique of Postcolonial Reason*, chap. 1; for a recent articulation of this critique from the point of view of queer theory, see Huffer, *Mad for Foucault*.
15. On this point, McCarthy, *Race, Empire and the Idea of Human Development*, 42–68.
16. Tully, "On Law, Democracy, and Imperialism," 148–149.
17. I borrow this way of using the pessimistic induction strategy from Kenneth Walden. See Walden, "Practical Reason Not as Such."
18. See ibid.
19. Given its reliance on this kind of transcendental argument, Forst's position could be aptly characterized, following Laden's critique of Habermas, as a combination of democratic politics and transcendental philosophy. See Laden, "The Justice of Justification," 141–144. Contra Laden, I think that Forst is a better candidate for this label than Habermas,

because describing Habermas's position in this way only makes sense if one plays down the role of his theory of modernity.

20. See Allen, Forst, and Haugaard, "Power and Reason, Justice and Domination."
21. Heidegger, *Being and Time*, sections 12–13.
22. As I discuss in detail in *The Politics of Our Selves*, chap. 5.
23. For the related claim that one cannot choose to be a practical reasoner for a reason, see Street, "Constructivism About Reasons."
24. On this point see Saar, "Power, Constitution, Discourse."
25. I discuss this issue in more detail, in relation to Judith Butler's theory of subjection, in Allen, *The Politics of Our Selves*, chap. 4.
26. Fanon, *Black Skin, White Masks*, xiv–xv.
27. Ibid., xviii, xii.
28. Contra Forst, JJ, 183.
29. See Taylor, *Sources of the Self*, although, to be sure, Taylor does not claim that the modern form of identity is ideological or bound up with relations of domination. This is where the communitarian critique and my more Foucaultian and Adornian critique of practical reason diverge.
30. In connection with this, it is perhaps worth noting that Forst's central concept, that of justification, emerges from a specific religious tradition, namely, the Christian tradition that stretches from the writings of the apostle Paul and St. Augustine to Martin Luther.
31. On this point, see Benhabib, *Situating the Self*; and Bernstein, *Recovering Ethical Life*.
32. See TP for elaboration of this idea; for insightful reconstruction of Forst's critique of the distributive paradigm of justice, see Laden, "The Practice of Equality."
33. As I discussed above and also in Allen, "The Power of Justification."
34. Hence, Forst's definition of power is a variation on Robert Dahl's classic definition: "A has power over B to the extent that he can get B to do something that B would not otherwise do." Dahl, "The Concept of Power," 203–204. Forst's modified Dahlian account defines power as "*the capacity of A to motivate B to think or do something that B would otherwise not have thought or done*" (NP, 5).
35. Allen, Forst, and Haugaard, "Power and Reason, Justice and Domination," 12.
36. Forst's attempt to demonstrate how the account of noumenal power can explain the power of "structures" confirms this suspicion. See NP, 8–12. However, Forst insists that the power of structures also ultimately rests on the "acceptance of the rules of these structures, as well as of certain justifications for them" (NP, 9).
37. Saar, "Power, Constitution, Discourse," 8.

38. Forst's recent protestations to the contrary notwithstanding; see JC, 1–6.
39. For compelling critical discussions of Rawls that foreground this issue, see Geuss, *Philosophy and Real Politics*; and Freyenhagen and Schaub, "Hat hier jemand gesagt."
40. Olson, "Complexities of Political Discourse," 97.
41. Bourdieu, *Practical Reason*, 136; cited in Olson, "Complexities of Political Discourse," 98.
42. Olson, "Complexities of Political Discourse," 98.
43. Spivak points out that even the use of the term "sati" to refer to this phenomena is problematic, since the term literally means "the good wife," and only gets applied to the self-immolating widow by means of the further assumption that throwing herself on the funereal pyre is what the good wife would do. See Spivak, *Critique of Postcolonial Reason*, 303. Henceforth cited parenthetically in the text as CPR.
44. Tully, "On Law, Democracy, and Imperialism," 159.
45. For an insightful analysis of how the "white women saving brown women from brown men" dynamics play out in some contemporary feminist movements, see Abu-Lughod, *Do Muslim Women Need Saving?*; and Mahmood, "Feminism, Democracy, and Empire." I discuss these issues in more detail in Allen, "Emancipation Without Utopia."
46. Spivak writes: "No account of Kant's universalism can account for this moment," namely, "the perspective of the 'native informant'" (CPR, 35).
47. On a related point, both Olson and Laden suggest that Forst's theory focuses too much on an idealized conception of the ways that individuals ideally would or should interact with one another in political contexts, rather than on their actual practices. See Olson, "Complexities of Political Discourse"; and Laden, "The Practice of Equality."
48. See Olson, "Complexities of Political Discourse," 98.
49. See Boltanski and Thévenot, "The Sociology of Critical Capacity" and *On Justification*.
50. Alternatively, one could take a more Humean line and argue that it may be possible to identify something like practical reason as such, but insist that whatever practical reason as such is, it is too thin and abstract a notion to supply the kind of normative content that Forst thinks he can get out of it. On this point, see Sharon Street, "Constructivism about Reasons."
51. On this point, see Hartsock, "Community/Sexuality/Gender," 39.
52. On this point, see Butler, "Contingent Foundations," 39.
53. See Linda Martín Alcoff, "The Problem of Speaking for Others."
54. For a compelling defense of this form of critique, see Honneth, "The Possibility of a Disclosing Critique of Society." On the role of world

disclosure in relation to critique more generally, see Kompridis, *Critique and Disclosure*.

55. I return to this issue in chapters 5 and 6.
56. I argue for this way of understanding the project of critical theory in "The Unforced Force of the Better Argument." Interestingly enough, Habermas himself comes closer to the view I am advocating—though not, as I argue, close enough—in his discussion of law in BFN. Forst explicitly distances himself from this aspect of Habermas's thought in chapter 4 of RJ; see especially RJ, 113–116.
57. Freyenhagen and Schaub, "Hat hier jemand gesagt," 464.
58. Chakrabarty, *Provincializing Europe*, 238.

5. FROM THE *DIALECTIC OF ENLIGHTENMENT* TO THE *HISTORY OF MADNESS*: FOUCAULT AS ADORNO'S OTHER "OTHER SON"

1. In the speech that he gave accepting the Adorno Prize in September, 2001, Jacques Derrida acknowledged his debt to Adorno and presented himself as an "heir to the Frankfurt School," even going so far as to refer to Adorno as his "adoptive father" (Derrida, "Fichus," 176 and 174). In this way, as Jean-Philippe Deranty argues, Derrida presents himself as Adorno's "other" son, a sibling rival to the contemporary philosopher more closely identified with Adorno's legacy, Jürgen Habermas (Deranty, "Adorno's Other Son"). For helpful discussions of the philosophical affinities between Adorno and Foucault, see Bernstein, *Recovering Ethical Life*, chap. 6; Butler, *Giving an Account of Oneself*; Dews, *Logics of Disintegration*; Pensky, "Introduction," in *The Actuality of Adorno*; and Wellmer, *The Persistence of Modernity*, 59–64.
2. See PDM, 126–130 (on Horkheimer and Adorno), and 276–281 (on Foucault).
3. Derrida, *Specters of Marx*, 54.
4. For the claim that Adorno is operating "outside ethics," see Geuss, *Outside Ethics*, 40–66. For the classic statement of the problem of normative confusion in Foucault, see Fraser, "Foucault on Modern Power."
5. See Allen, *The Politics of Our Selves*, esp. chap. 3.
6. Especially Bernstein, *Adorno*; and Freyenhagen, *Adorno's Practical Philosophy*.
7. Any discussion of the *Dialectic of Enlightenment* is complicated by the fact that this is a coauthored text. This raises complex interpretive questions that I unfortunately cannot take up here. In what follows, I will treat *Dialectic of Enlightenment* as if it is representative of Adorno's thinking; in so doing, I take Horkheimer and Adorno at their word when they say in their preface from 1969 that "no one who was not

involved in the writing could easily understand to what extent we both feel responsible for every sentence" (DE, xi). My decision to read *Dialectic of Enlightenment* alongside Adorno's later work in the philosophy of history and moral philosophy is further justified by the fact that Adorno's philosophy, unlike Horkheimer's, remained remarkably consistent throughout his career. Indeed, Adorno himself favorably references the argument of *Dialectic of Enlightenment* throughout his later work.

8. On this point, see Wellmer, *The Persistence of Modernity*, 1–35.
9. For helpful discussions of the positive epistemic and critical role of contradictions in Adorno's work, see Bernstein, "Negative Dialectic as Fate"; and O'Connor, "Adorno's Reconception of the Dialectic."
10. On this point, see Habermas, PDM, 106–130. Although Habermas recognizes the aporetic structure of the text, he suggests that Horkheimer and Adorno back into this aporia unwittingly because their attempt to engage in a totalizing critique of enlightenment rationality reduces such rationality to domination and thus leads them into a performative contradiction. In my view, Horkheimer and Adorno do not attempt a totalizing critique of enlightenment, nor are they unwittingly caught in this aporia; rather, their aim is to call attention to this aporia, and this is in service of an immanent rather than a totalizing critique of enlightenment rationality. I develop this point at greater length in Allen, "Reason, Power, and History." For a closely related reading, see Rocco, "Between Modernity and Postmodernity."
11. But note that there are good reasons for doubting whether or not Habermas's turn to communicative rationality really does constitute a "way out," at least on the terms specified by the *Dialectic of Enlightenment*. See Allen, "Reason, Power, and History."
12. For insightful discussion of this point, see Bernstein, "Negative Dialectic as Fate."
13. Compare Foucault's characterization of his own critical project as an attempt to articulate a "rational critique of rationality" that is also a "contingent history of reason." See CT/IH, 118.
14. Despite the fact that he uses Benjamin to formulate the problem with the concept of progress, Adorno is skeptical of Benjamin's notion of messianic time. For helpful discussion of this point, see O'Connor, "Adorno's Philosophy of History," 10–11; for a contrary, nonmessianic reading of Benjamin's philosophy of history, see Pensky, "Contributions Toward a Theory of Storms."
15. O'Connor, "Adorno's Philosophy of History," 186.
16. Finlayson, "Adorno on the Ethical and the Ineffable."
17. Ibid., 6.
18. For the critics, see esp. Habermas, PDM, 238–265. For the supporters, see esp. Huffer, *Mad for Foucault*. I offer an extended critical response

to Huffer's reading in Allen, "Feminism, Foucault, and the Critique of Reason."

19. For a related analysis of the connection between Foucault's late conception of critique and his early work—in this case, his thesis on Kant's anthropology and related early writings—see Allen, *The Politics of Our Selves*, chap. 2; and Rajchman, "Enlightenment Today."
20. On the importance of both contingency and complexity for Foucault's genealogical method, see Koopman, *Genealogy as Critique*, chap. 3.
21. Huffer, *Mad for Foucault*, 199.
22. On the importance of discontinuity in Adorno, see O'Connor, "Adorno's Philosophy of History."
23. For helpful discussion of this transformation in Foucault's historico-philosophical method, see Koopman, *Genealogy as Critique*, chap. 1.
24. On this point, see Young, *White Mythologies*, chap. 5.
25. For a discussion of the links between Foucault's approach to history and the political aim of his conception of critique, see ABHS, 222–223.
26. See O'Farrell, *Foucault*, 35. To be sure, Foucault may well be guilty of killing History as Sartre understands it. See Young, *White Mythologies*, chap. 3.
27. Here I agree with Leonard Lawlor, who is careful to distinguish unreason from madness and to link freedom only with the former. But he also suggests that freedom in the *History of Madness* means being unreasonable, whereas I draw the connection to freedom differently. See Lawlor, "Violence and Animality."
28. Thanks to Lynne Huffer for helpful discussion of this point.
29. Derrida, "Cogito and the History of Madness," 43. Henceforth cited parenthetically in the text as CHM.
30. See also PT, 137–139.
31. See, for example, CT/IH, 126.
32. Note that here Foucault distinguishes this approach explicitly from Habermas's rival approach, which focuses on "an investigation into the legitimacy of historical modes of knowing" (PT, 58).
33. On Foucault's relationship to utopian thinking, see Kelly, "Against Prophecy and Utopia"; and Allen, "Emancipation Without Utopia."
34. For a compelling defense of Adorno's negativism, see Freyenhagen, *Adorno's Practical Philosophy*.
35. See Wellmer, *The Persistence of Modernity*, 63.
36. I am deeply indebted to Nikolas Kompridis for my thinking here about the critical-utopian task of critical theory. See Kompridis, "Re-Envisioning Critical Theory" and, more generally, *Critique and Disclosure*. I reply to Kompridis's critique of my earlier work in Allen, "Normativity, Power, and Gender."

37. On this point, see, for example, Hohendahl, "Progress Revisited," 246; and Vázquez-Arroyo, "Universal History Disavowed," 458.
38. See also Adorno, "The Actuality of Philosophy," for an earlier version of this critique.
39. On this point, see Geuss, *Outside Ethics*, 153–160.
40. Again, see Koopman, *Genealogy as Critique*, chap. 3.
41. Ibid., chap. 2. See also Williams, *Truth and Truthfulness.*
42. Nietzsche, *On the Genealogy of Morals*, 20.
43. See Geuss, *Outside Ethics*, 158.
44. Nietzsche's work can be taken as a paradigm case of subversive genealogy; on this point, see Koopman, *Genealogy as Critique*, 73–83.
45. Koopman takes Williams's genealogies to be exemplary of the vindicatory approach; see ibid., 65–73. Elsewhere, I argue that Habermas's use of genealogy in his recent work is in the end a vindicatory one, and that this shows how far apart his use of this term is from Foucault's. See Allen, "Having One's Cake and Eating It, Too."
46. Note that implicit in these two quotations are two distinct but related senses of "problematization": the verbal sense, where the aim of genealogical critique is to problematize something, to put it into question, or to render it problematic, and the nominal sense, where a problematization is the object of genealogical inquiry. My focus here is on the former but both are crucial for understanding Foucault's use of the term. For helpful discussion, see Koopman, *Genealogy as Critique*, 98–103.
47. The genealogical element in Adorno should not be too surprising, given the heavy influence of Nietzsche on his work. For insightful discussions of Adorno's relation to Nietzsche, particularly with respect to method, see Rose, *The Melancholy Science*, chap. 2; and Menke, "Genealogy and Critique."
48. Bernstein, *Adorno*, 238–239.
49. See also MM, 151. Pensky notes the affinity between Adorno and Foucault on this point in *The Ends of Solidarity*, 34.
50. On this point, see Bernstein, "Negative Dialectic as Fate," 38. Here I part company with O'Connor, who presents negative dialectics as offering a transcendental account of the necessary and universal structures of experience. See O'Connor, *Adorno's Negative Dialectic.*
51. Saar, "Genealogy and Subjectivity," 236.
52. Lydia Goehr emphasizes the importance of exaggeration for Adorno's style; see Goehr, "Reviewing Adorno," xxiii–xxvi.
53. Saar, "Genealogy and Subjectivity," 239. For a related analysis of the *Dialectic of Enlightenment* as a form of critical world disclosure, see Honneth, PDCS.

54. For a related argument with respect to Adorno, see Freyenhagen, *Adorno's Practical Philosophy*, 82–83.
55. On this point, see also Saar, "Genealogy and Subjectivity," 233.
56. On this point, I part company with Koopman's and Geuss's readings of critique as problematization in Foucault. For details of my disagreement with Koopman, see Allen, "The Normative and the Transcendental."
57. Fabian Freyenhagen gives a compelling account of this under the heading of "living less wrongly." See Freyenhagen, *Adorno's Practical Philosophy*, 133–186.
58. For a discussion of modesty as one of the three virtues implicit in Adorno's ethics of resistance, see Finlayson, "Adorno on the Ethical and the Ineffable," 6–8. For a related account, though one that refrains from endorsing the term "virtue," see Freyenhagen, *Adorno's Practical Philosophy*, 175.
59. For insightful discussion of this point, see Saar, "Genealogy and Subjectivity."
60. For an argument to this effect, see Saar, *Genealogie als Kritik*.
61. Consider Adorno's sharp criticism of the very idea of transcendent critique: "Transcendent critique sympathizes with authority in its very form, even before expressing any content. . . . Anyone who judges something that has been articulated and elaborated—art or philosophy—by presuppositions that do not hold within it is behaving in a reactionary manner, even when he swears by progressive slogans" (H, 146; cf. PMP, 174–175). However, as Robyn Marasco argues, Adorno was also quite cognizant of the pitfalls of immanent critique, even as he hesitantly embraced this "more essentially dialectical" form. See Marasco, *The Highway of Despair*, 97; cf. Adorno, CCS, 31–34.
62. I suspect that Foucault would be much more skeptical than Adorno is about the possibility of progress in the future. For myself, I am won over by Adorno's argument that to conclude that progress in the future is impossible simply because it has not occurred up to now is to make a false inference. If x is actual, then it follows that x is possible; but from the fact that x is not actual, it does not follow that x is impossible. This is, of course, not to settle the extremely thorny question of how we could possibly determine what would count as historical progress in the future. I will attempt to address that metanormative question in the next chapter.
63. An admittedly partial list of other important works of postcolonial theory and studies that have been heavily though not uncritically influenced by Foucault would include Bhaba, *The Location of Culture*; Chakrabarty, *Provincializing Europe*; Chatterjee, *The Nation and Its Fragments* and *The Politics of the Governed*; Mahmood, *Politics of Piety*; Mignolo, *The Darker*

Side of Western Modernity; Scott, *Refashioning Futures*; and Young, *White Mythologies* and *Postcolonialism*.

64. See Young, "Foucault on Race and Colonialism."
65. Stoler, *Race and the Education of Desire*, 1.
66. For a helpful overview, see Nichols, "Postcolonial Studies and the Discourse of Foucault."
67. Stoler, *Race and the Education of Desire*, 5.
68. Young, "Foucault on Race and Colonialism," 57.
69. Hammer, *Adorno and the Political*, 5.
70. Gibson and Rubin, "Introduction," 14.
71. See, for example, Gilroy, *Postcolonial Melancholia*; Goswami, "The (M)other of All Posts"; Patke, "Adorno and the Postcolonial"; Spencer, "Thoughts from Abroad"; Varadharajan, *Exotic Parodies*; Vázquez-Arroyo, "Universal History Disavowed."
72. Goswami, "The (M)other of All Posts," 105–106.
73. Ibid., 108.
74. Chakrabarty, *Provincializing Europe*, 6.
75. See, for example, Spivak, CPR, 309.
76. Chakrabarty, *Provincializing Europe*, 94.
77. See especially Mignolo, "Delinking."
78. Chakrabarty, *Habitations of Modernity*, 36.

6. CONCLUSION: "TRUTH," REASON, AND HISTORY

1. On a related note, see Alcoff, *Real Knowing*, 205.
2. Bernstein, *Adorno*, 238. For a related argument, see Schweppenhäuser, "Adorno's Negative Moral Philosophy."
3. Menke, "Genealogy and Critique," 321–322.
4. Paradoxically, or at least counterintuitively, this might include being willing to question even the commitment to freedom itself, at least where this is understood as freedom as autonomy. I take it that something like this is the motivation behind Mahmood's *Politics of Piety*. For interesting critical discussion, see Weir, *Identities and Freedom*, chap. 5.
5. Jameson, *The Political Unconscious*, 9. For a related discussion, see Young, *White Mythologies*, chap. 6.
6. Chakrabarty, *Provincializing Europe*, 111.
7. Critical theory also needs a different conception of genealogy than the basically vindicatory conception endorsed by Habermas; on this point, see Allen, "Having One's Cake and Eating It, Too."
8. On this point, see Allen, "The Unforced Force of the Better Argument."
9. Menke, "Genealogy and Critique," 302. Henceforth cited parenthetically in the text as GC.

10. Mignolo, “Delinking,” 485.
11. Again, on the importance of both contingency and complexity as aspects of genealogical critique, see Koopman, *Genealogy as Critique*.
12. Chakrabarty, *Habitations of Modernity*, 36.
13. Butler, *Giving an Account of Oneself*, 103.
14. There are some subtle differences between their views, which I will discuss briefly below. But, for my purposes, these differences are less important than their shared commitment to a nonrelativistic, nonskeptical contextualism about epistemic justification.
15. Williams, *Unnatural Doubts*.
16. Ibid., 119.
17. Ibid., 113.
18. Alcoff, *Real Knowing*, 205. Henceforth cited parenthetically in the text as RK.
19. Another place where Alcoff and Williams differ is on the question of truth. Alcoff attempts to offer a coherentist account of truth that provides an alternative to metaphysical realism and Williams gives a more deflationary account of truth as semantic but sees his contextualism as compatible with metaphysical realism. But this isn't relevant for my purposes because I follow Habermas in thinking that when it comes to the normative domain what we aim for is not truth but rather normative validity or justification. See Habermas, DE.
20. For a related attempt to develop a metanormative contextualist position while avoiding relativism, but one that draws on a Wittgensteinian-pragmatist reading of Rawls, see Laden, “The Justice of Justification” and “Constructivism as Rhetoric.”
21. See Butler, “Contingent Foundations.” The approach described here could also be understood as a version of what Nancy Fraser and Linda Nicholson once called “Social Criticism Without Philosophy.”
22. On the need to resist epistemic authoritarianism, see also Cooke, *Re-Presenting the Good Society*.
23. On the compatibility of contingency and universality in normativity, see Koopman, *Genealogy as Critique*, chap. 7.
24. On this point, see the excellent discussion in Freyenhagen, *Adorno's Practical Philosophy*, 136–141.
25. Compare Freyenhagen, who claims that Adorno's negativism is objective. See ibid., 197ff.
26. See Boltanski and Thévenot, *On Justification*.
27. Here my view comes very close to Laden's radical Wittgensteinian reading of Rawls. See Laden, “Constructivism as Rhetoric.”
28. Chakrabarty, *Habitations of Modernity*, 36.
29. On this point, see Bernstein, “Negative Dialectic as Fate,” 40.
30. Laden, *Reasoning*. Henceforth cited parenthetically in the text as RASP.

31. Laden, "The Practice of Equality," 124.
32. For a related account, see Zerilli, "Toward a Feminist Theory of Judgment."
33. In this way, I think that Laden's social picture of reason fits together quite well with Boltanski and Thévenot's sociology of critique, inasmuch as both views envision the possibility of critique across spaces of reasons or orders of justification without appealing to some overarching conception of reason or justification as such that unifies all of these spaces or orders or assembles them into a hierarchy. See Boltanski and Thévenot, *On Justification*; and my discussion of their work above and in chapter 4.
34. I also think, though I don't have the space to go into it here, that it does so in a way that is preferable to the Heideggerian approach that Chakrabarty himself sketches out in *Provincializing Europe*, 249–255.
35. Thanks to Kevin Olson for pressing this point.
36. Thanks to both Dick Bernstein and Kevin Olson for pressing this point.
37. For a recent and forceful version of this criticism, see Chibber, *Postcolonial Theory and the Specter of Capital*.
38. A particularly influential version of this critique of postmodernism in critical theory is Habermas (PDM).
39. This suggests a way of responding to the reverse Orientalism charge; see, for example, Chibber, *Postcolonial Theory and the Specter of Capital*, 288–290.

BIBLIOGRAPHY

Abu-Lughod, Lila. *Do Muslim Women Need Saving?* Cambridge, Mass.: Harvard University Press, 2013.

Adorno, Theodor. "The Actuality of Philosophy." *Telos*, no. 31 (Spring 1977): 120–133.

——. "Cultural Criticism and Society." In *Prisms*, translated by Samuel M. Weber. Cambridge, Mass.: MIT Press, 1967.

——. "The Essay as Form." In *Notes to Literature*, vol. 1, edited by Rolf Tiedemann, translated by Shierry Weber Nicholsen. New York: Columbia University Press, 1991.

——. *Hegel: Three Studies*, Translated by Shierry Weber Nicholsen. Cambridge, Mass.: MIT Press, 1993.

——. *History and Freedom: Lectures, 1964–1965*. Edited by Rolf Tiedemann. Translated by Rodney Livingstone. Cambridge: Polity, 2006.

——. *Minima Moralia: Reflections on a Damaged Life*. Translated by E.F.N. Jephcott. London: Verso, 2005.

——. *Negative Dialectics*. Translated by E. B. Ashton. New York: Continuum, 1973.

——. *Problems of Moral Philosophy*. Edited by Thomas Schröder. Translated by Rodney Livingstone. Stanford: Stanford University Press, 2001.

——. "Progress." In *Critical Models: Interventions and Catchwords*, translated by Henry Pickford. New York: Columbia University Press, 2005.

Adorno, Theodor, and Max Horkheimer. *Dialectic of Enlightenment: Philosophical Fragments*. Translated by Edmund Jephcott. Stanford: Stanford University Press, 2002.

Alcoff, Linda Martín. "The Problem of Speaking for Others." *Cultural Critique* 20 (1991/1992): 5–32.

——. *Real Knowing: New Versions of the Coherence Theory*. Ithaca: Cornell University Press, 1996.

Allen, Amy. "Discourse, Power, and Subjectivation: The Foucault/Habermas Debate Reconsidered." *Philosophical Forum* 40, no. 1 (Spring 2009): 1–28.

——. "Emancipation Without Utopia: Subjection, Modernity, and the Normative Claims of Feminist Critical Theory." *Hypatia* (Summer 2015).

——. "Feminism, Foucault, and the Critique of Reason: Re-Reading the *History of Madness*." *Foucault Studies* 16 (September 2013): 15–31.

——. "Having One's Cake and Eating It, Too: Habermas's Genealogy of Post-Secular Reason." In Calhoun, Mendieta, and VanAntwerpen, *Habermas and Religion*.

——. "The Normative and the Transcendental: Comments on Colin Koopman's *Genealogy as Critique*." *Foucault Studies* 18 (October 2014): 238–244.

——. "Normativity, Power, and Gender: Reply to Critics." *Critical Horizons* 15, no. 1 (March 2014): 52–68.

——. *The Politics of Our Selves: Power, Autonomy, and Gender in Contemporary Critical Theory*. New York: Columbia University Press, 2008.

——. "The Power of Justification." In *Justice, Democracy and The Right to Justification: Rainer Forst in Dialogue*, edited by David Owen. London: Bloomsbury, 2014.

——. "Reason, Power, and History: Re-Reading the *Dialectic of Enlightenment*." *Thesis Eleven* 120, no. 1 (February 2014): 10–25.

——. "The Unforced Force of the Better Argument: Reason and Power in Habermas's Political Theory." *Constellations* 19, no. 3 (September 2012): 353–368.

Allen, Amy, Rainer Forst, and Mark Haugaard. "Power and Reason, Justice and Domination: A Conversation." *Journal of Political Power* 7, no. 1 (April 2014): 7–33.

Amin, Samir. *Eurocentrism*. 2nd ed. New York: Monthly Review Press, 2009.

Anderson, Kevin. *Marx at the Margins: On Nationalism, Ethnicity, and Non-Western Societies*. Chicago: University of Chicago Press, 2010.

Azmanova, Albena. *The Scandal of Reason: A Critical Theory of Political Judgment*. New York: Columbia University Press, 2012.

Bagnoli, Carla. "Constructivism in Metaethics." *Stanford Encyclopedia of Philosophy*, September 27, 2011. http://plato.stanford.edu/entries/constructivism-metaethics/.

Baynes, Kenneth. "Democracy and the Rechtstaat: Habermas's *Faktizität und Geltung*." In *The Cambridge Companion to Habermas*, edited by Stephen K. White. Cambridge: Cambridge University Press, 1995.

——. *The Normative Grounds of Social Criticism: Kant, Rawls, and Habermas*. Albany: State University of New York Press, 1991.

Beiser, Frederick. *Hegel*. New York: Routledge, 2005.

Benhabib, Seyla. *Critique, Norm, and Utopia: A Study of the Foundations of Critical Theory*. New York: Columbia University Press, 1987.

——. Review of Matthew Specter, *Habermas: An Intellectual Biography*. *Constellations* 18, no. 4 (December 2011): 589–595.

——. *Situating the Self: Gender, Community and Postmodernism in Contemporary Ethics*. New York: Routledge, 1992.

Benjamin, Walter. *Illuminations: Essays and Reflections*. Translated by Harry Zohn. New York: Schocken, 2007.

Bernstein, Jay. *Adorno: Disenchantment and Ethics*. Cambridge: Cambridge University Press, 2001.

——. "Negative Dialectic as Fate: Adorno and Hegel." In *The Cambridge Companion to Adorno*, edited by Tom Huhn. Cambridge: Cambridge University Press, 2004.

——. *Recovering Ethical Life: Jürgen Habermas and the Future of Critical Theory*. New York: Routledge, 1995.

Bhaba, Homi. *The Location of Culture*. New York: Routledge, 1994.

Bhambra, Gurminder. "Historical Sociology, Modernity, and Postcolonial Critique." *American Historical Review* 116, no. 3 (June 2011): 653–662.

——. *Rethinking Modernity: Postcolonialism and the Sociological Imagination*. London: Palgrave Macmillan, 2007.

Boltanski, Luc, and Laurent Thévenot. *On Justification: Economies of Worth*. Translated by Catherine Porter. Princeton: Princeton University Press, 2006.

——. "The Sociology of Critical Capacity." *European Journal of Social Theory* 2, no. 3 (1999): 359–377.

Bourdieu, Pierre. *Practical Reason: On the Theory of Action*. Cambridge: Polity, 1998.

Brown, Wendy. *Edgework: Critical Essays on Knowledge and Politics*. Princeton: Princeton University Press, 2005.

Buck-Morss, Susan. *Hegel, Haiti, and Universal History*. Pittsburgh: University of Pittsburgh Press, 2009.

Butler, Judith. "Contingent Foundations: Feminism and the Question of 'Postmodernism.'" In *Feminist Contentions: A Philosophical Exchange*, by Seyla Benhabib, Judith Butler, Nancy Fraser, and Drucilla Cornell, edited by Linda Nicholson. New York: Routledge, 1995.

——. *Giving an Account of Oneself*. New York: Fordham University Press, 2005.

——. *The Psychic Life of Power: Theories in Subjection*. Stanford: Stanford University Press, 1997.

Calhoun, Craig, Eduardo Mendieta, and Jonathan VanAntwerpen, eds. *Habermas and Religion*. Cambridge: Polity, 2013.

Chakrabarty, Dipesh. *Habitations of Modernity: Essays in the Wake of Subaltern Studies*. Chicago: University of Chicago Press, 2002.

——. *Provincializing Europe: Postcolonial Thought and Historical Difference*. Reissue ed. Princeton: Princeton University Press, 2008.

Chatterjee, Partha. *The Nation and Its Fragments*. Princeton: Princeton University Press, 1993.

——. *The Politics of the Governed*. New York: Columbia University Press, 2004.

——. "Subaltern Studies and *Capital*." *Economic and Political Weekly* 48, no. 37 (September 14, 2013): 69–75.

Chibber, Vivek. *Postcolonial Theory and the Specter of Capital*. London: Verso, 2013.

Cooke, Maeve. *Re-Presenting the Good Society*. Cambridge, Mass.: MIT Press, 2006.

Cornell, Drucilla. *Moral Images of Freedom: A Future for Critical Theory*. Lanham, Md.: Rowman and Littlefield, 2008.

Dahl, Robert. "The Concept of Power." *Behavioral Science* 2, no. 3 (July 1957): 201–215.

Deranty, Jean-Philippe. "Adorno's Other Son: Derrida and the Future of Critical Theory." *Social Semiotics* 16, no. 3 (September 2006): 421–433.

Derrida, Jacques. "Cogito and the History of Madness." In *Writing and Difference*, translated by Alan Bass. Chicago: University of Chicago Press, 1978.

——. "Fichus: Frankfurt Address." In *Paper Machine*, translated by Rachel Bowlby. Stanford: Stanford University Press, 2005.

——. *Specters of Marx: The State of the Debt, the Work of Mourning, and the New International*. Translated by Peggy Kamuf. New York: Routledge, 1994.

Dews, Peter. *Logics of Disintegration: Post-Structuralist Thought and the Claims of Critical Theory*. London: Verso, 1987.

Dudley, William C., ed. *Hegel and History*. Albany: State University of New York Press, 2009.

Duggan, Lisa. "The New Homonormativity: The Sexual Politics of Neoliberalism." In *Materializing Democracy: Toward a Revitalized Cultural Politics*, edited by Ross Castronovo and Dana Nelson. Durham: Duke University Press, 2002.

Dussel, Enrique. "Eurocentrism and Modernity." *Boundary 2* 20, no. 3 (Autumn 1993): 65–76.

Eagleton, Terry. "Postcolonialism and 'Postcolonialism.'" *Interventions* 1, no. 1 (1998): 24–26.

Edelman, Lee. *No Future: Queer Theory and the Death Drive*. Durham: Duke University Press, 2004.

Eisenstadt, S. N. "Multiple Modernities." *Daedalus* 129, no. 1 (Winter 2000): 1–29.

——. "Multiple Modernities in an Age of Globalization." *Canadian Journal of Sociology* 24, no. 2 (Spring 1999): 283–295.

Eng, David. *The Feeling of Kinship: Queer Liberalism and the Racialization of Intimacy*. Durham: Duke University Press, 2010.

Fanon, Frantz. *Black Skin, White Masks*. Translated by Richard Philcox. New York: Grove, 2008.

——. *The Wretched of the Earth*. Translated by Richard Philcox. New York: Grove, 2005.

Finlayson, James Gordon. "Adorno on the Ethical and the Ineffable." *European Journal of Philosophy* 10, no. 1 (2002): 1–25.

——. "Modernity and Morality in Habermas's Discourse Ethics." *Inquiry* 43 (2000): 319–340.

——. "The Persistence of Normative Questions in Habermas's *Theory of Communicative Action*." *Constellations* 20, no. 4 (December 2013): 518–532.

Forst, Rainer. *Contexts of Justice: Political Philosophy Beyond Liberalism and Communitarianism*. Translated by John M. Farrell. Berkeley: University of California Press, 2002.

——. *Justification and Critique: Towards a Critical Theory of Politics*. Translated by Ciaran Cronin. Cambridge: Polity, 2014.

——. "Justifying Justification: Reply to My Critics." In *Justice, Democracy and the Right to Justification: Rainer Forst in Dialogue*, edited by David Owen. London: Bloomsbury, 2014.

——. "Noumenal Power." *Journal of Political Philosophy*. August 11, 2014. DOI: 10.1111/jopp.12046.

——. *The Right to Justification: Elements of a Constructivist Theory of Justice*. Translated by Jeffrey Flynn. New York: Columbia University Press, 2012.

——. *Toleration in Conflict: Past and Present*. Translated by Ciaran Cronin. Cambridge: Cambridge University Press, 2013.

——. "Two Pictures of Justice." In *Justice, Democracy and the Right to Justification: Rainer Forst in Dialogue*, edited by David Owen. London: Bloomsbury, 2014.

——. "Zum Begriff des Fortschritts." In *Vielfalt der Moderne—Ansichten der Moderne*, edited by Hans Joas. Frankfurt: Fischer, 2012.

Foucault, Michel. "About the Beginning of the Hermeneutics of the Self: Two Lectures at Dartmouth." *Political Theory* 21, no. 2 (May 1993): 198–227.

——. *Aesthetics, Method, and Epistemology*. Vol. 2, *Essential Works of Michel Foucault*. Edited by James D. Faubion. New York: New Press, 1998.

——. "Critical Theory/Intellectual History." In *Critique and Power: Recasting the Foucault/Habermas Debate*, edited by Michael Kelly. Cambridge, Mass.: MIT Press, 1994.

——. *Ethics: Subjectivity and Truth*. Vol. 1, *Essential Works of Michel Foucault*. Edited by Paul Rabinow. New York: New Press, 1997.

——. "The Ethics of the Concern for Self as a Practice of Freedom." In *Ethics*, 281–301.

——. *History of Madness*. Edited by Jean Khalfa. Translated by Jonathan Murphy and Jean Khalfa. New York: Routledge, 2006.

——. "Nietzsche, Genealogy, History." In *Aesthetics, Method, and Epistemology*, 369–391.

——. "On the Genealogy of Ethics." In *Ethics*, 253–280.

——. "On the Ways of Writing History," in *Aesthetics, Method, and Epistemology*, 279–295.

——. "Polemics, Politics, and Problematizations." In *Ethics*, 111–119.

——. *The Politics of Truth*. Edited by Sylvère Lotringer. Translated by Lysa Hochroth and Catherine Porter. Los Angeles: Semiotext(e), 2007.

——. *Power*. Vol. 3, *Essential Works of Michel Foucault*. Edited by James D. Faubion. New York: New Press, 2000.

——. "Space, Knowledge, and Power." In *Power*, 349–364.

——. "The Subject and Power." In *Power*, 326–348.

——. *The Use of Pleasure*. Vol. 2, *The History of Sexuality*. Translated by Robert Hurley. New York: Vintage, 1985.

——. "What Is Enlightenment?" In *Ethics*, 303–319.

Fraser, Nancy. "Foucault on Modern Power: Empirical Insights and Normative Confusions." In *Unruly Practices: Power, Discourse, and Gender in Contemporary Social Theory*. Minneapolis: University of Minnesota Press, 1989.

——. *Justice Interruptus: Critical Reflections on the "Postsocialist" Condition*. New York: Routledge, 1997.

——. "What's Critical About Critical Theory? The Case of Habermas and Gender." In *Unruly Practices*.

Fraser, Nancy, and Axel Honneth. *Redistribution or Recognition? A Political-Philosophical Exchange*. London: Verso, 2003.

Fraser, Nancy, and Linda Nicholson. "Social Criticism Without Philosophy: An Encounter Between Feminism and Postmodernism." In *Feminism/Postmodernism*, edited by Linda Nicholson. New York: Routledge, 1989.

Freyenhagen, Fabian. *Adorno's Practical Philosophy: Living Less Wrongly*. Cambridge: Cambridge University Press, 2013.

Freyenhagen, Fabian, and Jörg Schaub. "Hat hier jemand gesagt, der Kaiser sei nackt? Eine Verteidigung der Geussschen Kritik an Rawls' idealtheoretischem Ansatz." *Deutsche Zeitschrift für Philosophie* 58, no. 3 (2010): 457–477.

Gabriëls, René. "There Must Be Some Way out of Here: In Search of a Critical Theory of World Society." *Krisis: Journal for Contemporary Philosophy* 1 (2013): 5–9.

Gaus, Daniel. "Rational Reconstruction as a Method of Political Theory Between Social Critique and Empirical Political Science." *Constellations* 20, no. 4 (December 2013): 553–570.

Geuss, Raymond. *The Idea of a Critical Theory: Habermas and the Frankfurt School*. Cambridge: Cambridge University Press, 1981.

——. *Outside Ethics*. Princeton: Princeton University Press, 2005.

——. *Philosophy and Real Politics*. Princeton: Princeton University Press, 2008.

Gibson, Nigel, and Andrew Rubin. "Introduction: Adorno and the Autonomous Intellectual." In *Adorno: A Critical Reader*. Oxford: Blackwell, 2002.

Gilroy, Paul. *Postcolonial Melancholia*. New York: Columbia University Press, 2004.

Goehr, Lydia. "Reviewing Adorno: Public Opinion and Critique." In *Critical Models: Interventions and Catchwords*, by Theodor Adorno, translated by Henry W. Pickford. New York: Columbia University Press, 2005.

Goswami, Namita. "The (M)other of All Posts: Postcolonial Melancholia in the Age of Global Warming." *Critical Philosophy of Race* 1, no. 1 (2013): 105–120.

Habermas, Jürgen. *Between Facts and Norms: Contributions to a Discourse Theory of Law and Democracy*. Translated by William Rehg. Cambridge, Mass.: MIT Press, 1996.

——. *Between Naturalism and Religion: Philosophical Essays*. Translated by Ciaran Cronin. Cambridge: Polity, 2008.

——. *Communication and the Evolution of Society*. Translated by Thomas McCarthy. Boston: Beacon, 1976.

——. "Concluding Remarks." In *Habermas and the Public Sphere*, edited by Craig Calhoun. Cambridge, Mass.: MIT Press, 1992.

——. "Constitutional Democracy: A Paradoxical Union of Contradictory Principles?" *Political Theory* 29, no. 6 (December 2001): 766–781.

——. "Discourse Ethics: Notes on a Program of Philosophical Justification." In *Moral Consciousness and Communicative Action*, translated by Christian Lenhardt and Shierry Weber Nicholsen. Cambridge, Mass.: MIT Press, 1990.

——. *The Divided West*. Edited and translated by Ciaran Cronin. Cambridge: Polity, 2006.

——. "Essay on Faith and Knowledge: Postmetaphysical Thinking and the Secular Self-Interpretation of Modernity." Unpublished manuscript on file with author.

——. *The Inclusion of the Other: Studies in Political Theory*. Edited by Ciaran Cronin and Pablo De Greiff. Cambridge, Mass.: MIT Press, 1998.

——. *Justification and Application: Remarks on Discourse Ethics*. Translated by Ciaran Cronin. Cambridge, Mass.: MIT Press, 1993.

——. *The Philosophical Discourse of Modernity: Twelve Lectures*. Translated by Frederick G. Lawrence. Cambridge, Mass.: MIT Press, 1987.

——. "A Postsecular World Society? On the Philosophical Significance of Postsecular Consciousness and the Multicultural World Society." Interview with Eduardo Mendieta. http://blogs.ssrc.org/tif/wp-content/uploads/2010/02/A-Postsecular-World-Society-TIF.pdf.

——. *Religion and Rationality: Essays on Reason, God, and Modernity*. Edited by Eduardo Mendieta. Cambridge: Polity, 2002.

——. "Reply to My Critics." Translated by Ciaran Cronin. In *Habermas and Modernity*, edited by Craig Calhoun, Eduardo Mendieta, and Jonathan VanAntwerpen. Cambridge: Polity, 2013.

——. *The Structural Transformation of the Public Sphere: An Inquiry Into a Category of Bourgeois Society*. Translated by Thomas Burger with the assistance of Frederick Lawrence. Cambridge, Mass.: MIT Press, 1989.

——. *Theory and Practice*. Translated by John Viertel. Boston: Beacon, 1973.

——. *The Theory of Communicative Action*. Vol. 1, *Reason and the Rationalization of Society*. Translated by Thomas McCarthy. Boston: Beacon, 1984.

——. *The Theory of Communicative Action*. Vol. 2, *Lifeworld and System: A Critique of Functionalist Reason*. Translated by Thomas McCarthy. Boston: Beacon, 1987.

Hammer, Espen. *Adorno and the Political*. London: Routledge, 2006.

Hartsock, Nancy. "Community/Sexuality/Gender: Rethinking Power." In *Revisioning the Political: Feminist Reconstructions of Traditional Concepts in Western Political Theory*, edited by Nancy J. Hirschmann and Christine Di Stefano. Boulder, Colo.: Westview, 1996.

Harvey, David. *Spaces of Capital: Towards a Critical Geography*. New York: Routledge, 2001.

Heath, Joseph. "Liberalization, Modernization, Westernization." *Philosophy and Social Criticism* 30, no. 5–6 (2004): 665–690.

Heidegger, Martin. *Being and Time*. Translated by Joan Stambaugh. Edited and revised by Dennis Schmidt. Albany: State University of New York Press, 2010.

Hesse, Barnor. "Racialized Modernity: An Analytics of White Mythologies." *Ethnic and Racial Studies* 30, no. 4 (July 2007): 643–663.

Hohendahl, Peter Uwe. "Progress Revisited: Adorno's Dialogue with Augustine, Kant, and Benjamin." *Critical Inquiry* 40, no. 1 (Autumn 2013): 242–260.

Honig, Bonnie. "Dead Rights, Live Futures: A Reply to Habermas's 'Constitutional Democracy.'" *Political Theory* 29, no. 6 (December 2001): 792–805.

Honneth, Axel. "Critical Theory." In *The Routledge Companion to Twentieth Century Philosophy*, edited by Dermot Moran. New York: Routledge, 2008.

——. *The Critique of Power: Reflective Stages in a Critical Social Theory*. Translated by Kenneth Baynes. Cambridge, Mass.: MIT Press, 1991.

——. *Freedom's Right: The Social Foundations of Democratic Life*. Translated by Joseph Ganahl. New York: Columbia University Press, 2014.

——. "The Irreducibility of Progress: Kant's Account of the Relationship Between Morality and History." In *Pathologies of Reason*.

——. "The Normativity of Ethical Life." Translated by Felix Koch. *Philosophy and Social Criticism* 40, no. 8 (October 2014): 817–826.

——. *Pathologies of Reason: On the Legacy of Critical Theory*. Translated by James Ingram. New York: Columbia University Press, 2009.

——. "The Possibility of a Disclosing Critique of Society: The *Dialectic of Enlightenment* in Light of Current Debates in Social Criticism." *Constellations* 7, no. 1 (2000): 116–127.

——. "Recognition as Ideology." In *Recognition and Power: Axel Honneth and the Tradition of Critical Social Theory*, edited by Bert van den Brink and David Owen. Cambridge: Cambridge University Press, 2007.

——. "Recognition between States: On the Moral Substrate of International

Relations." In *The I in We: Studies in the Theory of Recognition*, translated by Joseph Ganahl. Cambridge: Polity, 2012.

——. "Reconstructive Social Criticism with a Genealogical Proviso: On the Idea of 'Critique' in the Frankfurt School." In *Pathologies of Reason*.

——. "Replies." *Krisis: Journal for Contemporary Philosophy* 1 (2013): 37–47.

——. "The Social Dynamics of Disrespect: On the Location of Critical Theory Today." Translated by John Farrell. In *Disrespect: The Normative Foundations of Critical Theory*. Cambridge: Polity, 2007.

——. "A Social Pathology of Reason: On the Intellectual Legacy of Critical Theory." In *Pathologies of Reason*.

——. *The Struggle for Recognition: The Moral Grammar of Social Conflicts*. Translated by Joel Anderson. Cambridge, Mass.: MIT Press, 1995.

Honneth, Axel, and Hans Joas, eds. *Communicative Action: Essays on Jürgen Habermas's "The Theory of Communicative Action."* Translated by Jeremy Gaines and Doris L. Jones. Cambridge, Mass.: MIT Press, 1991.

Horkheimer, Max. *Critical Theory: Selected Essays*. Translated by Matthew O'Connell et al. New York: Continuum, 1972.

Huffer, Lynne. *Mad for Foucault: Rethinking the Foundations of Queer Theory*. New York: Columbia University Press, 2010.

Ingram, David. *Habermas: Introduction and Analysis*. Ithaca: Cornell University Press, 2010.

Iser, Mattias. *Empörung und Fortschritt: Grundlagen einer kritischen Theorie der Gesellschaft*. Frankfurt: Campus, 2008.

Jameson, Fredric. *The Political Unconscious: Narrative as a Socially Symbolic Act*. Ithaca: Cornell University Press, 1981.

Kant, Immanuel. "The Contest of the Faculties," In *Kant: Political Writings*, 2nd ed., edited by H. S. Reiss. Cambridge: Cambridge University Press, 1991. Originally published in 1798.

——. *Critique of the Power of Judgment*. Translated by Paul Guyer and Eric Matthews. Cambridge: Cambridge University Press, 2000.

——. "Idea for a Universal History from a Cosmopolitan Point of View." In *Kant: Selections*, edited by Lewis White Beck. New York: Macmillan, 1988. Originally published in 1784.

——. "On the Common Saying: 'This May be True in Theory but It Does Not Apply in Practice." In *Kant: Political Writings*, 2nd ed., edited by H. S. Reiss. Cambridge: Cambridge University Press, 1991. Originally published in 1793.

——. "Perpetual Peace: A Philosophical Sketch." In *Kant: Political Writings*, 2nd ed., edited by H. S. Reiss. Cambridge: Cambridge University Press, 1991. Originally published in 1795.

——. "What Is Enlightenment?" In *Kant: Selections*, edited by Lewis White Beck. New York: Macmillan, 1988. Originally published in 1784.

Kelly, Mark. "Against Prophecy and Utopia: Foucault and the Future." *Thesis Eleven* 120, no. 1 (February 2014): 104–118.

Kleingeld, Pauline. "Kant, History, and the Idea of Moral Development." *History of Philosophy Quarterly* 16, no. 1 (January 1999): 59–80.

Kompridis, Nikolas. *Critique and Disclosure: Critical Theory Between Past and Future*. Cambridge, Mass.: MIT Press, 2006.

——. "Re-Envisioning Critical Theory: Amy Allen's *The Politics of Our Selves*." *Critical Horizons* 15, no. 1 (2014): 1–13.

Koopman, Colin. *Genealogy as Critique: Foucault and the Problems of Modernity*. Bloomington: Indiana University Press, 2013.

Koselleck, Reinhart. "'Progress' and 'Decline': An Appendix to the History of Two Concepts." In *The Practice of Conceptual History: Timing History, Spacing Concepts*, translated by Todd Samuel Presner et al. Stanford: Stanford University Press, 2002.

Laden, Anthony Simon. "Constructivism as Rhetoric." In *A Companion to Rawls*, edited by Jon Mandle and David A. Reidy. London: Blackwell, 2013.

——. "The Justice of Justification." In *Habermas and Rawls: Disputing the Political*, edited by James Gordon Finlayson and Fabian Freyenhagen. New York: Routledge, 2011.

——. "The Practice of Equality." In *Justice, Democracy, and the Right to Justification*, edited by Rainer Forst. London: Bloomsbury, 2014.

——. *Reasoning: A Social Picture*. Oxford: Oxford University Press, 2012.

Lafont, Cristina. *The Linguistic Turn in Hermeneutic Philosophy*. Translated by José Medina. Cambridge, Mass.: MIT Press, 1999.

Larmore, Charles. "History and Truth." *Daedalus* 133, no. 3 (Spring 2004): 46–55.

Latour, Bruno. *We Have Never Been Modern*. Translated by Catherine Porter. Cambridge, Mass.: Harvard University Press, 1993.

Lawlor, Leonard. "Violence and Animality: On Absolute Freedom in Foucault." In *Foucault and Animals*, edited by Dinesh Wadiwel and Matthew Chrulew. New York: Fordham University Press, forthcoming.

Lear, Jonathan. "The Slippery Middle." In *Reification: A New Look at an Old Idea*, by Axel Honneth. Oxford: Oxford University Press, 2008.

Lloyd, Genevieve. *The Man of Reason: "Male" and "Female" in Western Philosophy*. 2nd ed. Chicago: University of Chicago Press, 1993.

Mahmood, Saba. "Feminism, Democracy, and Empire: Islam and the War of Terror." In *Women's Studies on the Edge*, edited by Joan Scott. Durham: Duke University Press, 2008.

——. *Politics of Piety: The Islamic Revival and the Feminist Subject*. Princeton: Princeton University Press, 2005.

Marasco, Robyn. *The Highway of Despair: Critical Theory After Hegel*. New York: Columbia University Press, 2015.

Marx, Karl. "The Eighteenth Brumaire of Louis Bonaparte." In *The Marx-Engels Reader*, 2nd ed., edited by Robert Tucker. New York: Norton, 1978.

Marx, Karl, and Friedrich Engels. "Manifesto of the Communist Party." In

The Marx-Engels Reader, 2nd ed., edited by Robert Tucker. New York: Norton, 1978.

McCarthy, Thomas. *The Critical Theory of Jürgen Habermas*. Cambridge, Mass.: MIT Press, 1978.

——. *Ideals and Illusions: On Reconstruction and Deconstruction in Contemporary Critical Theory*. Cambridge, Mass.: MIT Press, 1991.

——. *Race, Empire, and the Idea of Human Development*. Cambridge: Cambridge University Press, 2009.

McCormick, John. *Weber, Habermas, and the Transformations of the European State: Constitutional, Social, and Supranational Democracy*. Cambridge: Cambridge University Press, 2007.

McNay, Lois. "Social Freedom and Progress in the Family: Reflections on Care, Gender, and Inequality." *Critical Horizons* 16, no. 2 (2015).

Menke, Christoph. "Genealogy and Critique: Two Forms of Ethical Questioning of Morality." In *The Cambridge Companion to Adorno*, edited by Tom Huhn. Cambridge: Cambridge University Press, 2004.

Mignolo, Walter. *The Darker Side of Western Modernity: Global Futures, Decolonial Options*. Durham: Duke University Press, 2011.

——. "Delinking: The Rhetoric of Modernity, the Logic of Coloniality and the Grammar of De-Coloniality." *Globalization and De-Colonial Thinking*, special issue of *Cultural Studies* 21, no. 2/3 (March 2007): 449–514.

——. "The Geopolitics of Knowledge and the Colonial Difference." *South Atlantic Quarterly* 101, no. 1 (Winter 2002): 57–96.

Mitchell, Timothy. "The Stage of Modernity." In *Questions of Modernity*, edited by Timothy Mitchell. Minneapolis: University of Minnesota Press, 2000.

Moyn, Samuel. "The Continuing Perplexities of Human Rights." *Qui Parle* 22, no. 1 (Fall/Winter 2013): 95–115.

Muthu, Sankar. *Enlightenment Against Empire*. Princeton: Princeton University Press, 2003.

Nichols, Robert. "Postcolonial Studies and the Discourse of Foucault: Survey of a Field of Problematization." *Foucault Studies* 9 (September 2010): 111–144.

Nietzsche, Friedrich. *On the Genealogy of Morals*. Translated by Walter Kaufmann and R. J. Hollingdale. New York: Vintage, 1967.

O'Connor, Brian. *Adorno's Negative Dialectic: Philosophy and the Possibility of Critical Rationality*. Cambridge, Mass.: MIT Press, 2004.

——. "Adorno's Philosophy of History." In *Theodor Adorno: Key Concepts*, edited by Deborah Cook. Durham, UK: Acumen, 2008.

——. "Adorno's Reconception of the Dialectic." In *A Companion to Hegel*, edited by Stephen Houlgate and Michael Baur. London: Blackwell, 2011.

O'Farrell, Clare. *Foucault: Historian or Philosopher*. New York: St. Martin's Press, 1989.

Olson, Kevin. "Complexities of Political Discourse: Class, Power, and Justification in Rainer Forst's Political Theory." In *Justice, Democracy, and the Right to Justification*, edited by Rainer Forst. London: Bloomsbury, 2014.

——. "Paradoxes of Constitutional Democracy." *American Journal of Political Science* 51, no. 2 (April 2007): 330–343.

Owen, David. *Between Reason and History: Habermas and the Idea of Progress*. Albany: State University of New York Press, 2002.

Pandey, Gyanendra. "In Defense of the Fragment: Writing About Hindu-Muslim Riots in India Today." In *A Subaltern Studies Reader: 1986–1995*, edited by Ranajit Guha. Minneapolis: University of Minnesota Press, 1997.

Passerin d'Entreves, Maurizio, and Seyla Benhabib, eds. *Habermas and the Unfinished Project of Modernity: Critical Essays on The Philosophical Discourse of Modernity*. Cambridge, Mass.: MIT Press, 1997.

Patke, Rajeev. "Adorno and the Postcolonial." *New Formations* 47:133–143.

Pensky, Max, ed. *The Actuality of Adorno: Critical Essays on Adorno and the Postmodern*. Albany: State University of New York Press, 1997.

——. "Contributions Toward a Theory of Storms: Historical Knowing and Historical Progress in Kant and Benjamin." *Philosophical Forum* 41, no. 1/2 (2010): 149–174.

——. *The Ends of Solidarity: Discourse Theory in Ethics and Politics*. Albany: State University of New York Press, 2008.

Petherbridge, Danielle. *The Critical Theory of Axel Honneth*. Lanham, Md.: Lexington, 2013.

Pippin, Robert. "Hegel, Modernity, and Habermas." In *Idealism as Modernism: Hegelian Variations*. Cambridge: Cambridge University Press, 1997.

Puar, Jasbir. *Terrorist Assemblages: Homonationalism in Queer Times*. Durham: Duke University Press, 2007.

Quijano, Anibal. "Coloniality of Power, Eurocentrism, and Latin America." *Neplanta: Views from the South* 1, no. 3 (2000): 533–580.

Rajchman, John. "Enlightenment Today: Introduction to *The Politics of Truth*." In *The Politics of Truth*, by Michel Foucault, edited by Sylvère Lotringer, translated by Lysa Hochroth and Catherine Porter. Los Angeles: Semiotext(e), 2007.

Rawls, John. "Kantian Constructivism in Moral Theory." *Journal of Philosophy* 77 (1980): 515–572.

Rehg, William. *Insight and Solidarity: The Discourse Ethics of Jürgen Habermas*. Berkeley: University of California Press, 1994.

Rocco, Christopher. "Between Modernity and Postmodernity: Reading *Dialectic of Enlightenment* Against the Grain." *Political Theory* 22, no. 1 (1994): 71–97.

Rose, Gillian. *The Melancholy Science: An Introduction to the Thought of Theodor W. Adorno*. London: Verso, 1978.

Saar, Martin. *Genealogie als Kritik: Geschichte und Theorie des Subjekts nach Nietzsche and Foucault*. Frankfurt: Campus: 2007.

——. "Genealogy and Subjectivity." *European Journal of Philosophy* 10, no. 2 (2002): 231–245.

——. "Power, Constitution, Discourse." Unpublished manuscript, on file with the author.

Said, Edward. *Culture and Imperialism*. New York: Vintage, 1993.

——. *Orientalism*. 25th anniversary ed. New York: Vintage, 1994.

——. "Representing the Colonized: Anthropology's Interlocutors." *Critical Inquiry* 15, no. 2 (Winter 1989): 205–225.

Schaub, Jörg. "Misdevelopments, Pathologies, and Normative Revolutions: Normative Reconstruction as Method of Critical Theory." *Critical Horizons* 16, no. 2 (2015).

Scheuerman, William. "Between Radicalism and Resignation: Democratic Theory in Habermas's *Between Facts and Norms*." In *Habermas: A Critical Reader*, edited by Peter Dews. Oxford: Blackwell, 1999.

Schnädelbach, Herbert. "The Transformation of Critical Theory." In Honneth and Joas, *Communicative Action*.

Schweppenhäuser, Gerhard. "Adorno's Negative Moral Philosophy." In *The Cambridge Companion to Adorno*, edited by Tom Huhn. Cambridge: Cambridge University Press, 2004.

Scott, David. *Refashioning Futures: Criticism After Postcoloniality*. Princeton: Princeton University Press, 1999.

——. "The Traditions of Historical Others." *Symposia on Gender, Race, and Philosophy* 8, no. 1 (Winter 2012). http://web.mit.edu/sgrp.

Specter, Matthew. *Habermas: An Intellectual Biography*. Cambridge: Cambridge University Press, 2010.

Spencer, Robert. "Thoughts from Abroad: Theodor Adorno as Postcolonial Theorist." *Culture, Theory and Critique* 51, no. 3 (2010): 207–221.

Spivak, Gayatri. *A Critique of Postcolonial Reason: Toward a History of the Vanishing Present*. Cambridge, Mass.: Harvard University Press, 1999.

——. *In Other Worlds: Essays in Cultural Politics*. New York: Routledge, 2006.

Stahl, Titus. "Habermas and the Project of Immanent Critique." *Constellations* 20, no. 4 (December 2013): 533–552.

Stoler, Ann Laura. *Race and the Education of Desire: Foucault's History of Sexuality and the Colonial Order of Things*. Durham: Duke University Press, 1995.

Street, Sharon. "Constructivism About Reasons." In *Oxford Studies in Metaethics*, vol. 3, edited by Russ Shafer-Landau. Oxford: Clarendon Press, 2008.

Taylor, Charles. *Sources of the Self*. Cambridge, Mass.: Harvard University Press, 1989.

Therborn, Göran. "Entangled Modernities." *European Journal of Social Theory* 6, no. 3 (2003): 293–305.

Tully, James. "On Law, Democracy and Imperialism." In *Public Philosophy in a New Key*, vol. 2, *Imperialism and Civic Freedom*. Cambridge: Cambridge University Press, 2008.

——. "Political Philosophy as a Critical Activity." *Political Theory* 30, no. 4 (August 2002): 533–555.

Varadharajan, Asha. *Exotic Parodies: Subjectivity in Adorno, Said, and Spivak.* Minneapolis: University of Minnesota Press, 1995.

Vázquez-Arroyo, Antonio. "Universal History Disavowed: On Critical Theory and Postcolonialism," *Postcolonial Studies* 11, no. 4 (2008): 451–473.

Walden, Kenneth. "Practical Reason Not as Such." Unpublished manuscript, on file with the author.

Wallerstein, Immanuel. *World-Systems Analysis: An Introduction.* Durham: Duke University Press, 2004.

Warner, Michael. *The Trouble with Normal: Sex, Politics, and the Ethics of Queer Life.* Cambridge, Mass.: Harvard University Press, 1999.

Weir, Allison. *Identities and Freedom.* Oxford: Oxford University Press, 2013.

Wellmer, Albrecht. *The Persistence of Modernity: Essays on Aesthetics, Ethics, and Postmodernism.* Translated by David Midgley. Cambridge, Mass.: MIT Press, 1991.

Willett, Cynthia. *The Soul of Justice: Social Bonds and Racial Hubris.* Ithaca: Cornell University Press, 2001.

Williams, Bernard. *In the Beginning Was the Deed: Realism and Moralism in Political Argument.* Princeton: Princeton University Press, 2005.

——. *Truth and Truthfulness: An Essay in Genealogy.* Princeton: Princeton University Press, 2002.

Williams, Michael. *Unnatural Doubts: Epistemological Realism and the Basis of Skepticism.* Cambridge: Basil Blackwell, 1991.

Wilson, Bryan, ed. *Rationality.* Oxford: Oxford University Press, 1970.

Winch, Peter. *The Idea of a Social Science and Its Relation to Philosophy.* London: Routledge and Kegan Paul, 1958.

Wolf, Eric. *Europe and the People Without History.* 2nd ed. Berkeley: University of California Press, 2010.

Young, Robert J. C. "Foucault on Race and Colonialism." *New Formations* 25 (1995): 57–65.

——. *Postcolonialism: An Historical Introduction.* London: Wiley-Blackwell, 2001.

——. *White Mythologies.* 2nd ed. New York: Routledge, 2004.

Zerilli, Linda. "Toward a Feminist Theory of Judgment." *Signs* 34, no. 2 (Winter 2009): 295–317.

Zurn, Christopher. "Anthropology and Normativity: A Critique of Axel Honneth's 'Formal Conception of Ethical Life.'" *Philosophy and Social Criticism* 26, no. 1 (2000): 115–124.

——. *Axel Honneth: A Critical Theory of the Social.* Cambridge: Polity, 2015.

——. "Jürgen Habermas." In *The History of Continental Philosophy*, vol. 6, *Poststructuralism and Critical Theory's Second Generation*, edited by Alan Schrift. Durham, UK: Acumen, 2010.

INDEX

CPSIA information can be obtained
at www.ICGtesting.com
Printed in the USA
LVOW03s1955171017
552730LV00005B/21/P

9 780231 173254